T0370210

The Late Marx's Revolutionary Roads

Kevin B. Anderson is a Distinguished Professor of Sociology at the University of California, Santa Barbara, with courtesy appointments in Feminist Studies and Political Science. He is the author of *Foucault and the Iranian Revolution: Gender and the Seductions of Islamism* (with Janet Afary) and *Marx at the Margins: On Nationalism, Ethnicity, and Non-Western Societies*. He is also an editor of the forthcoming English edition of the late Marx's notebooks on non-Western and precapitalist societies.

The Late Marx's Revolutionary Roads

Colonialism, Gender, and Indigenous Communism

Kevin B. Anderson

VERSO
London • New York

First published by Verso 2025
© Kevin B. Anderson 2025

All rights reserved
The moral rights of the author have been asserted

1 3 5 7 9 10 8 6 4 2

Verso
UK: 6 Meard Street, London W1F 0EG
US: 207 East 32nd Street, New York, NY 10016
versobooks.com

Verso is the imprint of New Left Books

ISBN-13: 978-1-80429-687-5
ISBN-13: 978-1-80429-689-9 (US EBK)
ISBN-13: 978-1-80429-688-2 (UK EBK)

British Library Cataloguing in Publication Data
A catalogue record for this book is available from the British Library

Library of Congress Cataloging-in-Publication Data

Names: Anderson, Kevin, 1948- author.
Title: The late Marx's revolutionary roads : colonialism, gender, and
   indigenous communism / Kevin B. Anderson.
Description: London ; New York : Verso, 2025. | Includes bibliographical
   references and index.
Identifiers: LCCN 2024043605 (print) | LCCN 2024043606 (ebook) | ISBN
   9781804296875 (paperback) | ISBN 9781804296899 (ebook)
Subjects: LCSH: Marx, Karl, 1818-1883--Political and social views. |
   Imperialism. | Sex role. | Communism.
Classification: LCC HX39.5 .A5573 2025 (print) | LCC HX39.5 (ebook) | DDC
   335.4--dc23/eng/20241119
LC record available at https://lccn.loc.gov/2024043605
LC ebook record available at https://lccn.loc.gov/2024043606

Typeset in Minion by Biblichor Ltd, Scotland
Printed and bound by CPI Group (UK) Ltd, Croydon CR0 4YY

Contents

Abbreviations

CAP   Marx, *Capital*, Vol. I, trans. Ben Fowkes, London: NLB, 1976

EN   *The Ethnological Notebooks of Karl Marx*, transcribed and edited by Lawrence Krader, Assen: Van Gorcum, 1974

KOV   *Marx's notes on Kovalevsky on India and Algeria from the appendix to Lawrence Krader, *The Asiatic Mode of Production*, Assen: Van Gorcum, 1975

KOVLM   *Marx's notes on Kovalevsky on Latin America, from *Karl Marx über Formen vorkapitalistischer Produktion*, transcribed and edited by Hans-Peter Harstick, Frankfurt: Campus Verlag, 1975

MECW   *Marx-Engels Collected Works*, fifty volumes, New York: International Publishers, 1975–2004

MEGA2 I/25, II/10, etc.   *Marx-Engels Gesamtausgabe*, Berlin: Akademie Verlag, 1975–present

MEW   *Marx-Engels Werke*, forty-two volumes, Berlin: Dietz Verlag, 1964–73

MG	Lewis Henry Morgan, *Ancient Society*, New York: Henry Holt, 1878
MN	Henry Sumner Maine, *Lectures on the Early History of Institutions*, New York: Henry Holt, 1875
MSW	*Marx, *Notes on Indian History (664–1858)*, Moscow: Foreign Languages Publishing House, n.d., 1960, based on Sewell's book
SW	Robert Sewell, *The Analytical History of India*, London: W. H. Allen & Co., 1870
SHN	*Late Marx and the Russian Road*, edited by Teodor Shanin, New York: Monthly Review Press

Although I cite these sources as the most widely available, sometimes I have altered the translations based on the German or French original. Those marked with asterisks appeared 2024 in new versions in MEGA2 IV/27 and will appear in a new annotated English translation by several colleagues and me as part of a project to publish this material in English in the near future.

Introduction: Contours of the Late Marx

Two junctures at which Marx theorized a European revolution sparked from outside the core capitalist nations form the bookends to this work: the first centered on Ireland, at Europe's western edge, and the second on Russia, at its eastern edge.

In the winter of 1869–70, two years after the publication of *Das Kapital*, Marx wrote on several occasions that he was shifting his position on Ireland. He had looked to the British working class to initiate a wider revolution that would spread its liberating force elsewhere, including to less-developed Ireland, but he had come to believe that the wider European revolution could well begin in agrarian Ireland, among an increasingly restive peasantry that was coming under the influence of the democratically inclined, nationalist Fenian movement. A successful national uprising in Ireland would weaken Britain's dominant classes. This, along with an uprising in France, might help touch off a working-class revolution in Britain, at the time the only truly industrialized country.

A dozen years later, in 1882, Marx and Engels wrote in a preface to the *Communist Manifesto* that a revolution based upon the Russian peasantry, which still inhabited communal villages with less individualized social structures than their Western European counterparts, might lead to a communist revolution. A successful outcome would depend, however, on whether a Russian peasant revolution could link up with the proletarian communist movement in Western Europe, with the two complementing each other. In this sense, Russia would be the spark for a European revolution. At this juncture, Marx did not state explicitly that he was changing his position. But he was certainly doing so, since he had previously viewed Russia less as a revolutionary than a counter-revolutionary force in European politics.

In this book, I am considering the years 1869–82 as those of the late Marx.[1] I will be considering the following sets of writings and issues: (1) those on Ireland, in the 1869–70 writings mentioned above and in the 1879–82 excerpt notebooks; (2) his very extensive 1879–82 notebooks on South Asia, in which he took up colonialism, communal social formations, and social revolt; (3) related 1879 notes on Algeria and Latin America; (4) his 1879–82 notes on gender and the family in ancient and Indigenous societies across a wide geographical range, from Indigenous peoples of the Americas to ancient Greeks, Romans, and Celts; (5) other notes on social transformations in three agrarian societies: Russia, India, and ancient Rome; (6) the 1872–75 French edition of *Capital*, in which he modified the text in important ways that bear on the issues of center and periphery; and (7) theoretical sketches of modern, anti-statist communism in both *Critique of the Gotha Program* in 1875 and his writings on the Paris Commune of 1871.

This book will exclude Marx's other excerpt notebooks from 1869–82, which include: (1) his massive notes on world history, centering mainly on Europe up through 1648; (2) his extensive notes on landed property and agriculture in Russia, as well as the US and Western Europe; and (3) voluminous notes on mathematics and the natural sciences. The first two of these could have some relevance to this study but are inaccessible to me, while the last category is not very relevant here.

We will not need to bracket out work on the drafts of what became, under Engels's editorship, volumes two and three of *Capital*, which Marx in his lifetime referred to as the second volume of the work. This is for the simple reason Marx did little in the period under consideration to draft further material for those volumes, the vast majority of which he drafted in the mid-1860s, *before* the completion of volume one. However, Marx sometimes implies that he intends to use his data on Russia in a recasting of these volumes, and one can surmise that

---

1   Marx died in March 1883 after bouts of poor health, making 1882 the last year in which he was able to carry out intellectual and political work.

much of his other research in this period might also have been related to what was to become volumes 2 and 3. Of course, as mentioned above, he continued to work on the French edition of *Capital*, volume 1, published in serial form up through 1875.

Marx's relative lack of attention to volumes 2 and 3 after the publication of volume 1 has led generations of Marxists, beginning with Engels in the 1880s and then David Riazanov in the 1920s, to view Marx's last years as essentially unproductive, marred by ill health and digressions into areas far less important than the completion of *Capital*. As Engels complained in a letter of August 30, 1883, after he had gone through Marx's papers in the months following his comrade's death in March of that year:

> As soon as I am back, I shall get down to Volume 2 in real earnest and that is an enormous task. Alongside parts that have been completely finished are others that are merely sketched out, the whole being a *brouillon* [sketch] with the exception of perhaps two chapters. Quotations from sources in no kind of order, piles of them jumbled together, collected simply with a view to future selection . . . You ask why I of all people should not have been told how far the thing had got. It is quite simple; had I known, I should have pestered him night and day until it was all finished and printed. And Marx knew that better than anyone else.[2]

In assessing Marx's Nachlass, and during the remaining twelve years of his life, Engels focused his attention on *Capital*, as he painstakingly brought to press what became volumes two and three. But he paid little attention to other manuscripts, not even those that became famous later, such as the *1844 Manuscripts*, the *German Ideology*, or the *Grundrisse*, let alone the notebooks of the late Marx that are the focus of this study.

---

2 *Marx-Engels Collected Works* (hereafter MECW as an in-text reference), Vol. 47 (Moscow: Progress Publishers, 1995), p. 53. I will give page references to *Marx-Engels Collected Works* (MECW) where possible, but with letters I also give the date in text to allow them to be found more easily in any source. Similarly, with quotes from articles, essays, and books, I will give the title and its date in the text, again referring, when possible, to MECW. Translations are sometimes altered in light of German or French originals.

There was one exception to this neglect, however. Even before publishing the second volume of *Capital*, in 1885, Engels used parts of Marx's 1880–81 notes on the anthropologist Henry Lewis Morgan for his own classic study, *The Origin of the Family, Private Property, and the State* (1884). But, as we will argue in this study, Engels did not reach Marx's level in approaching these materials, especially on gender and the family. Nor did he connect them to colonialism and contemporary non-Western societies.

After Engels's death in 1895, the Marxists of the Second International did little to publish Marx's original writings, preferring instead popularizations of his work alongside their own efforts to theorize the present based on how they understood Marx. One exception was Marx's *Theories of Surplus Value*, but Karl Kautsky, the Second International's leading theorist, published this work with some serious omissions. This was even truer of Marx's correspondence, in which Second International editors deleted passages criticizing leading German socialists—Marx's successors.

After the Russian Revolution of 1917 created the first avowedly Marxist state, the government of Lenin and Trotsky funded what became the Marx-Engels-Lenin Institute, with responsibility for cataloguing and editing Marx's writings. The chief editor, David Riazanov, led a team that catalogued the whole and created the first *Marx-Engels Gesamtausgabe* (MEGA1), which included three separate sections for *Capital* and its drafts, other books and articles, and letters.

In a 1923 report to the Socialist Academy, Riazanov summarized the whole, only touching on the excerpt notebooks, which were not slated for inclusion in MEGA1. Among those he mentioned were notes on the 1857 economic crisis, those on European history through 1648, and mathematical notebooks. He reported that most of these materials did not warrant publication but would be useful for biographers, who would be interested in how Marx "worked systematically right up to his death" as a researcher:[3]

---

3   David Riazanov, "Neueste Mitteilungen über den literarischen Nachlass von Karl Marx und Friedrich Engels," *Archiv für Geschichte des Sozialismus und der Arbeiterbewegung* 11 (1924): 399.

If in 1881-82 he lost his ability for intensive, independent intellectual creation, he nevertheless never lost the ability for research. Sometimes, in reconsidering these Notebooks,[4] the question arises: Why did he waste so much time on this systematic, fundamental summary, or expend so much labor as he spent as late as the year 1881, on one basic book on geology, summarizing it chapter by chapter? In the 63rd year of his life—that is inexcusable pedantry. Here is another example: he received, in 1878, a copy of Morgan's work. On 98 pages of his very miniscule handwriting (you should know that a single page of his is the equivalent of a minimum of 2.2 pages of print) he makes a detailed summary of Morgan. In such manner does the old Marx work.[5]

This dismissal of many of the late Marx's notebooks as "inexcusable pedantry" reveals a certain attitude toward the last years.

Riazanov made some exceptions, however. Undoubtedly because Engels based his widely read *Origin of the Family* on Marx's notes on Henry Lewis Morgan's *Ancient Society* (1877), Riazanov took these notes more seriously, pointing to their "special importance," and related ones on Lubbock and Maine. He added that, at the end of the 1870s, Marx had occupied himself with "the history of feudalism and of landed property."[6] Thus, a few parts of the notebooks of the late Marx were worthy of study. But they would still not be included in MEGA1.

This is what Riazanov reported. But he did not report that, in his very last working years, 1879–82, Marx took voluminous notes on several societies impacted by colonialism: Indonesia, Latin America, Australia, Algeria, Egypt, and, at greatest length, India. The fact that Riazanov did not notice this even though one large notebook was devoted mainly to India, with several others also taking up that country, is particularly surprising given early Soviet Russia's emphasis on—and strong support for—anti-imperialist movements in Asia.

---

4   Later scholarship by Krader dates most of these notebooks as 1880–81 rather than 1881–82. Jürgen Rojahn and Emanuela Conversano, editor of MEGAdigital IV/27 (2024), date them "between the middle of December 1880 and June 1881." https://megadigital. bbaw.de/exzerpte/intro.xql?id=M3933891#heading-3, accessed March 4, 2024.

5   Riazanov, "Neueste Mitteilungen," p. 399.

6   Ibid., p. 399.

Did Riazanov revise his early dismissal of the late Marx as time passed and he and his colleagues had more time to examine these texts more carefully? The answer is no. In fact, Riazanov propagated a notion of the late Marx as having deteriorated to the point that he wrote and thought little of value. This can be seen in Riazanov's biography of Marx, which appeared four years later. There, like Engels, he complained of the lack of progress on *Capital* in the 1870s, but he attributed it to poor health, not only physical but also mental: "Any strenuous intellectual work was a menace to his overwrought brain," Riazanov wrote, as "Marx's life . . . was always threatened by a sudden stroke."[7] Riazanov adds: "After 1878 he was forced to give up all work on *Capital* in the hope he would be able to return to it at some more auspicious time. This hope was not fulfilled. He was still able to make notes."[8] Here, despite having begun to assess the wealth of material in the research notebooks of the late Marx, Riazanov fell back toward the conclusion of Franz Mehring, Marx's first biographer, that the last years were "really little more than a 'slow death.'"[9]

These pronouncements by authorities as eminent as Engels and Riazanov, the notion that Marx had lost his intellectual capacities and had produced nothing of value in his last years, became by far the dominant interpretation of his life and work for many decades afterward. It strongly influenced Marxist theorists and scholars of all stripes, as well as non-Marxist scholars of Marxism.

To be sure, it is true that, in the 1930s, the Stalinist apparatus undermined much of Riazanov's work and that of his colleagues, arresting almost all of them, with Riazanov meeting his death in a labor camp in 1942. Although Riazanov and his team of pioneering Marx scholars had been able to issue such major writings as the *1844 Manuscripts* and the *German Ideology*, and also prepared the *Grundrisse*, published by their successors in 1939, these early Marx scholars seriously underestimated the relevance—for their time and ours—of the late Marx.

The late Marx, as even Riazanov had acknowledged, continued to conduct research as recorded in his voluminous notebooks. Yet the

---

7 David Riazanov, *Karl Marx and Friedrich Engels: An Introduction to Their Lives and Work* (New York: Monthly Review, [1927] 1973), p. 205.

8 Ibid., p. 206.

9 Franz Mehring, *Karl Marx: The Story of His Life*, trans. Edward Fitzgerald (Ann Arbor: University of Michigan Press, [1918] 1962), p. 528.

narrow focus of Marx editors and scholars, beginning with Engels himself, on capital and class to the exclusion of other issues, seems to have made the rest of his work in this period opaque. In my previous book, *Marx at the Margins*, I tried to make a contribution to the overcoming of this limitation in Marxist scholarship, one that has left us open to attacks from postcolonial, decolonial, and other quarters in recent decades.[10] The present book is, in some sense, a sequel to that volume.

Not only are the topics the late Marx researched and wrote about of great interest for today, but they are also evidence of grueling intellectual labor. For example, by 1879, his knowledge of the Russian language, which he had begun teaching himself in 1869, was good enough to make detailed notes, mainly in German, on the anthropologist Maksim Kovalevsky's Russian-language book on the social structures of clans and villages in precolonial and colonial India, Algeria, and Latin America. Moreover, the notes on Morgan's English-language study show a detailed grasp of very complex kinship and gender relations among the Iroquois, the Aztecs, and the ancient Greeks and Romans. Are these kinds of studies less intellectually rigorous than the critique of political economy? Is their subject matter less significant for Marxism, or social theory more generally?

Read today, Riazanov's and Mehring's, and, to an extent, even Engels's strictures against the late Marx appear more like expressions of the Eurocentrism of these authors than persuasive arguments about limitations in Marx's own research and writing during his last years.

Moreover, these long-dominant interpretations of the late Marx not only minimize the importance of his research on non-Western societies, but they also fail to consider that, had he lived longer, these non-Western societies may have become more central to subsequent volumes of *Capital*. Already in the 1950s, the Russian-American philosopher Raya Dunayevskaya intoned, based on his attention to Russia and the US in his last years, that Marx may well have intended a different focus for these later volumes: "It is clear that Russia and America were to play the role in Vols. II and III that England played in Volume I."[11] Four

---

10 Kevin B. Anderson, *Marx at the Margins: On Nationalism, Ethnicity, and Non-Western Societies* (Chicago: University of Chicago Press, [2010] 2016).

11 Raya Dunayevskaya, *Marxism and Freedom: From 1776 until Today* (Amherst, NY: Humanity Books, [1958] 2000), p. 148.

decades later, David Norman Smith, editor of the forthcoming English edition of Marx's *Ethnological Notebooks*, suggested that Marx's 1879–82 notes on a number of non-European societies could have been related to the subsequent volumes of *Capital* because, as capitalism was extending itself more and more widely, "Now he needed to know concretely, in exact cultural detail, what capital could expect to confront in its global extension."[12]

The contents of the three Marx notebooks that bear most on the present book are listed below according to the cataloging system of the handwritten manuscripts at the Institute of Social History in Amsterdam; the newer notebook numbers are followed by the older ones. The descriptions of the sources are my own, as are the asterisks indicating texts that were published only in 2024, in MEGA2 IV/27.

Notebook B156/140 (begun around 1879)

Page Nos. in Marx's Handwritten Notebook	Text Marx Annotated
5–7	Robert Sewell's chronological history of India
8–11	*Karl Bücher's book on slave and plebeian uprisings in Rome
12–16	*Ludwig Friedländer's book on Roman culture
17–24	*Rudolf von Jhering's book on Roman law
26–47	Maksim Kovalevsky's book on communal land tenure in Algeria, India, and the Americas
48–65	Robert Sewell's chronological history of India
66–90	Maksim Kovalevsky's book on communal land tenure in the Americas, India, and Algeria
91–116	Robert Sewell's chronological history of India
117–140	*Ludwig Lange's book on the social and gender history of Rome

---

12   David Norman Smith, "Marx's *Capital* after the Paris Commune," *Marx and 'Le Capital': History, Evaluation, Reception*, ed. Marcello Musto (London: Routledge, 2022), p. 79.

Notebook B162/146 (December 1880–Spring 1881)

Page Nos. in Marx's Handwritten Notebook	Source Marx Annotated
4–101	Henry Lewis Morgan's book on clan societies and gender relations among the Iroquois, the Aztecs, and in ancient Greece and Rome
102–130	*J. W. B. Money's book on Indonesia under Dutch colonialism
131–157	John Budd Phear's book on village life in India and Sri Lanka
157–161	*Rudolf Sohm's article on Frankish and Roman law
162–199	Henry Sumner Maine's book on communal property in Ireland and India
200–203	*E. Hospitalier's book on electricity

Notebook B168/150 (1882)

Page Nos. in Marx's Handwritten Notebook	Source Marx Annotated
3–10	John Lubbock's book on preliterate societies around the world
11–18	*M. G. Mulhall's article on Egyptian finances and British colonialism

As can be seen above, the late Marx's notes on ancient Rome were published only in 2024, as with those on Indonesia or Egypt, and many of them are crucial to this book. (I have been able to draw upon these materials ahead of their publication, however, due to my earlier work with MEGA2 and the generous permission of its editors, MEGA2 general editor Gerald Hubmann, and the principal editor for these particular notebooks, Jürgen Rojahn.) It is also of interest that Marx intertwines his notes on Roman social history with those on India in notebook B156/140, suggesting a connection between his study of these two agrarian societies. During the years 1869–82, he also made voluminous notes on

Russian agriculture and society, almost none of them published and, as mentioned above, inaccessible to me. For many years, however, we have had in published form his letters sent to or drafted for Russian interlocutors, in 1877 and 1881, and his and Engels's 1882 preface to the Russian edition of the *Communist Manifesto*. Important letters and other texts on Ireland have also survived.

Marx's excerpt notebooks, including the 1879–82 ones that are at the center of this study, are much rougher in form than other posthumously published Marx writings such as the *Grundrisse* or the *1844 Manuscripts*. Unpolished and often ungrammatical in structure, they are notebooks in which Marx records or summarizes passages from books he is studying. But they show us Marx's own thinking in several ways. First, they include important comments in which Marx speaks in his own voice. Second, they show Marx as a "reader"; they contain his direct or indirect critique of the assumptions or conclusions of the authors he is studying and show how he connects or takes apart themes and issues in the texts he is reading. Third, they indicate which themes and data he found compelling in connection with these studies of non-Western, colonized, and precapitalist societies. In short, they offer a unique window into his thinking at a time when he was moving in new directions.

We cannot know with any certainty what Marx intended to do with the 1879–82 notebooks. One reason is that the epistolary record describing Marx's work becomes more limited after 1869, when Engels, his chief intellectual interlocutor, moved from Manchester to London. Before that period, we have many long letters from Marx to his closest comrade detailing his intellectual development. With the two of them now conversing in person almost daily, much less of a written record has survived.

Sadly, we are also deprived of what might have been an important alternative source for Marx's private thinking in his last years, at least on anthropology and non-Western societies: his dialogue with the young Russian anthropologist Maksim Kovalevsky, the person who introduced him to Morgan's *Ancient Society*. They saw each other frequently in London during 1875–77 and then Kovalevsky corresponded with Marx and continued to visit him after he moved from London in 1877 to assume a teaching position at Moscow University. In 1879, Kovalevsky published a book on communal land tenure among Indigenous peoples of the Americas and in India and Algeria, which Marx annotated and which I will discuss at length. In a letter of September 19, 1879, to Nikolai Danielson, the Russian translator of *Capital*, Marx called him "one of my 'scientific' friends" (MECW 45:209). As the historian James White recounts:

> As Kovalevsky stated in his reminiscences, on returning to Moscow he kept up correspondence with Marx. Unfortunately, Marx's letters to Kovalevsky have not survived. During one of his trips abroad Kovalevsky left his letters in the care of [Ivan] Ivanyukov, who burnt them, fearing his home would be searched by the police, a precaution which turned out to be unnecessary.[13]

This reduces further our source material on Marx's thinking concerning his 1879–82 notebooks. Some of Kovalevsky's letters to Marx have survived among Marx's papers in the International Institute of Social History in Amsterdam. Written in French, the language of educated Russians in this period, they do not indicate the nature of their dialogues about anthropology and communal social formations. Kovalevsky's attitude toward Marx seems to have been one of great esteem for his intellectual achievements, the young anthropologist addressing him in a letter of December 8, 1881, with the honorific "mon cher maître."[14]

With the rise of the Third World in the second half of the twentieth century and the publication in widely circulated form of the *Grundrisse*, with its substantial discussion of Asian societies, underestimations of the late Marx began slowly to fade, and, over time, interest in this period of Marx's writings grew. The currency of the term "late Marx" began in the 1980s and was seen as a counterpart to the widely used young Marx. Sometimes, the period was also referred to as Marx's last decade. Teodor Shanin's *Late Marx and the Russian Road*, a 1983 collection of Marx's writings on the Russian *mir* (communal village), and essays on them by several leading scholars, helped make both those writings and the term "late Marx" a common point of reference.[15] The previous year, Dunayevskaya's study of Rosa Luxemburg and Marx concluded with a chapter entitled "The Last Writings of Marx Point a Trail to the 1980s,"

---

13   James D. White, *Karl Marx and the Intellectual Origins of Dialectical Materialism* (New York: St. Martin's, 1996), p. 262.

14   The term does not, however, suggest that he saw Marx as a mentor rather than an older colleague.

15   Teodor Shanin, ed., *Late Marx and the Russian Road* [hereafter referred to in the text as SHN] (New York: Monthly Review Press, 1983).

bringing to a wider intellectual public his 1879–82 excerpt notebooks on
the Global South, Indigenous societies, and gender.[16] During the previous decade, some of these notebooks had been published in near
obscurity by the US anthropologist Lawrence Krader and also the
German historian Hans-Peter Harstick. Harstick stated succinctly that
by these last years, "Marx's gaze turned from the European scene . . .
toward Asia, Africa, and North Africa."[17] Some years later, the US
anthropologist Thomas Patterson took the notebooks up in a study of
Marx as anthropologist.[18] In 2010, in *Marx at the Margins*, I devoted the
final chapter to these notebooks, some related materials, and the late
writings on Russia. Two years later, Heather Brown focused two chapters
on the late Marx in her study of Marx on gender and the family.[19] In the
last few years, Marcello Musto published an intellectual biography of
Marx's last years that shows the multiplicity of his intellectual and political endeavors during that period, while the Japanese philosopher Kohei
Saito has launched a novel interpretation of the late Marx in terms of
ecology and communal societies.[20] Recently, the Brazilian Marxist Jean
Tible has summed up some of what is at stake here, writing that Marx,

> approaching sixty years of age, could dedicate himself to the study of
> Russian in order to better understand as specific a question as agrarian
> property . . . The shifts in his theoretical production coincide with . . .

---

16   Raya Dunayevskaya, *Rosa Luxemburg, Women's Liberation, and Marx's Philosophy of Revolution*, second edition (Urbana: University of Illinois Press [1982] 1991).

17   Lawrence Krader, *The Ethnological Notebooks of Karl Marx* [hereafter referred
to in the text as EN], second edition, transcribed, edited and with an introduction by
Lawrence Krader (Assen: Van Gorcum, 1974); Lawrence Krader, *The Asiatic Mode of
Production: Sources, Development and Critique in the Writings of Karl Marx* (Assen: Van
Gorcum, 1975)—appendix contains translation of Marx's notes on Kovalevsky on India
and Algeria [hereafter referred to in the text as KOV]; Hans-Peter Harstick, ed., *Karl Marx
über Formen vorkapitalistischer Produktion* (Frankfurt: Campus Verlag, 1977), p. ii—
contains transcription of Marx's notes on Kovalevsky on Latin America [hereafter
referred in the text as KOVLM].

18   Thomas C. Patterson, *Karl Marx, Anthropologist* (New York: Berg, 2009).

19   Heather Brown, *Marx on Gender and the Family: A Critical Study* (Leiden: Brill,
2012).

20   Marcello Musto, *The Last Years of Karl Marx, 1881–1883: An Intellectual Biography* (Stanford: Stanford University Press, 2020); Kohei Saito, *Marx in the Anthropocene:
Towards the Idea of a Degrowth Communism* (New York: Cambridge University Press,
2023); Kohei Saito, *Slow Down: The Degrowth Manifesto*, trans. Brian Bergstrom (New
York: Astra House, 2024).

anticolonial mobilizations, the Russian rural communes, the political organization of the Iroquois; through all these encounters we can observe Marx shedding his Eurocentric trappings.[21]

The writings of the late Marx have been increasingly accepted by scholars working in Marxist theory as an important area of inquiry for grasping his work as a whole and its importance for today.[22] In addition, a recent major biography by Gareth Stedman Jones is the first to consider at length the late Marx, although the author minimizes the originality of these writings or their relationship to the Global South.[23] Still, Stedman Jones's biography marks a kind of turning point in that the topic of the late Marx has forced its way out the confines of a specialist area in Marxology to one that any serious treatment of Marx's work as a whole would need to consider. In another sign of this change, Ryuji Sasaki's short introduction to Marx devotes an unprecedented one-third of its space to the late Marx.[24]

I would also like to state at the outset that none of what I put forward in this book is intended to displace the centrality of capital and class in Marx's writings. I still hold that *Capital,* Vol. I, is Marx's greatest work, the one in which his method and his analysis are at their most developed point. That said, the argument in *Capital* is sometimes very abstract, considering capitalism in general rather than specific variants or junctures. This use of what Marx called "the power of abstraction" is a necessary foundation for a work that for the first time really theorized the nature, structure, and internal contradictions of the capitalist system as a whole.[25] However, it must also be said that specific forms of

---

21 Jean Tible, "A Savage Marx," *Verso Blog* (Feb. 6, 2019).

22 See, for example, Luca Basso, *Marx and the Common: From Capital to the Late Writings* (Leiden: Brill, 2015); Harry Harootunian, *Marx after Marx: History and Time in the Expansion of Capitalism* (New York: Columbia University Press, 2015).

23 Gareth Stedman Jones, *Karl Marx: Greatness and Illusion* (Cambridge, MA: Harvard University Press, 2016). For an incisive critique, see Kohei Saito, "Confining Marx to the Nineteenth Century: On Gareth Stedman Jones," *International Marxist-Humanist* (online Oct. 26, 2016).

24 Ryuji Sasaki, *A New Introduction to Karl Marx* (New York: Palgrave Macmillan, 2021).

25 Marx. *Capital,* Vol. I [hereafter referred to in the text as CAP], translated by Ben Fowkes (London: Penguin, [1890] 1976), p. 90. While I will be citing other editions of *Capital* in English, German, and French, I will usually give a reference to this edition as well, the best and most widely cited English version in recent decades.

capitalism—Irish, US, Indian, Chinese, German, and so on—exbibit important variants, in which race, gender, colonialism, and other issues not directly related to the dialectic of labor and industrial capital come to the fore, and in a multiplicity of ways. This kind of variety is even more important when one considers the loci of resistance to capital, and of revolution. In this sense, Marx was not becoming an empiricist in the narrow sense, although he did rely upon a wealth of empirical data, whether anthropological or statistical. Instead, he remained a follower— and a critic—of his intellectual mentor, Hegel, whose dialectic pointed to the fullness of human emancipation at the most abstract level of the absolute spirit, while at the same time rooting itself in concrete historical circumstances, from those of the Greco-Roman slave to the French revolutionaries of his youth.

This work is divided into six chapters.

1. Communal Social Formations and Their Vicissitudes: Marx's discussion ranges from precolonial North America, where the Iroquois shared all but the most personal property, to the ancient Germans and precolonial Ireland, which were moving toward creating class societies out of the Indigenous clans, and to the Incas of South America and the Mughals of precolonial India, where communal property in land under-girded a rigid class hierarchy dominated by small ruling groups. For Marx, nineteenth-century Russia was a particularly important example of an economy based upon communal villages underneath a despotic ruling class, here in a contemporary society that had not yet been pene-trated very much by capitalism. Other nineteenth-century societies more directly dominated by European colonialism, like those of Latin America, Algeria, and India, retained vestiges of communal structures underneath the more individualized social relations imposed by capital via colonialism.

2. Temporalities and Geographies of Gender, Kinship, and Women's Empowerment: Engels's *Origin of the Family, Private, Property, and the State* (1884), published a year after Marx's death, offered what many have considered to be too schematic a view of gender and the family. Engels based his book upon a single late Marx notebook, on evolutionary anthropologist Lewis Henry Morgan's *Ancient Society* (1877). According to Engels, early preliterate societies that were egalitar-ian along gender lines were succeeded in many parts of the world by the rise of social classes, private property, the state, and unmitigated male domination. Ancient Greece and Rome as well as Native American societies served as his prime examples. Marx's notes concerning gender—drawn from Morgan but also from other writers—show a wider range of topics and sources, including anthropology and social history on colonial India and Algeria, ancient Greece and Rome, Native American groups, and Ireland. Also in contrast to Engels, Marx's notes develop a subtler interpretation of Morgan and other anthropologists and social historians. On the one hand, Marx differs with Engels and Morgan in discerning more elements of gender inequality and other forms of incipient hierarchy in preliterate societies, thus avoiding Engels's almost Rousseauian idealization. On the other hand, Marx sees a later patriarchal domination that is more permeable, here in contrast to Engels's simplistically Hegelianized concept of a world historic defeat of the female sex. Another key issue is whether vestiges of female social power remain in the contemporary peripheral societies that Marx was analyzing in his last years.

3. Multilinear Concepts of Historical and Social Development: In his early writings, Marx put forth a sequence of modes of production and predominant types of social labor: "primitive" (hunter-gatherers), ancient (enslaved laborers), feudal (enserfed peasants), and "bourgeois" (wage laborers). In the *Grundrisse* (1857–58), he incorporates an "Asiatic" mode of production, suggesting that precolonial Asian societies were on a different trajectory. But it is only in his late writings that Marx makes this change explicit. For example, he attacks vehemently those who imported European-based categories to characterize Mughal India as feudal. In the French edition of *Capital* (1872–75), a version of the book that is getting increasing attention, he adopts a similarly multilinear perspective as he rewrites some key passages to state that societies outside Western Europe will not necessarily follow the British pathway of development.[26] He repeatedly refers to this change in his late writings on Russia.

4. Colonialism and Resistance: While the *Communist Manifesto* of 1848 and his 1853 *New York Tribune* writings on India portrayed British colonial rule as a painful but necessary form of modernization, Marx's late writings offer scathing accounts of British rule in India and French rule in Algeria, the latter with a gender dimension. In his 1879 notes on India, he covers the Sepoy Uprising of 1857–59 with great enthusiasm,

---

26 Marx, *Das Kapital*, Vol. I, ed. Thomas Kuczynski (Hamburg: VSA, 2017); Marcello Musto, ed., *Marx and* Le Capital.

while at the same time pointing to remnants of communal social relations as possible loci of anticolonial resistance. In his 1879 notes on Latin
America, he describes Spanish annihilation and enslavement of the
Indigenous population in the early sixteenth century, but he also notes
that the lessening of that exploitation under Church pressure led to
another type of exploitation, the mass importation of enslaved Africans.
Fourteen years before his death, in 1869, Marx also reversed his earlier
position that Ireland's liberation depended upon the success the British
labor movement. He now argued that British workers, increasingly
bound to the dominant classes by colonialist ideology, would not be able
to achieve much for themselves until Ireland was free of British rule.

   5. **Rome, India, and Russia: Three Agrarian Societies in Flux**: In his
late writings and notebooks, Marx gives particular attention to three
precapitalist societies: contemporary Russia, India, and, in a very different historical period, ancient Rome. India under the British and Rome
under the Republic had undergone, albeit in different ways, the uprooting of their earlier, more communal and egalitarian social structures at
the village level. By the early nineteenth century, India had seen the
large-scale destruction of these communes at the hands of British colonialism, while ancient Rome experienced during its republican period
the decline of its free peasant population in the face of large estates
worked by slave labor. The hostility of free plebeians toward the enslaved
population, which Marx saw as akin to modern racism, forestalled a
social revolution. In Russia in the 1870s and 1880s, pressure from
Western European capitalism was undermining the communal villages.
Ancient Rome and contemporary Russia each had some features that
could have led toward capitalism, but to Marx their differences from
capitalism were even more striking. Above all, he now denied the inevitability of an evolution toward capitalism in Russia and probably other
non-capitalist lands as well. This represented a move away from the
somewhat teleological framework of the *Communist Manifesto*, wherein
all societies around the world were moving in the same direction, with
some further behind than others.

   6. **New Concepts of Revolutionary Change and of Alternatives to
Capitalism**: The late Marx concretized and developed his concept of
revolution, specifying and bending the general theory of a workers'
uprising in a highly developed capitalism with which he ended *Das
Kapital* in 1867. In 1869–70, Marx writes that a British workers' uprising

might be sparked from outside by the revolutionary movement in Ireland being led by the peasant-based Fenian nationalist movement. Inside Britain, English prejudice and condescension toward the Irish permeated the working classes and undercut the formation of class consciousness. However, Irish independence would shake up what Marx saw as the quasi-racist anti-Irish animus of English workers, helping the largest and most organized contemporary working class to see more clearly what he regarded as its true interests. During this same period, Marx clarifies and deepens his concept of communism in the *Civil War in France* (1871), and in the *Critique of the Gotha Program* (1875), in which he sketches non-statist forms of free and associated labor that go beyond the more centralist and statist notions put forward earlier in the *Communist Manifesto*. Similarly, in his 1877–82 writings on Russia, Marx suggests that uprisings in its communal villages against capitalist encroachments could lead to a form of modern communism, if these uprisings could link up with the Western European labor movement. On Algeria and India, his notes on communal village structures and anti-colonial resistance imply something similar. Another important issue to consider is to what extent his notes on gender impacted his new concepts of revolution.

Work on this book was assisted by my access to the transcriptions of several hundred pages of Marx notebooks before their 2024 publication. This results from my participation over a decade ago in a group working on an edited volume of his 1879–82 excerpt notebooks as part of a US National Endowment for the Humanities–supported Collaborative Research Grant connected to the *Marx-Engels Gesamtausgabe* (MEGA2). I would like to thank the MEGA2 editors, particularly Gerald Hubmann and Jürgen Rojahn, for access to material that appeared in 2024 in MEGA2 IV/27, which several others and I intend eventually to publish in English. I would also like to thank David Norman Smith for access to his forthcoming annotated English translation of Krader's multilingual edition of Marx's *Ethnological Notebooks*. In addition, I am grateful to the American Council of Learned Societies for a one-year fellowship in 2020, which allowed me to complete a rough draft of all the chapters.

1

Communal Social Formations and Their Vicissitudes

During his last working years, 1869–82, Marx's long-standing interest in communal social formations and their vicissitudes intensifies. It is crucial to note that he is interested in something broader here than communal property, which is too superficial a category for his investigations. He focuses on communal social formations or forms, for two reasons: (1) some of the societies Marx considers not to have developed much in the way of property, communal or otherwise; and (2) in terms of Marx's theorization of social formations and modes of production from the 1840s onward, the defining feature is the form of social labor used to sustain society rather than property forms, which are a secondary characteristic. For example, as early as 1844, in his essay on alienated labor, he maintains: "Private property is therefore the product, the necessary result, of alienated labor."[1] And, in a celebrated line three years later in *The Poverty of Philosophy*, Marx views the type of labor as the determinant of what he is later to call modes of production: "The hand-mill gives you society with the lord [*suzerain*]; the steam-mill, society with the industrial capitalist" (MECW 6: 166).[2] As the American anthropologist and Marx

---

1 Marx, "Economic and Philosophical Manuscripts," trans. Tom Bottomore, in Erich Fromm, *Marx's Concept of Man* (New York: Ungar, 1961), pp. 105–6.

2 French original: Marx, *Oeuvres, Économie* I, ed. Maximilien Rubel (Paris: Éditions Gallimard, 1963), p. 79. The latter does not contain the term "feudal" as a modifier of "lord" [*suzerain*], giving Marx's point a wider range.

scholar Lawrence Krader sums up, in Marx's work, "the relation of property is subordinate to the mode of production" (EN: 120).

In his 1879–82 notebooks, Marx delves deeper into the communal institutions found among preliterate societies. In this sense, he is exploring the origins of property alongside those of class, the state, and gender subordination.

But in another sense, he is looking at his own time with new eyes. As will be discussed in chapter 6, he theorizes the Paris Commune of 1871 as a modern social revolution that went a long way toward substituting a communal form of governance for the modern centralized state, a struggle he sees as a model for future working-class revolutions. By 1882, in his last published text, he views the long-standing village communes of the Russian peasantry as the social base for a modern revolution that could link up with the Western proletariat. In these senses and others, he was rethinking his concept of the communal, of what he sometimes called primitive communism.

Before the 1870s, Marx views premodern communal social formations less affirmatively, as either props for harsh forms of domination or as vestiges of a somewhat attractive but long-dead past. In "British Rule in India," a June 25, 1853, *New York Tribune* article criticized for its Eurocentrism by Edward Said and many others, he writes:[3]

> We must not forget that these idyllic village-communities, inoffensive though they may appear, had always been the solid foundation of Oriental despotism, that they restrained the human mind within the smallest possible compass, making it the unresisting tool of superstition, enslaving it beneath traditional rules, depriving it of all grandeur and historical energies. (MECW 12: 132)

Here, in 1853, the communal formation is conceptualized as a barrier to human progress. These kinds of social forms, as Marx sees it, are also present in Russia, a society whose political structures were formed by an "Oriental despotism" originally forged under "Asiatic" Mongol rule. He

---

3 Edward Said, *Orientalism* (New York: Vintage, 1978). While acknowledging Marx's early Eurocentrism and even favorability toward aspects of colonialism, Gilbert Achcar makes a nuanced Marxist response to Said in his *Marxism, Orientalism, Cosmopolitanism* (Chicago: Haymarket, 2013).

sees Tsarist Russia, a regime founded upon communal property in the villages, as more dangerous to human progress than the Indian village commune, which merely blocked progress. For Russia's communal villages formed the economic foundation of a state that was the most reactionary power in Europe, as seen in both its internal despotism and its multiple counterrevolutionary military interventions. For Marx and his generation, Russia's massive 1849 intervention not only saved the Austro-Hungarian Empire from the democratic revolution but also constituted a decisive blow against the overall European revolution, whose defeat sent Marx into exile in London.

Over a decade later, in the commodity fetishism section of *Capital*, Marx theorizes premodern communal forms in less pejorative language. Nonetheless, he sees them as products of an earlier stage of humanity with no relevance to modern communism:

> Those ancient social organisms of production are much more simple and transparent than those of bourgeois society. But they are founded either on the immaturity of the human individual who has not yet been torn loose from the umbilical cord of a natural species-connection with other human beings, or on direct relations of domination and servitude. They are conditioned by a low level of development of the productive powers of labor and correspondingly restricted human relationships within the process of creating and reproducing their material life. (CAP: 172–3)

Thus, to the extent that contemporary Russian or Indian communal villages represented social relations different from modern capitalism, they were simply archaic social forms that were no longer viable amid capitalist modernity.

Marx moves away from this kind of framework in his last years. Beginning around 1879, he studies a wide variety of preliterate stateless societies intensively. These societies fell into various types, across wide geographic and temporal boundaries. As discussed above, the term "communal property" is often applied to these societies in Marxist theory. But that term is inexact, because, as mentioned above, several of the societies Marx investigates in his last years had little in the way of property of any kind, save small amounts of personal property. Other societies, or later stages of the same ones, developed property as an institution, albeit still in communal forms, along with greater social hierarchy. These early forms of communal property often included landed property and slave property. At a later point, many of these societies developed social classes and individually held private property, but several had not done so, even by Marx's own era. Let us look now at how Marx studies these kinds of communal social organizations and property forms during his last years.

Classless Clan Societies among Native Americans

In 1879–82, Marx studies several Native American groups, and, very briefly, Australian Aborigines, as examples of preliterate societies that lack much in the way of even communal property. These societies also lack clear-cut social classes. The prime example he considers is the Iroquois of North America, who engage in communal labor and social organization at a fairly low technological level. While they demarcate hunting territories, they develop neither landed nor slave property. Marx's principal source for the Iroquois is American anthropologist Henry Lewis Morgan's *Ancient Society* (1877), which he annotates at great length, also making many favorable comments. In the Morgan notes, he also covers the Aztecs as his other prime example of a clan society, albeit one at a higher level of technological development.

Let us begin with the theoretically sophisticated framework Marx found in Morgan's *Ancient Society*. Krader estimates in his introduction to the *Ethnological Notebooks* that Marx's notes on Morgan were composed in late 1880 or early 1881, about a year after those on Kovalevsky's book on communal property in Latin America, India, and Algeria (EN: 87–9). As the Brazilian anthropologist Lucas Parreira Álvares notes, Marx reorders Morgan's data and argument by moving the discussion of "government" in his notes from near the beginning to the end, a procedure that Engels also follows in *Origin of the Family*.[4] This probably reflects Marx's anti-statist position, as opposed to that of an anthropologist who was also a US civil servant.

---

4 Lucas Parreira Álvares, "On Karl Marx's 'Ethnological Notebooks,'" *Critique* 49: 3–4, p. 219.

In *Ancient Society*, Morgan analyzes the Iroquois as his prime example of a classless clan society with little in the way of property, a procedure Marx follows in his notes. However, the Iroquois were further on the way toward a class society than were the much simpler societies to be mentioned below. In Morgan's language, they had already passed from the stage of "savagery"—a hunter-gatherer society in contemporary usage— to the "lower status of barbarism"—a semi-agricultural society in later usage—at the time when they encountered European colonialism.

Marx begins his notes on Morgan by delineating—and sometimes criticizing—the American anthropologist's identification of four stages of social development, up through early Greco-Roman society. The first of these is exemplified by hunter-gatherer or "savage" societies, which Morgan covers only briefly: "Property of savages inconsiderable; rude weapons, fabrics, utensils, apparel, implements of flint, stone, and bone and 'personal ornaments' their chief items of property," also noting the absence of the "passion for possession" (EN: 128).[5] Property in land, such as it is, is demarcated territory held in common.

Marx then moves into a second stage of development, semi-agricultural societies like the Iroquois, who were, in Morgan's schema, in the "lower status of barbarism." Marx singles out in his notes the material basis of this stage of development: "Principal inventions: art of pottery, finger weaving, and the art of cultivation" of maize (EN: 128; MG: 528). With the clan or gens now dominant, this institution—rather than the biological children—inherits the personal property of the deceased. Marx quotes Morgan on this as the "first great rule" of inheritance, a point he emphasizes with a checkmark in the margin of his notebook (EN: 128; MG: 528). He also emphasizes the matrilineal aspects of clan-based inheritance at this stage, to be discussed more in chapter 2.

The third stage is exemplified by agricultural village societies like the Aztecs, who, having developed systems of irrigation and adobe houses with some walls for defense, were in what Morgan calls the "middle status of barbarism." These societies also create, at their top layers, a priesthood and an "aristocratic element" among the clan "chiefs, civil

---

5   See also Lewis Henry Morgan, *Ancient Society* [hereafter MG, with page references directly in the text], second and corrected edition (New York: Henry Holt, 1878), p. 527. Here and elsewhere when quoting Marx's notes, I have left intact his sometimes rough and ungrammatical language rather than, for example, adding verbs or creating subject-object agreement when it is missing. Italics mostly represent Marx's own underlining.

and military," albeit "in feeble forms" (EN: 131; MG: 534). However, they did not develop either chattel slavery or flocks of domestic animals as expressions of wealth. The absence of large flocks is conditioned by the paucity in the Western Hemisphere of domesticable animals like horses, sheep, or cows, leaving only dogs and llamas available for this purpose. In their gender relations, these Native American societies retained some matrilineal elements but were moving toward structures of patrilineal descent. Marx seems to appreciate the multilinear aspects of Morgan's analysis here, especially his rejection of Western European–based categories like feudalism as descriptive of Aztec society. Thus, Marx seems to be in accord with the anthropologist's critique of the "inextricable confusion" of early Spanish accounts, which "saw a feudal estate," with chiefs akin to landowning "feudal lords," rather than developing an accurate picture of the "land owned in common" (EN: 133; MG: 537).

Early Greco-Roman society represents an example of a fourth stage, Morgan's "upper status of barbarism." Here, while some land is beginning to be held privately, most of it is still held in common. At this juncture, Marx makes three telling critiques of Morgan. First, he points to what he considers to be Morgan's rushing to conclusions about the development of private property in land as far back as the Mycenaean Greeks of Homer's *Iliad*, writing that "Morgan errs when he believes that the mere presence of fencing proves private property in land" on any significant scale. Marx expresses a second point of difference with the anthropologist here, as Morgan also sees this ostensible privatization as a form of "progress" (EN: 134; MG: 542). Third, Marx questions Morgan's account of the sixth-century BCE Athenian lawgiver Solon as establishing "testamentary" inheritance to replace the clan-based system (EN: 138; MG: 549). Thus, Marx seems to believe that Morgan is jumping the gun on the development of private property, also disagreeing with his view of this development as a form of progress.

Marx seems, however, to align with Morgan's theories concerning chattel slavery as a major factor in the origin of property during early Greco-Roman society: "Slavery originates in this status; it stands directly connected with the production of property" (EN: 133; MG: 540). This is a theme to which Marx will return. Slaveholding also spurs the development of aristocratic rule, not least because slave labor gains for those who appropriate its social product a huge advantage over free commoners dependent upon the far more meager product of their own labor.

Also important at this stage are large flocks of domestic animals, to Morgan the prime form of wealth in the era before landed property. Marx records and seems in accord with Morgan's statement that "their possession revealed to the human mind the first conception of wealth" (EN: 135; MG: 542–3). This point is a bit complicated because, as discussed above, enslaved people also constituted an early form of property, and the temporal relation of these two developments is unclear. Again disagreeing explicitly with what he seems to view as another of Morgan's anachronistic interpretations, Marx distances himself from the importance the anthropologist gives to money in gold at this early stage (EN: 135; MG: 542–3).

Marx ends his notes on this part of Morgan by appearing to identify with the American anthropologist's conclusions about the deleterious effects of what was in that period launched as the "property career" of humankind. To Morgan, this "is not the final destiny of mankind." Instead, Morgan, as recorded by Marx, looks forward to

> the termination of a career of which property is the end and aim; because such a career contains the elements of self-destruction . . . It (a higher plan of society) will be a revival, in a higher form, of the liberty, equality and fraternity of the ancient gentes [clans].[6] (EN: 139; MG: 552)

This opens the way for Marx's admiring account of the Iroquois, albeit with reservations not found in Morgan, or for that matter, in his comrade Engels's *Origin of the Family*.

Let us look more closely at Marx's detailed investigations of these technologically underdeveloped Native American societies, investigations that seem to have begun not with the study of Morgan's book, but with his 1879 notes on Kovalevsky. Marx appears to have first read and annotated his young friend Kovalevsky's *Communal Landownership: The Causes, Course, and Consequences of Its Dissolution* in September 1879, shortly after the Russian anthropologist gifted him a copy of the book (EN: 343). Although its title is sometimes translated from the Russian as "Communal Property," the book's focus is not on communal

---

6   Morgan, Marx, and Engels often used the Roman Latin term *gens* (also *gentes*, gentile) more generally to refer to clans in societies across the world.

property in general, but communal land tenure in particular, since its Russian title, *Obscinnoe zemlevladenie*, could also be translated as "Communal Land Tenure." Kovalevsky takes only slight account of Morgan's analysis published two years earlier, giving little attention to the American anthropologist's emphasis on gender and kinship.

In a passage Marx records in his notebook, Kovalevsky stresses the lack of private property among some of the least technologically developed Native American societies:

> On the American continent the *Eastern Dakota* of North America and the *Botocudos of Brazil* are found in this relatively oldest form. The *Dakota* (*Waitz*) migrate constantly from place to place in the *hunt for buffalo* . . . (28) Among them the products of the hunt *not private property* but *communal goods of the whole group of hunters*. Everybody obtains his "equal" share. *No domestication of animals*. Therefore even *food originally not private property*. (29) . . . Among the *Dakota* only the *clothing* he wears counts as *private property* and those *more or less primitive weapons* that *serve* him as *tools in the fight with organic and inorganic nature*. Similarly among the Botocudos private property only: *weapons* (or tools), *clothing* and *ornament*. Everything else among them *communal goods* of one or several *families communally living together and interrelated*. (KOVLM: 22)[7]

It is striking that even the food supply is not very individualized in these societies, with weapons, tools, clothing, and ornaments the only really personal property. For his part, Marx may be expressing a bit of skepticism here, adding his own scare quotes to the term "equal" in Kovalevsky's phrase "equal shares." He will continue to make these kinds of inserts or remarks, often suggesting that social hierarchies may have emerged earlier than his anthropological sources are indicating. And, as will be taken up later, Engels, in his *Origin of the Family*, did not exhibit this degree of skepticism toward his main source, Morgan's *Ancient Society*.

---

7   I will be giving in-text references to the transcription of Kovalevsky's notes on Latin America by Harstick, which was until recently the only published version. But for all of Marx's notes on Kovalevsky, I will be quoting the forthcoming MEGA IV/27 version, transcribed and edited by Norair Ter-Akopian, Georgi Bagaturia, and Jürgen Rojahn, in the annotated translation prepared for later publication by Charles Reitz and me, with assistance from Lars Lih for Russian terms.

Hunting and fishing form the material base of these kinds of societies, with some agriculture in small plots, in what Kovalevsky refers to as the primal horde stage, and which is today usually termed a hunter-gatherer society. As Marx records material on this from Kovalevsky, he inserts in brackets or parentheses some clarifying remarks:

> During the oldest period of the horde form—nomadic, not sedentary, living only from *hunting wild animals and fishing*—oldest form of property (*'immovables'* do not yet exist) *possession in common,* because *cooperation is indispensable* in their battle with nature, *only through united powers can they wrest from her* that which is necessary for life (1.c.) [[The products themselves as communal *product* are property of the *horde.*]] (KOVLM: 23–4)

Marx, like Kovalevsky, is also interested in the transition to a more property-oriented society, which both see as emerging alongside settled agriculture. He annotates a passage in Kovalevsky giving Morgan's materialist interpretation of this transition:

> *Morgan (Systems of consanguinity* etc. p.173) remarks that as a *consequence of population increase with no possibility of a corresponding expansion of the territory occupied,* the Dakota just like *most of the American tribes, must either change to agriculture* and livestock husbandry *as the chief occupations* or disappear from the face of the earth (38 N. 4) This the case in North, Central, South America. (1.c.) (KOVLM: 25)

This takes these societies toward more hierarchical forms, albeit fluid ones, as in the following passage Marx records from Kovalevsky:

> Associated with such a *transition to agriculture as main occupation* a *settling down* of this or that people at first for *longer or shorter periods* but over time *definitively* at the chosen *abiding place.* This latter *"usually"* appears not uninhabited, but already occupied for a long time by *foreign tribal populations,* which give up their settled (cultivated?) lands only under compulsion; these become mere *class of slaves* at first, *dependent on the conquerors;* over time they acquire for themselves, bit by bit, *equality of rights with the ruling tribe;* often

forming from the beginning the numerical majority, increasing from time to time through new groups of enslaved prisoners of war, the subjugated tribe obtains sometimes, *finally*, after century-long efforts, a more favorable reorganization of the land and property relations. Quite varied *forms of landed property* arise from this. (KOVLM: 25)

This marks the transition to societies like the Aztecs and the Incas, to be discussed below. As before, Marx inserts quotation marks around a word, "usually," suggesting that Kovalevsky is softening his account by implying that such territories are sometimes empty. His parenthetical question "cultivated?" seems to be about whether these conquered societies were also agricultural, and it appears to be a complaint about a lack of clarity in Kovalevsky's account.

Marx's notes on Morgan concentrate heavily on the society to which Morgan himself devotes the most attention, the Iroquois of North America, which Marx, quoting Morgan, describes as practicing "communism in living" (EN: 115). Marx also records in his notes the clan (gentile) foundation of this society, with two or more clans forming a phratry and several phratries a tribe, and with the powerful Iroquois Confederacy becoming a structure uniting five tribes. It lacked a state, social classes, or property in land. At an economic level, it was at an early agricultural stage of development (Morgan's "lower status of barbarism"), with some farming but also hunting and gathering.

Iroquois society exhibits many democratic features that Morgan admires. Marx does so as well, albeit with a dose of skepticism. In this system, clans elect male sachems (peace chiefs) as well as war chiefs, but these offices are not hereditary. The highest decision-making body within a tribe is the council of chiefs representing the various clans. The council meets in public, with non-chiefs having the right to speak, thus incorporating a wide public opinion. This includes women's voices, but with some limitations to be discussed in the next chapter. Another democratic feature lies in the fact that chiefs and sachems can be deposed. Since the clans are matrilineal, sons of leaders do not succeed them, as the son would have been from a different clan. This undercuts the possibility of monarchy and also attenuates the development of patriarchal hierarchies.

Nonetheless, trends in the direction of hierarchy are present. Theoretically, the Iroquois tribes were at war with all other societies around them, unless a peace treaty was in effect, as was the case within the Iroquois Confederacy itself. As wars were not a constant feature of social life, the post of war chief was not initially a permanent one, as was that of sachem or peace chief. However, there was some evolution after the beginning of European contact in the direction of a supreme war chief with stronger powers. Morgan writes: "The introduction of this office as a permanent feature in the government was a great event in the history of human progress" (MG: 146). In his notes, Marx highlights this passage but rewords it in a way that both rejects Morgan's progressivist evolutionism and views extremely negatively any such evolution in the direction of state formation: "The introduction of this office as a permanent feature disastrous [verhängnisvoll][8] event in human history" (EN: 173). This passage dramatically illustrates Marx's deepening antagonism toward the state in his late writings, as will be discussed in chapter 6.

Iroquois wars took place for many reasons, one of which was to obtain captives to replenish tribal ranks. Marx gives some emphasis to Morgan's report that "slavery . . . was unknown among tribes" in societies like the Iroquois (EN: 148). Instead, captives were either burned at the stake, or if more fortunate, adopted with the status of brothers or sisters of clan members. However, this meant that to survive the captives were forced to adopt and perform such social roles.

Marx also records Morgan's data about the conquest of entire tribes by more powerful ones, here looking at another society at a similar level of development to the Iroquois, the Athabascans of the Pacific Northwest. In so doing, he speculates about such conquests as the origin of caste hierarchies from within the more egalitarian clan [gentile] societies. Adopting the dialectical language of transformation into opposite, Marx writes that since clans or gentes practiced endogamy, these kinds of exclusions could, in the hierarchical context of such a conquest, "get into conflict with the gentile principle and harden the gens into its opposite, caste" (EN: 183). Krader calls this "the most explicitly dialectical of all of Marx's formulations" in his notes on Morgan (EN: 15). It strongly demarcates Marx's reflections from Morgan's more unilinear evolutionism. In terms of Marx's own theorization of caste, as Krader also remarks, Marx by now sees caste not as a vestige of very early, almost

---

8   Could also be translated, slightly less ominously, as "fatal," but the negative charge of the word "disastrous" seems closer to Marx's meaning.

"natural" distinctions, as he had in *Capital* and his early writings, but as a later development on the road toward social class that could have even been enacted explicitly via legal arrangements (EN: 404n160).

Marx records text from Morgan on how, when societies like the Iroquois grow larger as more widespread agriculture supports a bigger population, the practices of hunter-gatherer society recede. Cultivated land is still held in common, with maize as the staple crop. At the same time, however, individual possessory rights to specific plots of land emerge. Still, the development of property is blocked by the fact that these allotments are inherited through the clan and not the individual (EN: 129).

A far more populous and technologically developed form of clan society arose in in the Valley of Mexico under the seven tribes of the Aztec Confederacy in the early fifteenth century. Here, Marx relies on Spanish accounts from the sixteenth century, reading them critically via his deeper knowledge of Iroquois society, gleaned from both his own research and that of other observers of Iroquois daily life and institutions. In Morgan's schema, Aztec society exemplifies the "middle status of barbarism," while the Iroquois remain at the "lower" stage of this status. Marx records Morgan's point concerning higher technological development among the Aztecs, as exemplified by "mechanical engineering" feats like a causeway across Lake Texcoco, "one of the greatest achievements of the Aztecs" (EN: 188). The Aztecs possess more advanced weapons than the Iroquois, a writing system, a very accurate solar calendar, a priesthood to maintain it, and, at a political level, a paramount war chief.

Despite this, Marx considers Aztec political development to have been below that of the Iroquois, who achieved a relatively stable, substantially democratic society and, more importantly in this context, the ability to integrate conquered people. He writes: "The Aztec confederacy—in plan and symmetry—lower than that of the Iroquois" (EN: 190). He judges them here in somewhat harsher fashion than Morgan, who writes more circumspectly, "The government they formed probably not equal in plan and symmetry with that of the Iroquois" (MG: 196). Unlike the Romans who assimilated subject peoples, albeit in an inferior status, the Aztecs allowed conquered peoples to keep their own chiefs and clans, while at the same time forcefully subjugating them and demanding sacrificial victims. As Marx records Morgan, this led to "holding these tribes under burdens, inspired by enmity and always ready to revolt" (EN: 189).

Marx also adapts Morgan's division of these stateless societies into three stages in terms of treatment of captives: (1) sacrificial death or adoption (Iroquois); (2) sacrifice (Aztecs); and (3) chattel slavery (Greco-Romans). Morgan writes of these practices as exemplifying three stages of "barbarism," with slavery only coming to an end with difficulty, as "civilization and Christianity combined were required for its displacement" (MG: 193). With a different stress, Marx incorporates the latter passage into his notes, but with the phrase "so-called" modifying the word "civilization" (EN: 189). Something more is going on here than Marx's disparagement of Morgan's sugarcoating of more than two millennia of widespread chattel slavery in Western "civilization," much of it under Christianity. For it is likely also connected to Marx's theorization of slavery as a prime example of the emergence of property, as discussed above.

As mentioned above, Marx also records approvingly Morgan's critique of Spanish accounts of Aztec society as resembling European feudalism. While a permanent war chief existed, this office was not hereditary. Moreover, Aztec clans, based in different districts of the city or in rural areas, appear to have retained a somewhat democratic internal structure. Some chieftaincies were hereditary, but land was held in common and could not be alienated from the clans. Some evidence also existed of a council of chiefs as an administrative body. In these senses, Aztec society is an example of a communal social structure, albeit more developed technologically and much more hierarchical than that of the Iroquois, but similar in most respects.

In his 1879 notes on Kovalevsky, Marx also takes up Aztec society, but, apparently not yet having read Morgan, he places less stress on the clan element and more on the creation of an aristocracy, which Kovalevsky ties to a precolonial version of feudalism. Of course, this "feudal" notion was something Morgan and Marx regarded as a misreading of the evidence, a critique Marx was to apply with vehemence to Kovalevsky's analysis of India. One important society covered in these notes on Kovalevsky—but not found in those on Morgan or in Morgan's book—is the Inca Empire of South America.

Despite his "feudal" analysis, Kovalevsky stresses the clan structure of precolonial Mexico and Peru. Marx's notes on Kovalevsky also stress the "clan-obshchina, clan-commune" as the foundation of these societies, here using *obshchina*, a Russian term for village commune, alongside the

German one, *Gemeinde*, for these Amerindian societies (KOVLM: 26). This suggests that he sees connections between these two social institutions. These communes of precolonial America hold the land, which cannot be alienated by individuals or individual families. In Inca society, a ruling group has by now appeared, as in this description Marx records from Kovalevsky:

> The communes, *so far free from any dues* to anybody, become, in Peru, bound to *payments in kind* to the *government* on the one hand, and to the *priesthood* on the other; and indeed to each of these two, 1/3 of the product of the lands belonging to them. This led to the *assignment of certain lands* within the borders of each commune, *one for the Sun God, and the other for the Inca*. (KOVLM: 27)

In this respect, the notes on Kovalevsky give a clearer explanation than Morgan of the relations of domination in highly developed precolonial societies of the Americas. But to Marx, Kovalevsky's account is also marred by an attempt to fit them into a feudal model.

In one of the rare discussions to date of Marx's notes on Kovalevsky on the Americas, the Bolivian Marxist Álvaro García Linera has tied them to the prospects of a different type of revolution:

> Against this "feudalist" position, Marx was concerned with grasping the real nature of societies with extensive communitarian relations, because that communitarian aspect, still widely surviving under colonization and industrial capitalism, was for him the key and the possibility for socialist revolution in those countries, without being obligated to pass through the complete proletarianization of society.[9]

Garcia Linera's interpretation is similar to the one put forward in the present book concerning a number of societies Marx took up in his last years, from the Americas to India and from Russia to North Africa.

---

9   I would like to thank Patrick Cabell for allowing me to cite his forthcoming translation from the Spanish of Garcia Linera's 1989 analysis of Marx's notes on Kovalevsky.

Ancient Greco-Roman Clan Society

Marx next considers Morgan's treatment of ancient Greco-Roman society at its early, pre-class stage of development, sometimes called the archaic period. Morgan and Marx treat Greco-Roman society on the whole as a single social formation. To be sure, they note that it is technologically more advanced in some ways than the Aztecs, and markedly more so than the Iroquois. Nonetheless, Morgan and Marx find numerous affinities between these early European societies and Native American ones, especially the Iroquois, in this sense reading or rereading very early Greco-Roman institutions through the lens of Iroquois ones. Because Morgan and Marx lack contemporary accounts of the egalitarian clan and gender structures they find in this early history, they search them out via deconstructions of later sources written from more class-bound and patriarchal perspectives. This produces key insights on the transition from clan to class structures and the profound changes in gender relations during the same period; the latter issue will be discussed more in chapter 2. Given that Marx knew vastly more about Greco-Roman than Native American societies, here he often intersperses his notes on Morgan with additions from original Greek and Latin sources. Marx also quotes key nineteenth-century authorities on ancient Greco-Roman society like Theodor Mommsen, Barthold Niebuhr, and George Grote, whom he often criticizes for their patriarchal assumptions, which he sees as having been refuted or undermined by Morgan's new interpretation. This represents a changed attitude toward these historians, for, as Paola Foraboschi underlines, Marx "used extensively and esteemed" Niebuhr in his treatment of precapitalist economic formations in the *Grundrisse*.[10]

In Morgan's interpretation, which Marx views as a major innovation, the archaic Greek societies of the era portrayed in the *Iliad* were not kingdoms, but rather chieftaincies based upon clans or gentes. Thus, Agamemnon, the commander of Greek (Achaean) forces during the Trojan War as recounted in the *Iliad*, is not a king (as Homer writes) but a paramount war chief appointed on a temporary basis. Entitled the

---

10   Paola Foraboschi, "The Ethnological Notebooks on Karl Marx. Some Remarks," *Beiträge zur Marx-Engels Forschung*, New Series (Berlin: Argument Verlag, 1994), p. 108.

basileus, this office is now seen by Morgan as analogous to the Iroquois or Aztec war chief. Thus, the power of the *basileus* was restricted, as he had to contend with both a council of chiefs or *boulé* and an assembly of the citizens or *agora*.

Marx offers a long comment on this in the context of the war chief Achilles's debate with Agamemnon over the distribution of booty after a battle in which Achilles played a key part. Here is an excerpt:

> Considering that the Greeks appeared before Troy only qua army, things in the agora go on democratically enough. Achilles, when he speaks of "gifts," i.e. distribution of booty, constantly appoints as dispenser, not Agamemnon, not any other Basileus, but "*the sons of the Achaeans*," the people. (EN: 207)

Marx also notes that evolution toward aristocracy or monarchy was very slow, even though the communal groups that included those like Achilles were themselves overlords dominating a plebeian population. For even as the *basileus* gained more authority, taking over priestly and judicial as well as military functions, "he appears never to have exercised civil functions," Marx writes, here recording a passage from Morgan (EN: 189; MG: 250). Thus, the transition to a real aristocracy was blocked at this point by Greek society's deeply rooted clan structure.

In reading Greek history in this manner, Morgan and Marx are seeking to penetrate the monarchist, patriarchal veneer of texts like those of Homer, written centuries after the events they describe. As David Smith notes, such a critique of "authority fetishism" runs throughout the late Marx: "Often, Marx pauses to criticize scholars and colonists who imagine that they see the hand of the patriarch or the feudal lord in social relations that are inherently nonpatriarchal and nonfeudal."[11]

For his part, Morgan makes a detailed list of the rights of Greek clans or gentes drawn from Grote, who, wrongly in his view, saw these as artificial or even contrived. Grote's list, as adapted by Morgan and summarized by Marx, includes (1) common religious ceremonies; (2) a common burial place; (3) mutual rights of inheritance; (4) reciprocal defense and right of retribution against foes; (5) rules concerning

---

11 David Smith, "Accumulation and the Clash of Cultures: Marx's Ethnology in Context," *Rethinking Marxism* 14: 4 (2002), p. 8.

intermarriage with other clans or gentes; (6) "possession in some cases at least of common property"; (7) patrilineal descent; (8) prohibition (with some exceptions) of marriage within the clan or gens except in the case of heiresses to large property holdings; (9) right to adopt strangers; and (10) right to elect and depose chiefs (EN: 198). Morgan and Marx see points seven (patrilineal descent) and eight (allowing heiresses rather than clan to inherit) as aspects of the overthrow of the ancient, more egalitarian clan structures.

In the middle of enumerating these key features of archaic Greek clan society, Marx remarks, "Through the Grecian gens the savage [*die Wilde*][12] (for example, Iroquois) also peers through unmistakably" (EN: 198). Marx is here emphasizing the need to peel away layers of ideological distortion on the part of the cultural representatives of the new class-bound and patriarchal "classical" Greek society to glimpse the older, more communistic one. In so doing, Marx sharpens and makes more precise the more circumspect language of Morgan, who writes: "The similarities between the Grecian and the Iroquois gens will at once be recognized" (MG: 222).

In terms of how deep that peeling away needed to go, Marx again sharpens a criticism by Morgan of Grote, writing that the British historian fails to realize "that although the Greeks took their gentes from mythology, the former are themselves more ancient than their self-created mythology with its gods and demi-gods" (EN: 200). Thus, as Marx sketches it from Morgan's study—since no accounts still existed of its structure in its older, fuller form—the archaic Greek clan or gens could be discerned by what remnants of clan or gentile structures still persisted.

Theseus and Incipient Class Divisions

In Morgan's study, the figure of Theseus, a mythical Athenian ruler from the period supposedly some centuries after that of the Trojan War, is seen as having begun the transition from a society structured by clans to

---

12 Could also be translated as "wild state." It should be noted that the term "savage" was often viewed positively by Marx and his contemporaries, and his use of it here is probably more analogous to Rousseau's "noble savage" than to the ideologies of settler colonialism or modern racism. Even today, a spontaneous or wildcat workers' strike is termed a "wilde Streik" in German (and similarly in French, a "grève sauvage").

one by social classes. Marx seems to accept from Morgan the notion that the figure of Theseus represents "the name of a period or a series of events," not a historical individual as in Greek semi-mythical accounts (EN: 209). Relying heavily on Plutarch's account of Theseus, Marx writes that the efforts of the latter, or rather the social processes the legend about him represented, constitute the first attempt to replace the clan or gentile structure of society with a ruling class based upon wealth. This would have resulted in three major classes that would have cut across the old clans or gentes: aristocrats, farmers, and artisans. Morgan remarks that this effort seemed to wither because it was ahead of its time:

> This scheme of Theseus died out, because there was in reality no transfer of powers from the gentes, phratries and tribes to the classes, and because such classes were inferior to the gentes as the basis of a system. (MG: 260)

Thus, Morgan is suggesting that most elements of Athenian society wanted to hold onto the more egalitarian clan or gens structure. Morgan acknowledges that society was changing, but not this fast. He writes that a more complex, more urbanized Athenian society needed judges, written laws, and other developments on the road toward a state. In short, it needed a system of governance based upon territory rather than kinship, which Morgan from the beginning of his book conceptualizes as helping to form the advent of "political society" as opposed to clan or gentile society (MG: 7). He therefore sees the rise of the state in prag- matic and evolutionary terms.

Marx differs markedly from Morgan on this point, developing a dia- lectical rather than an evolutionary argument, similar to the one he made earlier concerning the possible rise of a caste system out of the subjugation of one clan by another. As Marx sees it, Theseus is a *basileus* who, on the one hand, is the representative of an incipient aristocracy, but on the other hand, a representative of the people, the plebeian element. Thus, the person of Theseus embodies or represents a deep social contradiction within clan/gentile society, as the clan chiefs are beginning to develop in the direction of an aristocracy. In analyzing this part of Morgan, Marx goes back directly to the American anthro- pologist's source, Plutarch's second-century CE biography, in which the Greco-Roman historian writes of Theseus and Athens:

The common folk and the poor quickly answered to his summons; to
the powerful he promised government without a king and a democracy, in which he should only be commander in war and guardian of
the laws, while in all else everyone should be on an equal footing . . .
Desiring still further to enlarge the city, he invited all men thither on
equal terms, and the phrase "Come hither all ye people," they say was
a proclamation of Theseus when he established a people, as it were, of
all sorts and conditions. However, he did not suffer his democracy to
become disordered or confused from an indiscriminate multitude
streaming into it, but was the first to separate the people into noblemen and husbandmen and handicraftsmen. To the noblemen he
committed the care of religious rites, the supply of magistrates, the
teaching of the laws, and the interpretation of the will of Heaven, and
for the rest of the citizens he established a balance of privilege, the
noblemen being thought to excel in dignity, the husbandmen in
usefulness, and the handicraftsmen in numbers. And that he was the
first to show a leaning toward the multitude, as Aristotle says, and gave
up his absolute rule, seems to be the testimony of Homer also, in the
Catalogue of Ships, where he speaks of the Athenians alone as a
"people."[13]

Summarizing Morgan but also bringing in Aristotle via Plutarch, whom
Morgan does not cite on this point, Marx declares that Theseus appeals
to the plebeian elements, also giving up his power as *basileus*:

That he at first, as Aristotle says, "was leaning toward the people" and
gave up absolute rule [*Alleinherrschaft*], which Homer also seems
attest . . . The remark of Plutarch "that the lowly [common people]
and poor eagerly followed the summons of Theseus," and the remark
cited by him by Aristotle that Theseus "was leaning toward the
people," seems, however, despite Morgan, to suggest that the chiefs
of the gentes etc. due to wealth etc. already gotten into conflict of
interest with the masses of the gentes, was inevitable with private
property in houses, lands, herds combined with monogamous family.
(EN: 210)

---

13   Plutarch, "Life of Theseus," *Parallel Lives*, trans. Bernadotte Perrin, New York:
Loeb Classical Library, 1914, ¶24–25, penelope.uchicago.edu.

In this sense, the egalitarian clan/gentile society, as it was developing some incipient class contradictions, brought forth the figure of Theseus. As Marx sees it, Theseus reaches toward a different type of society: more centralized, with a uniform law code, and with an explicit class hierarchy based upon wealth rather than birth or clan membership.

This passage in Marx's notes on Morgan has evoked discussion, as it alludes to a key turning point in the move from communal or clan/gentile society toward one based upon social classes, private wealth, and the patriarchal monogamous family. Engels, the first reader and commentator on these notes by Marx, stresses in *Origin of the Family* that a growing population of "inhabitants, although they were fellow countrymen, did not belong to these [clan] bodies and, therefore, were outsiders in their own place of abode" (MECW 26: 213). Engels adds that this resulted in a more centralized governance by the "coalescence into a single people" of the Athenians, a class division within that people, and "the irreconcilable antagonism between gentile society and the state" (MECW 26: 214). Unlike Marx, Engels places the rise of social classes later, in the following centuries, in the period up to the time of the sixth-century BCE Athenian reformer Solon. Most importantly, Engels highlights the contradiction between the clans/gentes and the area residents who lacked membership in them. Unlike Marx, he mentions neither that Theseus had a following among the poor and lowly, nor that internal contradictions within the clans might themselves have emerged by the time of Theseus. Nor does he even hint at a critique of Morgan on the era of Theseus. Thus, Engels interprets Theseus's time as one of conflict between the clan/gentile principle and that of the state and social classes, in effect romanticizing the clan/gens as a model of democracy and equality.

For his part, Krader highlights Marx's differences with Morgan over the period of Theseus, noting that Marx, against Morgan, writes of "the division developing within the Greek gentile society," adding that "the criterion of property fell way from Morgan's analysis of the dissolution of the gens" (EN: 21, 22). In keeping with the overall tone of his introduction, Krader politely refrains from an explicit criticism of Engels here. Krader notes at a general level, however: "Marx's strictures upon Morgan were generally passed over by Engels" (EN: 78).

Dunayevskaya takes it a step further, both on dialectics and in sharpening the critique of Engels. She sees the discussion of the era of Theseus by Marx as a window into the dialectical method of his last years. Disagreeing with what she terms "Engels's uncritical acclaim of Morgan" as a fellow "historical materialist," she writes:

> Marx was showing that it is *during* the transition period that you see the duality emerging to reveal the beginnings of antagonisms, whereas Engels always seems to have antagonisms at the end, as if class society came in very nearly full blown *after* the communal form was destroyed and private property was established . . . Marx demonstrated that, long before the dissolution of the primitive commune, there emerged the question of ranks *within* the egalitarian commune. It was the beginning of a transformation into opposite—gens into caste. That is to say, within the egalitarian communal form arose the elements of its opposite—caste, aristocracy, different material interests. Moreover, these were not successive stages, but *co-extensive* with the communal form . . . *In a word, though Marx surely connects the monogamous family with private property, what is pivotal to him is the antagonistic relationship between the chief and the masses.*[14]

Thus, as with Marx's perception of incipient caste relations among the Iroquois, discussed above, the dialectical concept of transformation into opposite of the clan/gens itself is again at work here, rather than a simpler antagonism between the communal structure and moves toward a class society. That a figure like Theseus, a *basileus* or war chief, would lead the "masses" as part a move from communal toward class society is not surprising. His reported social base among the poor and lowly had some resemblance to how later Greek "tyrants," so labeled by Aristotle and others, restructured society. Violating social norms for leaders, they gained key support from the plebeians against their fellow aristocrats.

All this may have led Engels to add a footnote in 1888, five years after Marx's death, to the celebrated opening sentence of the *Communist Manifesto*, which read: "The history of all hitherto existing society is the history of the class struggle." Engels's footnote read:

14　Raya Dunayevskaya, *Rosa Luxemburg, Women's Liberation, and Marx's Philosophy of Revolution*, second edition (Urbana: University of Illinois Press [1982] 1991), pp. 180, 181, 182.

That is, all *written* history. In 1847, the pre-history of society, the social organization existing previous to recorded history, was all but unknown. Since then, August von Haxthausen (1792–1866) discovered common ownership of land in Russia, Georg Ludwig von Maurer proved it to be the social foundation from which all Teutonic races started in history, and, by and by, village communities were found to be, or to have been, the primitive form of society everywhere from India to Ireland. The inner organization of this primitive communistic society was laid bare, in its typical form, by Lewis Henry Morgan's (1818–1881) crowning discovery of the true nature of the gens and its relation to the tribe. With the dissolution of the primeval communities, society begins to be differentiated into separate and finally antagonistic classes. I have attempted to retrace this dissolution in *Origin of the Family, Private Property, and the State*, second edition, Stuttgart, 1886. (MECW 6: 482)

Based on the above discussion about Theseus and incipient class divisions inside the clan, Engels's footnote seems at variance with Marx's own thinking as expressed in his notes on Morgan. It should also be mentioned that Marx did not attempt to add anything like this to the 1882 edition of the *Manifesto*, which featured a new preface that took account of the Russian communal village and was written about a year after he made his notes on Morgan. For her part, Dunayevskaya charged that "Engels thereby modified the dialectical structure" of the *Manifesto*.[15] One could say the same about his interpretation of the notes on Morgan.

From Greece to Rome

In these same pages of Marx's notes, he also takes issue, at least implicitly, with Morgan's fulsome praise of the Athenian democracy that eventually emerged once class society was established. Marx skips over passages like these:

We shall draw nearer the truth of the matter by regarding Theseus, Solon and Cleisthenes as standing connected with three great movements of the Athenian people, not to found a democracy, for Athenian

---

15   Ibid., p. 196.

democracy was older than either, but to change the plan of government from a gentile into a political organization. Neither sought to
change the existing principles of democracy which had been inherited
from the gentes. They contributed in their respective times to the great
movement for the formation of a state, which required the substitution
of a political in the place of gentile society. (MG: 273)

Where Morgan here minimizes Athenian slavery, Marx incorporates
into his notes a passage from the German historian August Böckh on the
topic of Attica, the region comprising Athens: "The *population of Attica*
(*Böckh*) in the time of its flowering about 1/2 million; of that, more than
2/3, that is, *365,000 slaves*, besides perhaps 45,000 resident foreigners,
leaving for the *free citizen population—90,000!*" (EN: 209).

As Marx traces the pathway of Athens from a communal clan/gentile
social order to a class-bound and slaveholding democracy, he keeps to
the theme of growing internal inequality as the key explanation of the
overthrow of the communal/clan system: "Disregarding locality: the
property difference within the same gens had transformed the unity of
the members' interests into antagonism; besides that, next to land and
cattle money capital became decidedly important, with the development
of slavery" (EN: 213). Here, he expresses an explicit difference with
Morgan's emphasis on issues like constant warfare preserving the clans/
gentes beyond what would have been their relevance and his notion that
the proliferation of free, non-clan-member residents put pressure on the
clan-based political system. It is also noteworthy that Marx again ties
the rise of inequality of property to the rise of a slaveholding stratum.

In his 1879–82 notebooks, Marx also traces similar processes in
Rome. In contrast to the Greeks, Roman class society continues to refer
to clans for a longer period, at least in terms of status honor. At the same
time, Marx notes that even less evidence has been preserved in Rome of
the social structure of the early clan/gentile period. As Marx's contemporary and noted historian Theodor Mommsen writes, "Fewer traces
comparatively of the primitive state of things have been preserved in the
case of the Italians, and of the Romans in particular, than in the case of
any other Indo-Germanic race."[16] The late Marx's study of Roman clans/

---

16   Theodor Mommsen, *History of Rome*, Vol. 1, trans. W. P. Dickson (New York: E.
P. Dutton, 1868), p. 148.

gentes seems to begin about a year before his notes on Morgan, with social historian Ludwig Lange's *Römische Alterthümer* [Ancient Rome], first published in 1856. Marx adds his notes on Lange at the end of the notebook that includes those on Kovalevsky's book on communal land-holding, but the fact that they appear at the end of that notebook leaves open the possibility that Marx read Lange after Morgan. However, the most likely date of the notes on Lange is late 1879 or early 1880, six months to a year before those on Morgan.[17]

The Lange notes begin with Marx recording text from Lange on pre-literate Roman tribes:

> The site of Rome and the Roman territory inhabited long before the "organization of the state," i.e., the so-called founding of Rome, set by *Varro* 753 (BC). [p. 63] *District communes in Latium (pagi)*, basis for the more tightly unified community; continued to exist in the *region surrounding Rome* after the subsequent political division into *rural tribes* [tribus rusticae] . . . In the most ancient period—when the pagi were *not yet* unified *into a city—Capitoline Hill* nonetheless fortified in order to protect the ancient places of worship and refuge for the flocks. *Rome's* location favored the *conduct of inland trade between* Latium and the neighboring regions, and *export trade* with *Greek and Carthaginian sea merchants; protected* against *piracy; possessing the only harbor on the coast of Latium,* which was *nearby at the mouth of the Tiber.* Was trade center . . . *Carthaginian trade agreement.* [[508 BC]] . . . In addition, because of its location, a natural fortification of *Latium against Etruria* . . . *Landowners* of the *pagi the gentes* of the Romili etc., many of whom are known only through the names of the later rural tribes recognized as masters because of the *clients* they obtained *through their first conquest, merchants from Latium* and *Tuscan refugees* who trespassed into their territory. [p. 66][18]

---

17 The possibility that Marx annotated Lange after the Morgan notes is raised by the fact that Marx does not mention Lange's very detailed history of the Roman family in the notes on Morgan, even when he is taking up Rome. The Lange notes also contain a few critiques by Marx on gender and the family that are based upon Morgan's 1877 book. But these critiques are not systematic. Therefore, it is more likely that Marx possessed some general knowledge of Morgan's book before reading Lange but did not make a detailed study of *Ancient Society* until afterward.

18 Marx's Lange notes, along with his other never previously published 1879 notes on Rome, also covering books by Bücher, Friedländer, and Jhering, were published in the

Marx here seems to be in accord with Lange's general description of early Roman clan/gentile society. He appears to disagree, however, with the German historian's anachronistic assumption of the existence of private property at this early stage by adding the word "gentes" to the term "landowners" above. Marx also takes explicit issue with Lange's assumption that communal property would have faded by the time of sedentary agriculture: "Mr. Lange thinks 'communal [*gemeinschaftliches*]' property impossible (!), given sedentary agriculture." Marx sees this as obviously false based upon his studies during the same period of communal property in the villages of India, which will be discussed in the next section of this chapter.

As will be discussed in the next chapter, he differs even more sharply with Lange's assumption that nuclear families existed from earliest times. Referring to the *ager publicus*, a form of Roman communal property held by a town or village, Marx objects in some bracketed comments: "*Ager publicus*. [[A falsification runs throughout all of Lange's discussion, in that he views the individual family to be earlier than the gens etc., individual property as the starting point, etc., distorting his whole discussion.]] That *land conquered by the state in war* [[this presupposes the state *before* communal property!]]."

Marx's more extensive ruminations on very early Roman society's communal social forms can be found in the notes on Morgan. Romulus, the legendary founder of Rome, is seen by Morgan and Marx as representing, like Theseus, a period of dramatic social change rather than an individual person. Unlike with Theseus, however, Romulus's founding of Rome in 753 BCE as an incipient class society is presented as a successful effort to overcome a clan/gens-based communal system. In the mythical year 753 BCE, Romulus formed the Romans into a single city rather than a confederacy of tribes. The political structure preserved key features from clan/gentile society, however, with a senate

---

Marx-Engels Gesamtausgabe (MEGAdigital IV/27) in 2024, edited by the late Georgi Bagaturia, Jürgen Rojahn, and Emanuela Conversano, on the basis of an initial transcription by the late Norair Ter-Akopian. MEGAdigital IV/27 is part of an NEH-supported project that is to include an all-English edition of some of Marx's 1879–82 notebooks, translated and annotated by Charles Reitz, Gerhard Schutte, the late Heinz D. Osterle, Danga Vileisis, and me, in collaboration with David Norman Smith. This edition will include the Rome notes. Here and in subsequent chapters I will be quoting from this forthcoming edition of Marx's notes on Rome, but without providing specific page references, as yet unavailable.

(comparable to a council of chiefs), a *comitia curiata* (popular assembly), and a *rex* (war chief).

Marx shows particular interest in the persistence of clan/gentile practices in many aspects of Roman social life after this period. Clans/gentes organized or restricted the following social practices: inheritance, burial places, religious rites, marriage (prohibited within the same clan/gens), common lands, reciprocal defense, right to the clan/gentile name, adopting strangers, electing and deposing chiefs. Amplifying Morgan's term "close parallelism," Marx writes, "fully parallel to the Iroquois—gens, tribe, confederacy" (EN: 222; MG: 292). Many of these clan practices are superseded by the Law of the Twelve Tables of 451 BCE: rather than running through the clan, inheritance becomes lineal via the male line and land allotments accrue to individual families. Significantly, obligations of mutual defense are the "first to disappear" as state law takes over and establishes, if not a monopoly of violence in the Weberian sense, control over crime and punishment in many spheres. Clans/gentes can now simply "mourn" the imprisonment of one of their members (EN: 222). Some older practices remain, hidden beneath newer patriarchal/class relations, perhaps in the selection of the city's religious leader, the pontifex. As status markers, however, clans persist as a form of social honor well into the Imperial Period, as seen in how Emperor Claudius (r. 40–54) barred Romanized foreigners from adopting Roman names, especially those of the ancient clans/gentes. Marx also sees the Tribunate, a powerful office that represented the plebeians, as "literally the equivalent of the old tribal chief" (EN: 226). Was there a connection between this persistence of the clan/gens at least as a status group and that of female power in Roman class society, certainly as compared to Greek practices during roughly the same period? Those issues will be addressed in the next chapter, but first I will explore other communal social formations, particularly in India. These remained prominent into Marx's time, and after.

The Persistence of Communal Formations in India

While Morgan says very little about clan and communal social forms in Asia and Africa, Marx researches these issues extensively in his last years via Kovalevsky's book, as well as other sources. Kovalevsky demonstrates important changes over time in the Indian communal social forms, but he also shows their persistence over several thousand years under class societies, right up to the late nineteenth century.

In the next few pages, I will go into these stages—as recorded by Marx in his notes—to give readers a better grasp of the extent to which he has by now broken with his 1850s notions of an unchanging, stagnant Indian village.

What particularly interests Kovalevsky and Marx about India is the huge variety of communal forms found across the Subcontinent, with very ancient ones coexisting at the margins along with newer ones. In this vein, Marx records a summary passage:

> In no country more than India such variety in the forms of land and property relationships. Besides the *commune based on kinship* the *neighbor-based* or *rural* ones; the *system of periodic* and *equal distribution of arable and meadow lands* involving also the *rotation of dwellings* hand in hand with the *system of lifelong, unequal allotments,* the size of which is determined through *laws of succession* or *factual possession at the time of the last distribution; communal exploitation* coincides with *private; communal cultivation* in some places, in others *mere communal* resources (like forest, pasture, etc.); here *permission for all inhabitants of the community to utilize the communal lands,* there the *right of utilization limited to small number of families of the earliest settlers;* and besides these *communal property forms* of all types and categories, *peasant property in parcels,* and lastly *ownership of enormous estates,* often encompassing entire districts. (74) (KOV: 346)

The very earliest nomadic hunter-gatherer social forms were exceptions, as they seemed no longer present by 1879.

Kovalevsky and Marx attempt to discern the nature and structure of these very early communal social forms that preceded settled agriculture and communal landholding and property, but doing so entailed reading critically even the most ancient written law, which came afterward. Marx records Kovalevsky's rhetorical question concerning this problem: "Why the oldest collections of legal traditions such inadequate sources for research on the oldest forms of social life? How should historical research on the oldest forms proceed?" (KOV: 346). The goal was to unearth evidence or at least speculate knowledgeably about the nature of the very oldest groups, before settled agriculture. While there is some slippage in

Kovalevsky on this point, as he occasionally assumes a much earlier emergence of private property in these preliterate societies, Marx remains firm on this issue, here chiding Kovalevsky for such a slippage:

> Yet this is not consistent with what was said earlier; according to which there was [cooperation] among *nomadic and even savage peoples before the existence of landed property*—communal or private—necessitated through the conditions of the hunt, etc. (KOV: 357)

Little was known about these very early "savage" or hunter-gatherer societies on the Indian Subcontinent. In trying to discern the structure and social practices of this very ancient stage in India, Marx, like Kovalevsky, is distrustful of the evidence provided by much later systematic jurisprudence, like the Code of Manu. Although this code is dated by scholars today around the first century CE, nineteenth-century estimates placed it about a millennium earlier. For his part, Kovalevsky argues that real social practices can be better discerned via "*customary law (local)* [which] is almost entirely excluded from the *legal codes*" (KOV: 355).

Marx also expresses some skepticism about the results of Kovalevsky's attempts to puzzle out the hunter-gatherer stage. Kovalevsky, like Marx, assumes an early kin-based community with some kind of clan structure. But, at one point, Kovalevsky seems to assume the warlike character of these early clans, writing of "the *original settlement by the clan* within the boundaries of the *territory it conquered.*" Marx records this in his notes, but he remarks, questioning the assumption of violent seizure of territory, "that clan communities necessarily settle on *foreign, conquered* territory is an *arbitrary* assumption of Kovalevsky" (KOV: 147). Beyond this kind of debate, little is developed in terms of analysis of this stage in terms of India.

Kovalevsky seems to disregard this sketchy, very early stage, going on to create a five-part schema of successive communal forms in Indian village life, in which the completely kin-based, settled, communal village constitutes a first stage, with the land held entirely in common, a social form still in existence in some parts of the Subcontinent in 1879, in what are today the Northwest Frontier Provinces of Pakistan:

> *Oldest Form* (still in existence): *kinship commune*, whose members *live with one another inseparably*, *working* the *land in common*, and meeting

their needs from the communal/general income. With respect to this
form one of the *resolutions of the Privy Council* declares: "*No member
of the kinship group* can refer to personal possession of this, whether
as *property*, or even in terms of *his temporary utilization of this or that
sector of the communal lands.* The products of the communal economy
go into the common fund and serve to meet the needs of the entire
community." This *form of communal property* has only been preserved
in *a few places in northern and northwestern India.* (KOV: 346)

Although this form was very rare in India by 1879, it was important both
logically and historically as the first communal social form involving
permanent settlement on the land.

The evolution of this extremely egalitarian consanguineal community
toward more individualized property ownership and social differentiation based upon closeness of kinship forms a second stage, as seen in this
passage Marx records:

*As a result of the tendency toward individualization in the property
relations within the boundaries of particular settlements (villages)* the
indivisible property of the kinship group dies out more and more and
new property form emerges. In the majority of the provinces during
the epoch of the English takeover, the *indivisible kinship commune*
disappeared; only the remnants of later systems of landownership still
existed within *these communities under condition* of the *use* by individual families of *unequal allotments in terms of their size,* and where
the size of the allotments in each case is determined either *by how
closely related* its owners are to the real or fictive clan founder [*Stammvater*][19] of the community, or through *factual cultivation*; in *other
communities* under *condition of the periodic distribution of the communal lands in equal allotments.* (77, 78) (KOV: 348)

At this second stage, inequality in the ownership of private property is
coming to the fore and kinship relations are developing forms of inequality as well.

Two successive subforms emerge at this second stage. The "oldest"
subform greatly preserves communal landholdings even in the face of

---

19   *Stammvater* could also be translated as "clan ancestor."

the development of private property (KOV: 348). Marx incorporates this passage, a combination of text from another British report quoted by Kovalevsky and the latter's own summary:

> The allotments of arable land determined in this manner may be described neither as determined *for life* nor *hereditary*. They remain at the disposal of this or that family until such time as the necessity of fashioning new allotments for descendants or those distant in time appears to the members of the kinship group as a warrant for a new distribution of the communal arable land. (KOV: 349)

However, such land distribution is not completely egalitarian, according to what Marx records from another part of the same report as cited by Kovalevsky: "The closer or more distant proximity to the clan founder of this or that member of the commune determines the size of the plot that is at his disposal" (KOV: 349). Thus, degree of kinship has emerged as a key marker of social hierarchy.

The next subform of stage two arises as communities grow and armed conflict develops, disrupting the older communal social relations:

> The *determination of the degree of relatedness to the clan founder* is more and more *difficult* as time goes on with the numerical multi-plication of the members of the kinship group, and *impossible* just as soon as *violent* changes occur; *stability of the gens* is disrupted through war with neighboring clans, many clan communities are wiped out, their portion of land sometimes stolen, or falls into disuse. (KOV: 350)

With population growth and generational succession, kinship ties have become less determinate, while armed conflict alters many social boundaries. It reaches the point where Marx, using the Russian word for village commune, *obshchina*, quotes a British report cited by Kovalevsky and the latter's comments:

> "We find in the *obshchina* no constant allotments. Each owns *the plot worked on / cultivated by him* as long as it remains cultivated. As soon as *this or that tract of land* remains untended, it enters the communal 'waste lands' and can *be occupied* by any member of the community, under *condition that it be worked and the tax that falls upon this land*

is paid." (81) The *inequality of the allotments* leads often to squabbles among the members of the community. (KOV: 351)

This leads to the third stage, which features the periodic reassignment of allotments by a process within the village.

At the third stage, the old communal forms exist in contradiction with newer ones based upon private property, and, periodically, a village council meets to make a new distribution of land allotments. Here, villagers with weaker kinship ties to the purported clan ancestor come to the fore, according to the same British report that Marx incorporates, as again quoted and analyzed by Kovalevsky:

> "The individuals, who are demanding a redistribution, insist on *equal-sized parcels* (allotments) and are just as *opposed to the system of determining allotments in terms of the degree of kinship*, as against the system sanctioning factual possession." *The equal distribution of the common land, repeated in definite periods of time and often yearly,* appears *therefore to be a relatively late form in the history of Indian forms of landownership.* (KOV: 351)

In his notebook, Marx draws a line in the margin next to the last sentence in the above, suggesting its particular importance to him. By this stage, considerable social conflict has emerged over property. When land allotments are realigned, village members resist giving up better for poorer land. Built structures are defended even more strongly as private property, per a British report cited by Kovalevsky that Marx records:

> When required to relinquish their previous dwelling places, the village inhabitants clear away their farmstead for the time being and leave vacant and uncultivated stretches in the places of their earlier settlement and in this manner clearly protest against the duty prescribed by custom to transfer to others the results of their own labor. (KOV: 353)

Here, communal forms coexist and conflict with later ones involving private property. These periodic, sometimes even annual, redistributions are seen, according the British report cited by Kovalevsky and recorded by Marx, as having arisen *"from the desire to remove any inequality,* might arise from the assignment of land for more or less permanent utilization" (Marx ([1879] 1975: 354). In this sense, communal social relations retain considerable strength even as they are being eroded by the expansion of private property rights in land and farmsteads.

A fourth stage features the diminution of communal property to the point where it becomes secondary to private property in land. On this point, Marx records Kovalevsky writing that such villages thus came to resemble Western European ones in the era of feudalism:

> In the process of dissolution, the *rural community* of India ultimately advanced to the stage of development that prevails in Germany, England, and France during the Middle Ages and still exists today in the entire territory of Switzerland, namely: arable soil and also hayfields have become private property of the various members and only the so-called *resources* remain as their *common* property; these are called "sayer" in the Northwest Provinces and include: a) uncultivated land rich in grass, underbrush, or forests; b) natural and artificial reservoirs of water, like springs and swamps which are used for irrigation; c) groves and gardens, with fruit trees and firewood; d) *residential sites* not occupied by the commune members if these receive special rents because of the dwellings and buildings built upon them; e) wastelands that contain *saltpeter or iron* whose exploitation is the occupation of commune members or outside leaseholders; f) lastly, the *charges assessed during the annual market or fair* and *payments from persons* who settle within the commune to engage in this or that form of craft. (KOV: 354–55)

These are by now rather limited forms of communal property, as opposed to earlier systems wherein the land as a whole was seen as communal.

Even at this stage, however, when compared to the communities of Western Europe, the Indian village was more inclusive of all its members. Marx records Kovalevsky on this point:

> What was *characteristic of the Indian system* however—as a result of its greater proximity to the earliest forms of communal property: Even the citizens of the commune who are *landless* for one reason or another take part in the "*commons.*" (KOV: 355)

This issue of inclusion is also extremely important to Marx's notion of communal social relations as more fundamental than communal property.

Marx now records, with a brief addition of his own on the South Slavs, a long summary of these four stages by Kovalevsky, who has by now added a fifth one that informs the reader of the contemporary situation in most of the Subcontinent:

> *Thus the following sequence*: 1) *First kinship commune with indivisible property in land and communal agriculture.* 2) The *kinship commune* divides, each according to the number of kinship branches, into a larger or smaller number of *familial communes* [[in the manner of the south Slavs.]] In the end undivided property in land and cultivation in common are also lost. 3) *System of inheritance based on degree of kinship and therefore unequal allotments.* War, artificial colonization, etc. alter the nature of the kinship commune and thereupon the extent of the allotments. *The earlier inequality* grows; and has 4) its foundation no longer in the degree of relatedness to the leader of the clan but instead in factual ownership which is expressed in the manner of cultivation itself. Opposition occurs; hence: 5) *system of the more or less periodic distribution of the communal lands*, etc. At first only of equally apportioned *living areas* (with accompanying equipment), *arable soil, and hayfields*. In the ensuing changes just the *living area* (with the fields belonging to the farm, etc.) is differentiated as *private property*; later ditto *arable soil, and hayfields*. From the old *system of communal property* the exquisite remains [*beaux restes*] are: the *common land* [[i.e. this in the sense of the contradiction to that transformed into private property]] [[or those things which were earlier only resources]] and on the other hand *the familial communal property*, and this family is reduced more and more through the historical process to the *private family / individual family* in the modern sense. (86, 87) (KOV: 355)

In the above, it is also noteworthy that Marx makes use of the dialectical term "contradiction" in a bracketed summary comment. Up to now, Marx's notes present these successive stages as internally driven, from antagonisms within the village commune. He adds his own summary: "discord *when allotment disparities become great*; over time other kinds of inequality, of wealth, of entitlement, etc. come to imply much other social disparity, which in the estimate of those who are thus in fact privileged, calls forth the tendency *to entrench* themselves as possessors"

(KOV: 358). This seems to accord with how he approached the Iroquois and Homeric Greek communal forms, where he saw differentiation within the commune itself toward greater hierarchy and incipient class division as the primary drivers of change, rather than outside pressure or intervention. One major difference, however, is that the Iroquois and Greek clans enjoyed self-rule within a given territory. That is not the case with the communal structures of the Indian Subcontinent, which existed for millennia under state rule.

Indian Communes and the State

The first two forms of state rule, that of the Indian rajahs and then a series of Muslim empires and sultanates in the Subcontinent, did not radically change the communal structures at the village level. British rule did so, however. I will now take up Marx's reading of Kovalevsky on the Indian village under Hindu and then Muslim rule.

Marx begins by recording how pre-Islamic Hindu legal texts reflect how, under the Indian rajahs, the communal forms lost some of their political power, and he inserts his own bracketed summary comment:

In the legal codes of both *Yajnavalkya* and *Narada*, the members of the rural communities are *charged* by the central authorities—in the name of communal associations or *convocations of kin—with police and judicial functions*, that is to say with keeping the peace. This means: These kinship associations and communes are already *transformed* from *organs* having these functions *independently* into the *lowest-level police and security authorities of the state*. [[The *social functions* they originally possessed—judiciary and police—now appear as something the state entrusts, assigns, or requires.]] The *solidarity* or *collective responsibility* that has bound them together since ancient times, from this moment on becomes *their general accountability to the state;* a *whole series of regulations* appears in those codes that determines accountability for breaches of the peace occurring within the boundaries of the *kinship groups.* (KOV: 355)

Thus, the state not only rules from a distance, but it also partially transforms communal institutions into its instruments. And the new system of collective responsibility also involves obligations to collect and transfer "taxes to the state" (KOV: 359).

Yet, as Marx records from Kovalevsky, communal institutions retain great strength and stability even under state overlordship, as the ancient Hindu legal codes

> confirm *the appointment of the communal elders* (leaders) *by the communes themselves*; both advise choosing these from among persons who understand their obligations and adhere to them, who are unselfish and pure in spirit; the members of the commune are assigned unconditional subordination to the members of the commune in accordance with the *ordinances/regulations* of those thus selected. (101) (KOV: 361)

But two different types of commune, kin-based and residency-based, eventually appear, with Marx here recording Kovalevsky on the Institutes of Narada, a legal code in force as late as the first millennium CE, until just before the Muslim conquests:

> In several articles *Narada* calls the members of the communal assemblies *"kin,"* in others just *"those who live together"* (sharing a home, neighbors, living together in one residence).[20] Thus even back then two types of communes *"kinship communes"* and *"rural communes."* The existence of the *first* as early as *4th century B.C.* (KOV: 361)

The difference between these two types of communes is one of Kovalevsky's core themes.

The antiquity and persistence of communal property form another of Kovalevsky's core themes, as do the communal social forms at a more general level for Marx. Like those of the ancient Greeks and Romans, written records describe communal institutions and social practices indistinctly if at all. This is the case in India even though these forms persisted well into the modern era. One important reason for this, at least in terms of legal codes, is explained by Kovalevsky in a comment that Marx records:

---

20 "Communal assemblies" is Marx's phrase, seeming to emphasize similarities of Indian institutions to Greco-Roman and Iroquois ones.

> In *none of the legal compendia* [is] *direct description of the communal*
> *form of property* because the *relationships among the communal prop-*
> *erty owners* are regulated not through the law, but through local
> custom. Thus [the legal code] *Pita Maha* demands that judgments be
> rendered directly on the basis of local custom in disputes between
> village inhabitants, shepherds, etc. and the binding power of local
> custom is recognized in all of the newest commentaries, etc. The
> customs are enforced through the communal courts. (KOV: 365)

Thus, unwritten customary law lies at the center of what is preserved
from the communal forms of social organization and action.

While Marx seems in accord with the above, he takes issue with
Kovalevsky's attempts to push back the origins of private property to
the very early stage of the oldest surviving legal text, the Code of
Manu. Specifically, he takes issue—in a bracketed comment in the
extract below—with Kovalevsky's assumption that written records
about the delineation of boundaries inform us about what kind of
property relations, communal or private, were prevalent at a given
stage:

> Kovalevsky *finds traces in* [the Code of] *Manu* (see the citations from
> the French translation by *Loiseleur Deslongchamps*) "of both *the*
> *communal possession of land* and the simultaneous emergence of
> *private landownership—*whether through the *exclusion of individual*
> *allotments from the communal land,* or through *new settlers* who seized
> upon this or that plot of communal wasteland and forest, bringing
> them under cultivation—this only occurs *with the provisional consent*
> *of the communal kinship associations."* (90, 91) [[The citations about
> the *boundaries* of the villages do not point directly to communal
> property in the villages.]] (KOV: 356)

This critique is similar to the one Marx made of Morgan concerning the
fencing off of land in Mycenaean Greece as evidence of private property,
as discussed above.

Besides the state, Marx, amplifying Kovalevsky with a parenthetical
remark, sees the rising power of the priestly Brahmin caste as a key
impetus to the undermining of communal and joint familial property,
which was inalienable according to ancient communal practices:

The individualization of immovable property strengthened through the *increased ease of division within the family* and *increased freedom to dispose not only of self-acquired property, but also property of the kinship group,* particularly when bestowing some nice little advantages of wealth upon the members of the priestly caste, the Brahmins. (113) The *priestly* rabble [*Pack*][21] thus plays a central role in the *process of the individualization of family property.* (113) *The main characteristic of indivisible family property—its inalienability.* In order to get at it the system of law that was developing under the influence of the Brahmins had to attack especially this *bulwark* more and more. *Manu* recognizes *no sale* of indivisible family property; neither does *Narada.* Among the most recent ones—like Vyasa and Chintamani *this kind of sale is allowed,* on *condition of common consent of all co-owners.* This condition pains the priest because "presents" do no harm. [[*Disposition through gifts* everywhere the *priestly hobbyhorse!*]] (KOV: 366)

In such an agrarian society, "immovable property" is almost always landed property. In a comment, Marx generalizes this point about the role of clerics in establishing private property in land, here referring to the Franks of early medieval Europe: "Other peoples too, for instance the Germano-Roman world (see Merovingians, Carolingians) the same hierarchy—*gift-giving to the priest* the first *form of the alienation of immovable property* preceding all others" (KOV: 367). Here, Marx's more universal framework differs from the way Kovalevsky concludes this section by stressing the persistence of communal property in India, in contrast to Western Europe.

Moving to the period of Muslim rule, Marx records at length from Kovalevsky an account of how various Muslim conquerors left the land in the hands of its previous occupants. The new rulers' use of the institution of *iqta* (a system of benefices) saw subordinates (*iqtadars*) charged with providing military service in exchange for land. While *iqta* became widespread, the land so distributed was usually confined to wasteland, abandoned land, and only a very small fraction of the land controlled by

---

21 Marx's "Pack" versus Kovalevsky's neutral "priestly estate." In this sentence, Marx also adds the word "central" to Kovalevsky's language about the role of the Hindu priests. Throughout these notes, Marx's discussions of clerics are laden with sarcasm.

the conquered people. Despite efforts on the part of *iqtadars* over the centuries, a feudal system did not emerge, in part because Muslim rulers frequently took back these land grants and redistributed them.

Precolonial Algeria

Marx next makes notes on Kovalevsky's far briefer account of Algeria prior to French colonial rule. Here, Marx records Kovalevsky on Algeria's many similarities to India, including the former's preservation of communal forms preceding the arrival of French colonialism in the 1830s, but persisting until at least 1873, when French law establishes private property in land as the norm:

> Algeria has, after India, *the most remnants of the archaic form of land-ownership*. Here the prevailing types of landholdings are *clan* and *undivided familial property*. Centuries of Arab, Turkish, and finally French rule were unable—except in most recent times, officially since *law of 1873*—to defeat the *consanguineal organization* and principles based thereupon of *indivisibility* and *inalienability* of landed property. (197) (KOV: 400)

Thus, Algeria retained until very late a significant number of communal social forms. To be sure, ancient Roman law influenced the development of some forms of private alongside communal property.

But one Algerian ethnic group, the Kabyles, retained the most ancient type of communal forms, those based upon kinship. Marx records Kovalevsky on how this resulted from the Arab conquests that followed the collapse of Roman rule:

> Among the Berbers some—called *Kabyles,* living in the *north on the shore of the Mediterranean* etc. who up to now live in undivided families with strict observance of *inalienability of family property*, thus preserving many remnants of *kinship property and communal property*. The largest portion of the Berbers took on the Arab language, way of life and *characteristic features of landholding*. (197, 198) The collective forms of landed property, above all *kinship property*, were undoubtedly *introduced by the Arabs*. (KOV: 400)

Since the patriarchal, patrilineal family also existed among the Kabyles, communal and familial property were merged, resulting in communal structures based to a great extent upon, as indicated above, "features of landholding" introduced by the Arabs.[22]

Individual property was strictly limited, with little personal (as opposed to familial/communal) property, as noted in this passage Marx records from Kovalevsky, along with a parenthetical reference to the South Slavs:

> The *family* supplies each one of its members the *instruments of work, guns, the capital needed for trade or handicraft.* Every member of the family must dedicate his labor to it—i.e., put into the hands of the head of the family all revenues he receives—under pain of expulsion from the family. With regard to *individual property*, that is *movables*, limited to *clothing* alone among *males*; among *females* to *cloth* . . . and *jewelry*, which they receive as *dowry* (rather *gift*) on their wedding day; exceptions only for *luxury clothing and valuable necklaces*; these remain *communal property of the family and* may only be *used individually* by one or another of the women. (cf. *South Slavs*). *In terms of immovable property*, which a *member* has received through *gift or bequest*, it is acknowledged as his *individual property*, yet develops into a *possession* (*vladenie*) of the entire family. (l.c.) If the family composed of not many members, then *dining at a common table and the function of the cook* becomes in succession the responsibility of every woman member. (KOV: 402)

In the above, Marx writes the Russian word *vladenie* next to the German *Besitz* [possession], his translation of it into German. He is thus bending his notes toward possession, something less than outright ownership (*Eigentum* in German), since *vladenie* carries the meaning of both ownership and possession. In keeping with this, he also records a briefer passage from Kovalevsky: "If therefore the *Kabyles acquainted with private property in land*, this only as an *exception*. Here as everywhere

---

22   Recently, the persistence of these kinds of communal social relations in Arab villages, despite attempts to eradicate them by the Ottomans, the British, and the Israelis, has been noted at the other end of Mediterranean, in twenty-first-century Gaza. And again, these social relations are forming loci of resistance. See Peter Linebaugh, "Palestine and the Commons," *Counterpunch* (March 6, 2024).

else this occurs among them *as a product of the gradual process of the dissolution of clan, communal, and familial property* (204)" (KOV: 403). After studying Morgan more closely, as he did in the next year, Marx would likely have questioned Kovalevsky on whether clans rather than extended families constitute the prime institution here. Be that as it may, Marx is noting the persistence of communal, collective forms, not only in property but also in social practices like common meals.

Marx also records material on the development of private property in land in Algeria under Ottoman rule (1515–1830), when two main factors pushed this forward: (1) confiscation and sale of the land of rebellious clans, and (2) a policy of turning land over to religious institutions:

> The *Turkish government* also forcefully facilitated the *concentration of private property in land in the hands of religious and benevolent associations*. The ease with which it moved to confiscate and its tax pressures often caused *private owners* to transfer their *property titles* over to such institutions. (KOV: 404)

Still, communal land tenure persists on a large scale up to the period around 1873, when large amounts of land were confiscated by the French for their massive settler population. This contrasted with India, which was not a settler colony, a factor in the greater prevalence of communal social forms there. At the same time, it should be noted, based on his later writings as well, that Marx did not idealize this kind of communal system, any more than he had with the Greeks or the Iroquois. For example, in a visit to Algiers for convalescence just before his death, Marx, on the one hand, expresses great admiration for the personal dignity with which Muslim Algerians carried themselves on the streets, but, on the other hand, warns, "Nevertheless, they will go to rack and ruin without a revolutionary movement" (Letter to Laura Lafargue of April 13–14, 1882, MECW 46: 242).

Overall, though, Marx in these notes seems to be stressing the similarities rather than the differences between Algeria and India. Nor is he conceptualizing a European–non-European divide as the prime factor. Not only does he leave aside material from Kovalevsky to that effect, but he also inserts comments linking India and Algeria to early medieval Europe and to the communal forms found among the South Slavs in his own era. As with the Morgan notes, where he seems to follow Morgan, albeit critically, in reading Greco-Roman society through the lens of the Iroquois, Marx is here reading Western Europe through India and Algeria, finding communal social forms where he had not seen them before, or had not thought them to be as important as he now did.

For this reason, it is important also to examine his ruminations about communal social forms in three European contexts besides those of Greece and Rome: the ancient Germans, precolonial Ireland, and Russia.

Ancient German and Precolonial Irish Communal Societies

Already in a letter of March 14, 1868, to Engels, Marx reports that he is rethinking the relationship of communal social organization to Western Europe after reading the work of social historian Georg Ludwig von Maurer:

> Old Maurer . . . demonstrates at length that private property in land only arose later, etc. . . . . The idiotic . . . opinion . . . that the Germans settled each by himself, and only afterward established villages, districts, etc., is completely refuted. It is interesting just now that the *Russian* manner of re-distributing land at certain intervals (in Germany originally annually) should have persisted in some parts of Germany up to the 18th century and even the 19th. The view I put forward that the Asiatic or Indian property forms everywhere mark the beginning in Europe receives new proof here . . . the Russians . . . still maintain forms long abandoned by their neighbors. (MECW 42: 547)

As Japanese Marx scholar Tomonaga Tairako notes, these reflections on Maurer began soon after the publication of the first German edition of *Capital* in 1867. They led Marx to see ancient "Germanic communal property" as more collectivist than before, no longer "consisting of independent farmers."[23] In a subsequent letter to Engels dated March 25,

---

23   Tomonaga Tairako, "A Turning Point in Marx's Theory on Pre-Capitalist Societies: Marx's Excerpt Notebooks on Maurer in MEGA IV/18," *Hitotsubashi Journal of Social Studies* 47 (2016), p. 1.

1868, again ruminating on Maurer, Marx conceptualizes forms of communal social organization underneath the European feudal institutions of lord and serf, linking these "primitive" social relations to "the socialist trend" of his own time (MECW 42: 557). Moreover, he perceives traces of these communal forms in isolated rural areas of contemporary Germany. It is doubtful that Marx thought all this to be of merely historical interest. It would therefore follow that the German peasantry of his own time, some of which was maintaining these vernacular communist practices, was in a new sense a potential ally of the socialists and the working class. In Russia, where these communal forms persisted more widely, its peasantry constituted a larger and more important potential ally. Be that as it may, it is clear that Marx in 1868 sees communal social organization as a core theme in need of study, in both European and non-European contexts, and this surely motivates his further investigation of European societies in this regard.

At the end of the notes on Morgan, Marx goes beyond Morgan's text to examine anew the communal social forms of the ancient Germans, as delineated by contemporary Roman observers Julius Caesar and Tacitus. When encountered by Caesar in the first century BCE, the Germanic tribes were at a stage of development similar to that of the Homeric Greeks. Lacking a written language, they recorded their history via songs. In Caesar's account from around 50 BCE, their communal social structure and practices allowed them to eschew landed property:

> They do not pay much attention to agriculture, and a large portion of their food consists in milk, cheese, and flesh; nor has any one a fixed quantity of land or his own individual limits; but the magistrates and the leading men each year apportion to the tribes and families, who have united together, as much land as, and in the place in which, they think proper, and the year after compel them to remove elsewhere. For this enactment they advance many reasons—lest seduced by long-continued custom, they may exchange their ardor in the waging of war for agriculture; lest they may be anxious to acquire extensive estates, and the more powerful drive the weaker from their possessions; lest they construct their houses with too great a desire to avoid cold and heat; lest the desire of wealth spring up, from which cause divisions and discords arise; and that they may keep the common people in a

contented state of mind, when each sees his own means placed on an equality with [those of] the most powerful. (EN: 240)[24]

Particularly notable in Caesar's description is not only the Germans' lack of landed property but also their outright opposition to the class divisions their establishment might stir up. Recording a remark from Tacitus, who wrote 150 years after Caesar, Marx leaves open the possibility that holdings in livestock were starting to foster economic inequality, incorporating into his notes the notion that cattle were "their sole wealth, which they value the most" (EN: 239).

As to political structure, Marx goes deeper into Tacitus than Morgan, recording the following passages showing a semi-democratic structure among the Germans:

> They choose their kings for their noble birth, their commanders for their valor. The power even of the kings is not absolute or arbitrary. The commanders rely on example rather than on the authority of their rank—on the admiration they win by . . . pressing forward in front of their own troops . . . On matters of minor importance only the chiefs debate; on major affairs, the whole community . . . The Assembly is competent also to hear criminal charges, especially those involving the risk of capital punishment . . . These same assemblies elect, among other officials, the magistrates who administer justice in the districts and villages. Each magistrate is assisted by a hundred assessors chosen from the people to advise him and to add weight to his decisions. (EN: 240)[25]

Marx finds the German arrangements similar to those of the Iroquois as described by Morgan.

By this time, around 100 CE, the Germans seem to have developed the beginnings of landed property, on which Marx again quotes Tacitus:

> The employment of capital in order to increase it by usury is unknown in Germany; and ignorance is here a surer defense than any prohibition.

---

24 See also Julius Caesar, *Commentaries on the Gallic Wars*, trans. W. A. McDevitte and W. S. Bohn, n.d. Book 6, Ch. 22, Internet Classics Archive, classics.mit.edu.

25 See also Publius Cornelius Tacitus, *The Germany and the Agricola*, c. 98 CE, Oxford Translation, revised, gutenberg.org.

Lands proportioned to their own number are appropriated in turn for tillage by the whole body of tillers. They then divide them among themselves according to rank; the division is made easy by the wide tracts of cultivable ground available. These ploughlands are changed yearly, and still there is enough and to spare. (EN: 241)[26]

Again, the fact that Marx, in his above-cited 1868 letters on Maurer, notes that some of these structures persisted in parts of Germany until almost his own time, suggests that these reflections were of more than historical importance to him. In the above-cited letter to Engels of March 25, 1868—as in these notebooks—Marx also takes issue with how important German scholars of the nineteenth century like the Grimm brothers misread and "mistranslated the simplest Latin sentences" in Caesar and Tacitus due to their prejudices, which led them to find private property where it did not exist, and to miss the fact of "communal land" (MECW 42: 558).

In his 1879–82 notebooks, a second non-Greco-Roman European people Marx studies closely with a focus on communal social forms is the Irish. Near the end of the notes on Morgan, he records this point about Celtic peoples: "The Celtic branch of the Aryan family (except that in India) held onto their gentile organization longer than any others" (EN: 238; MG: 357). He also refers to British anthropologist Henry Sumner Maine's theory—as mentioned by Morgan—to the effect that ancient Celtic communal structures survived among the medieval French *villeins*, a class of semi-free peasants (EN: 238). This seems to have taken Marx directly to Maine's writings.

Maine, a high British colonial official in India and simultaneously an Oxford and Cambridge professor, was the subject of Marx's ire throughout his notes on the British anthropologist's *Lectures on the Early History of Institutions* (1875). Marx's strictures center on two issues: (1) what he considered to be Maine's negative attitude toward communal social structures, and (2) his failure to realize, as had Morgan, that early communal societies tended to lack patriarchal families. On the first of these issues, Marx already attacked Maine in his 1879 notes on Kovalevsky on India, characterizing him not as a real scientist or scholar but a mere "publicist" for British colonialism:

---

26 See also ibid.

> The English officials of India and the publicists they supported, like
> *Sir Henry Maine*, etc., interpret the decline of communal property in
> Punjab – despite the tender loving care bestowed by the English upon
> the archaic form—as the simple outcome of *economic progress*, while
> they themselves are the *main* (active) *contributors* to this—to their
> own danger. (KOV: 394)

Note also how Marx suggests that the undermining of communal property would stir up things and destabilize British rule. On the second
point, gender and the family, Marx sees Maine's perspective as largely
refuted by Morgan's research, a topic to which I will return in the next
chapter.

Marx's lengthy notes on Maine's *Lectures on the Early History of
Institutions* are, judging from internal evidence, from at least as late as
June 1881, three months after the letter to Vera Zasulich, and thus constitute his last detailed set of notes on communal social forms. In
discussing precolonial Irish communal forms, Maine writes that these
formations block social progress, an argument that Marx records and
ridicules as an ideological expression:

> This ludicrous fellow . . . continues: "to the principle of several and
> absolute property in land [which existed overall more in Western
> Europe than in England] I hold this country to be committed . . . there
> can be no *material advance in civilization* unless landed property is
> held by groups at least as small as Families." . . . Oh you philistine!
> (EN: 294)

Maine is referring specifically to the precolonial Irish law of Gavelkind,
whereby property was divided equally among sons, as opposed to the
English law of primogeniture.

Thus, unlike in the Morgan notes, in those on Maine, Marx feels the
need to subject his source to critique at almost every point, while, at the
same time, incorporating his insights and data. This is critical appropriation of a most critical type.

Nonetheless, there are some issues on which Marx seems ready to
record Maine without too much derogation, most commonly around the
growth of hierarchy within the ancient clans. In a nomadic pastoral
society, where landed property had not really emerged as a major form

of wealth, herds of cattle were a chief form of wealth. On this, Marx records a passage from Maine without comment:

> The difficulty—in ancient Ireland—not to obtain land, but the means of cultivating it. The great owners of cattle were the various Chiefs, whose primitive superiority to the other tribesmen in this respect was probably owing to their natural functions as military leaders of the tribe. On the other hand it appears to follow from the Brehon laws that the Chiefs pressed by the difficulty of finding sufficient pasture for their herds. Have their growing power over the waste land of the particular group over which they presided, but most fruitful portions of the tribal territory probably those which the free tribesmen occupied. Hence the system of giving and receiving stock. (EN: 297)[27]

Such wealth in cattle lies at the origin of the financial term "stock."

This led to a system whereby chiefs were able to reduce some clan members to a dependent status, as in this passage Marx records from Maine:

> He is meanwhile the military (leader) of his tribesmen, and probably in that capacity has acquired great wealth in cattle. It has somehow become of great importance to him to place out portions of his herds among the tribesmen, and they on their part occasionally find themselves through stress of circumstance in pressing need of cattle for employment in tillage. Thus the Chiefs appear in the *Brehon law* as perpetually "*giving stock*" and the tribesmen as *receiving* it. By taking stock the *free Irish tribesman* becomes the *Ceile* or *Kyle*, the vassal or man of his Chief, owing him not only rent but service and homage. The exact effects of "commendation" are thus produced. The *more stock* the tribesman accepts from his Chief, the lower in status he sinks. (EN: 298; MN: 157–8)

At a later stage, this relation became more generalized and developed even among chiefs and high chiefs. Thus, "to 'give stock' came to mean

---

27 See also Henry Sumner Maine, *Lectures on the Early History of Institutions* [hereafter MN, with page references directly in the text] (New York: Henry Holt, 1875), p. 152.

the same thing as [feudal] 'commendation'" or vassalage. As an illustration, some legends recounted a high king of Ireland accepting stock from the Roman emperor as a form of connection that conveyed status within Ireland (EN: 300; MN: 165).

Another route toward greater hierarchy was the use by chiefs of *fuidhir* or "stranger tenants," those without clan membership but who could be absorbed as dependents without full rights. Placed onto wastelands controlled directly by the chiefs, these dependents could also be used to secure those parts of the wastelands that were also borderlands. As Marx again records Maine:

> On the "waste"—common tribeland not occupied—portions continuously brought under tillage or permanent pasture by settlements of tribesmen, and upon it cultivators of servile status are permitted to squat, particularly toward the border. It is the part their territory over which the authority of the Chief tends steadily to increase, and here he settles his "*fuidhir*," or stranger-tenants, a very important class—the outlaws and "broken" men from other tribes who come to him for protection are only . . . connected with their new tribe by their dependence on its chief, and through the responsibility which he incurs for them. (EN: 289–90; MN: 93)

If giving out cattle made free clan members into dependents of the chiefs, giving out wasteland to non-clan members secured for the chiefs a class of dependents with no real ties to the clan save through their relationship to them.

As Ireland was increasingly beset by both internal conflict and invasions from the Vikings and the English, the number of these "broken men" increased with a concomitant hardening of these incipient class hierarchies:

> And causes at work, powerfully and for long periods of time, to increase the numbers of this class: *Danish piracies, intestine feuds, Anglo-Norman attempts at conquest*, the existence of the Pale, and the policy directed from the Pale of *playing off against one another the Chiefs beyond its borders*. Through this civil war etc. tribes *far and wide broken up*, this implies a *multitude of broken men*. (EN: 303; MN: 183)

The increased power of Irish war chiefs would also have been a factor.

Marx chides Maine additionally for reading back into ancient times that succession of property and of office would follow from father to son in a patrilineal line. Not only does this miss the fact that most property was not yet held individually, but Maine overlooks the clan as the basis for succession, as Marx argues here:

> It is a *modern* prejudice, which springs from the notion of *testamentary inheritance* that the *division* of property has to occur specifically *after death*. Ownership of land, for example, was held in common even after its *transformation into the property of a private family*, in particular as the common property of this family, with every member having a morally determined [*ideellen*] share, and this remains after the death of the chief, whether the family stays together or whether it actually *separates*. (EN: 308–09)

Thus, succession went through the clan, not the individual family. Marx adds:

> And now Maine finds himself in a new difficulty, stemming from his lack of knowledge of the nature of the gens, namely that instead of the eldest son *the eldest male relative of the deceased* inherits . . . or that *neither the succession of the eldest son nor that of* the eldest *relative could take effect without election or confirmation by the members of the aggregate group to which they belong* . . . It is also a fiction of Mr. Maine that the *war chief* is originally the tribal chief. On the contrary, those chosen were elected on the basis of their individual capacities. (EN: 310)

In these ways, Marx avers the importance early on of communal social forms, often carrying out an immanent critique of Maine.

This is also true when it comes to the persistence of these communal social forms. As seen below, Marx reads Maine against the grain concerning *rundale* property, an ancient Irish form of village common land:

> Rundale holdings in part of Ireland; now most common form: *arable land held in severalty* (this describes the thing falsely!), while pasture and bog are in common. But as recent as 50 years ago, *cases were frequent* where the arable land divided in farms which *shifted* among

the *tenant-families* periodically, and sometimes annually. (101) According to Maine "the Irish holdings 'in rundale' are *not forms of property*, but *modes of appropriation*," but the fellow himself remarks: "*archaic kinds of tenancy* are constantly evidence of *ancient forms of proprietorship.*" (EN: 290)

Here, Marx is arguing that Maine's evidence, once separated from his interpretation, shows the persistence of communal forms into their own century. Moreover, rundale property seemed to be a remnant of something like the version of communal property found in India where, as discussed above, allotments were periodically re-allocated. As Eamonn Slater and Eoin Flaherty suggest, "the rundale agrarian commune" can be seen most clearly through the lens of "Marx's concept of the primitive communist mode of production" (2009: 24).[28] Is Marx also coming to see these vestiges of communal forms as linked to the implacable resistance of the contemporary Irish peasant to British colonialism and capitalism?

The Russian Communal Village

Marx was thinking in those very terms when he considered the case of the Russian communal form. There is considerable evidence in his correspondence after 1870 of his increasing interest in Russia and in its agrarian relations, but all that has attained published form besides these letters are the long drafts of an 1881 letter to Russian revolutionary Vera Zasulich and a brief discussion in the 1882 preface he and Engels contributed to a new Russian edition of the *Communist Manifesto*.[29] The

---

28   Eammon Slater and Eoin Flaherty, "Marx on Primitive Communism: The Irish Rundale Agrarian Commune, Its Internal Dynamics and the Metabolic Rift," *Irish Journal of Anthropology* 12: 2 (2009), p. 24.

29   Marx also took extensive notes during the years 1876–82 from Russian sources, particularly on agriculture and landed property, but this material has not yet been published. (It will eventually appear in Part IV of MEGA2, devoted to his excerpt notebooks.) The only notes on Russia to which I have had access appear in MEGAdigital IV/27 along with the notebooks discussed in this chapter. These notes on Russian sources cover: (1) Nikolai Kostomarov's book on Stenka Razin's early eighteenth-century Cossack uprising in Russia's eastern borderlands, and (2) an 1880 article on Russian banking and agriculture. However, neither of these two sets of notes deals with communal social structures and will therefore not be discussed in this study.

most substantial of these texts are the four fairly lengthy drafts for a brief March 8, 1881, letter to Zasulich, in reply to hers of February 16, on whether the communal social formations found in the Russian village might have some revolutionary possibilities in the coming period. In that letter of March 8, Marx alludes to his Russian studies, mentioning in passing "the special study I have made" of the Russian "rural commune," during which he "sought to obtain [*cherché*] original source material" (SHN: 124; MEGA I/25: 241).[30]

What is the temporal relationship of the Zasulich material to the notes on communal social forms discussed up to now in the present chapter? Since a remark near the end of Marx's notes regarding Maine on Ireland is dated June 1881 and Ireland is not mentioned in the February–March 1881 Zasulich materials, it is clear that Marx wrote the latter to Zasulich before he completed his study of Maine's book. He likely composed the Zasulich materials not long after he completed his notes on Morgan, to whom he refers obliquely in the first draft of the letter to Zasulich as "an American writer who, supported in his work by the Washington government, not at all to be suspected of revolutionary tendencies" but who nonetheless appreciated many features of communal social forms (SHN: 107; MEGA I/25: 220). He also discusses the ancient Germans in the Zasulich materials in similar terms to those he employs at the end of the Morgan notes. The notes on Kovalevsky, particularly those on different forms of communal social relations in India, to which he also refers in the Zasulich materials, but without naming him, were made about eighteen months earlier, probably in fall 1879. There is also a brief reference to the decline of the Roman Empire, possibly related to his notes on Rome from the same notebook in which the Kovalevsky notes can be found.

It should be underlined that the Zasulich materials are entirely Marx's words, drafts, and a letter rather than excerpt notebooks in which his own point of view is sometimes harder to discern. Marx's main purpose in this 1881 letter and its drafts is to defend the possibility of a Russian revolution based upon the village communes, a topic that will

---

30 In my discussions of the Zasulich letter and drafts, I will be citing Patrick Camiller's translation in the best English edition, that of Shanin in 1983 [SHN], but I will sometimes—as here—alter it slightly on the basis of the MEGA2 edition of 1985, which reproduces the text in its original French. Marx was trilingual, writing with ease in German, French, and English.

be taken up in later chapters. But his drafts also elaborate some general ideas about the history and nature of communal social forms based upon the kinds of research evidenced by his notebooks discussed above. In this sense, then, the Zasulich materials, at about 9,000 words, represent the closest thing we have to a systematic treatment on Marx's part of his thinking on communal social forms in his very last working years, 1879–82. However, one important gap lies in the fact that Ireland is not included, as it seems to have come up a bit later, in the notes on Maine.

At the outset, it is important once again to note that Marx is concerned here not only with communal property in the Russian village but also—and more fundamentally—with the communal mode of production, as seen in the first draft of his letter: "It is immediately apparent that one of its fundamental characteristics, common landownership, forms the natural basis of collective production and appropriation," this in a period prior to Marx's time (SHN: 113; MEGA I/25: 227).

Marx theorizes a number of issues concerning communal social formations in the drafts for the Zasulich letter, some of which are clearly connected to his study of Kovalevsky and Morgan. In the second draft of the Zasulich letter, he makes an analogy to the earth's geological layers, while placing the Russian village commune in the context of the other communal forms he has been studying:

> The archaic or primary formation of our globe itself contains a series of layers from various ages, the one superimposed on the other. Similarly, the archaic formation of society exhibits a series of different types, which mark progressive epochs. The Russian rural commune belongs to the most recent type in this chain. Already, the agricultural producer privately owns the house in which he lives, together with its complementary garden. This is the first element that dissolves the archaic form, and which is unknown to the older types. (SHN: 103; MEGA2 I/25: 233)

Thus, the Russian communal form represents an evolution from earlier types, now including communally owned farmland in the village, but also a degree of private property, in both a dwelling and a small plot of land for a garden. The is a first and major difference from older forms.

Moreover, even the far larger primary farmlands of the commune are not worked collectively, but by individual families: "The landed property is communal, but each peasant cultivates and works his field on his own account, like the small Western peasant" (SHN: 104; MEGA2 I/25: 233). Here, in the first draft of his Zasulich letter, Marx contrasts this to the ancient Germanic commune he took up a few months before in the notes on Morgan, but without mentioning the American anthropologist:

> We know nothing of the life of the commune after Tacitus, nor how and when it actually disappeared. Thanks to Julius Caesar, however, we do at least know its point of departure. In Caesar's time, the land was already distributed on an annual basis—not yet, however, among individual members of a commune, but among the gentes and tribes of the Germanic confederations. The agricultural rural commune therefore emerged in Germania from a more archaic type; it was the product of spontaneous development rather than being imported ready-made from Asia. It may also be found in Asia—in the East Indies—always as the final term or last period of the archaic formation. (SHN: 108; MEGA2 I/25: 223)

This earlier Germanic form had a more collectivist structure in terms of land distribution than the nineteenth-century Russian one.

Marx adds a second element of differentiation from the oldest communal forms, which is found in the residential rather than kinship-based foundation of the communal ties in the Russian village: "On the other hand, these older types all rest upon natural kinship relations between members of the commune, whereas the type to which the Russian commune belongs is emancipated from that narrow bond" (SHN: 103; MEGA2 I/25: 233).

As to the future prospects of the village commune, Marx challenges the notion that it is inevitably doomed to extinction: "What threatens the life of the Russian commune is neither a historical inevitability nor a theory; it is state oppression, and exploitation by capitalist intruders whom the state has made powerful at the peasants' expense" (SHN: 103; MEGA2 I/25: 233). In this vein, he also refers to Maine, but apparently to his earlier *Village-Communities in the East and West* (1871), rather than the work Marx was soon to annotate, *Lectures on the Early History of Institutions* (1875). In an attack on Maine as basically an ideologue, he writes:

> When reading the histories of primitive communes written by bourgeois authors, one should be on guard. They do not shrink even from

falsehood. Sir Henry Maine, for example, who enthusiastically collab-
orated with the English government in its violent destruction of the
Indian communes, hypocritically assures us that all the government's
noble efforts to maintain the communes failed against the spontaneous power of economic laws! (SHN: 107; MEGA2 I/25: 230)

In so doing, Marx is also reading beneath the surface of authors like
Maine to argue for the persistence and durability of communal forms not
only in past history, but right up to the present.

In this regard, he also refers to his previous reflections on Maurer,
suggesting that communal forms persisted even in Germany, where they
had been mostly undermined by feudalism:

> Scattered examples survived all the episodes of the Middle Ages and
> have maintained themselves up to the present day—e.g. in my own
> home region of Trier. More importantly, however, it so stamped its
> own features on the commune that supplanted it—commune in
> which arable land became private property, while forests, pastures,
> wastelands, etc., remained communal property—that Maurer, in deci-
> phering the commune of secondary formation, could reconstruct the
> archaic prototype. Thanks to the characteristic features inherited from
> the prototype, the new commune which the Germans introduced into
> every conquered region became the only focus of liberty and popular
> life throughout the Middle Ages. (SHN: 107–8; MEGA2 I/25: 223)

While this was a more evolved form of the commune, with many admix-
tures of private interest and private property, important remnants of the
deeper kind of commune from pre-feudal days survived in the communal
property that still constituted something important in the German village.

In Russia, however, these survivals were wider and deeper, for it had
not gone through Western feudalism. Russia's communal forms were
older and more genuinely communistic. And, while Russia was experiencing pressure from the new capitalist economies of Western Europe,
it still had choices in terms of avoiding capitalism, in no small part
because it was not directly ruled by a capitalist colonial power like
Britain in India.

This takes us to areas that will be discussed in later chapters: how
Marx saw the Russian commune's future prospects and its relation to a

wider European revolution that he also was conceptualizing right up to the end of his life.

But before going there, I would be highly remiss not to discuss an aspect of communal formations and their successor class societies that loomed very prominently in Marx's notebooks. Only touched on so far, this is the issue of gender and the family, to which the next chapter is devoted.

2

Temporalities and Geographies of Gender, Kinship, and Women's Empowerment

Prologue: Some Weaknesses of Engels's *Origin of the Family*

Before getting into the substance of this chapter, it is necessary to step back and develop a critique of the most celebrated Marxist discussion of gender and kinship, Engels's *Origin of the Family, Private Property, and the State*. Engels wrote it based on his understanding of Marx's notes on the American anthropologist Lewis Henry Morgan, which he studied soon after his friend's death in March 1883. *Origin of the Family*, which appeared in 1884, was the first major work Engels published or edited in the wake of Marx's death, aside from the 1883 third German edition of *Capital*, Vol. I, which was nearly ready for publication at Marx's death. In the preface to *Origin of the Family*, Engels wrote that he was fulfilling a "legacy [*Vermächtnis*]"[1] left to him by Marx, who had

> planned to present the results of Morgan's researches in connection with his own—in certain limits I might say our own—materialist study of history [*materialistische Geschichtsuntersuchung*][2] and only

---

1 Could also be translated as "bequest" or "at Marx's behest."
2 The terms "materialist conception of history [*materialistische Anschauung der Geschichte*, or *materialistische Geschichtsauffassung*]" or "historical materialism," which

thus to make clear their whole significance. For Morgan rediscovered in America, in his own way, the materialist conception of history that had been discovered by Marx forty years ago and . . . was led by this conception to the same conclusions, in the main points, as Marx. (MECW 26: 131; MEW 21: 27)

Engels offers no evidence that Marx agreed with his view that Morgan used the same historical and materialist method, or that Marx had transmitted a "legacy" to him. It is, of course, possible that Marx did so in conversation with Engels, or even with Engels and Kovalevsky, who had introduced Marx to Morgan's book. But Marx's own notes on Morgan, with their frequent criticisms of Morgan, suggest that Engels was vastly simplifying matters here.

As the Italian philosopher Emanuela Conversano notes, however, Engels was, in a sense, right to concentrate on Morgan, since Marx saw Morgan as far more profound than the other anthropologists he studied during this period, enabling him to use Morgan to critique their "ideological naturalization of the monogamian family."[3] But that is not the same thing as amalgamation.

Engels's amalgamation of Marx with Morgan was, however, strongly connected to something else, at least conceptually, his equally problematic assimilation of Marx to Charles Darwin, as seen in his March 1883 speech at Marx's funeral: "Just as Darwin discovered the law of development of organic nature, so Marx discovered the law of development of human history" (MECW 24: 467). The common thread here, whether it concerns Darwin or Morgan, is an attempt to endow Marx's theorization of capitalism with the prestige of a great scientific

---

one might have expected Engels to have used here, seem not yet to have solidified in the Marxist lexicon. Six years earlier, in *Anti-Dühring* (MECW 25:254; MEW 20:248), Engels had written of "the materialist conception [*Anschauung*] of history," but that term seems not yet to have been standardized, even in his own mind. Nor was the term's English translation standardized as yet as "materialist conception of history," which can in any case be translated in a more open sense as the "materialist approach to history." Marx himself employed neither "materialist conception of history" nor "historical materialism," though he did on occasion refer to his approach as "materialist" or as one using the "dialectical method."

3 Emanuela Conversano, "Ethnological Notebooks," in *Marx: Key Concepts*, ed. by Riccardo Bellofiore and Tommaso Redelfi Riva (Cheltenham: Edward Elgar, 2024), p. 236.

discovery. Marx himself was more critical of the perspectives of natural science than has often been supposed—definitely more so than was Engels—as seen in an often overlooked footnote to *Capital* on the British biologist: "The weaknesses of the abstract materialism of natural science, a materialism which excludes the historical process, are immediately evident from the abstract and ideological conceptions expressed by its spokesmen whenever they venture beyond the bounds of their own specialty" (CAP: 494).

The fact that Morgan was a Darwinian may also have influenced Engels's uncritical acceptance of his findings. As Conversano suggests, Marx

> has reservations about Morgan's general theory of history. The latter's concept of development is an evolutionist account of the progress from barbarism to civilization so that all peoples should achieve, according to the "plan of Supreme Intelligence," which Marx cannot accept, as the systematic omissions in his notes on Morgan's book silently testify.[4]

For this reason, one needs to pay attention not only to Marx's comments and insertions but also to those passages and whole areas of argument that he, to use Conversano's formulation, "silently" skips over. The Italian social theorist Marcello Musto makes a similar point about the notes on Morgan, which also speaks to the rough, exploratory character of Marx's studies of communal social forms:

> Engels's thesis posited an overly schematic relationship between economic conflict and gender oppression that was absent from Marx's—fragmentary and highly intricate—notes . . . Whereas, in comparison with the Darwinist oracles, Marx's voice might seem uncertain and hesitant, he actually escaped the trap of economic determinism into which many of his followers and ostensible continuators tended to fall.[5]

---

4   Emanuela Conversano, "Marx, Hegel, and the Orient. World History and Historical *Milieus*," *Philosophica* 54 (2019), p. 75.

5   Marcello Musto, "A Reappraisal of Marx's *Ethnological Notebooks*: Family, Gender, and Individual vs. State and Colonialism," *Inter-Asia Cultural Studies* 24: 1 (2023), pp. 120, 124.

Nonetheless, partly because of Engels's funeral speech, although Engels himself never said any such thing, weakly sourced accounts were repeated for nearly a century, to the effect that Marx intended to dedicate Vol. II of *Capital* to Darwin. This myth was demolished only in the 1970s. In fact, all Marx ever did in this regard was to send Darwin a copy of the 1872–73 second German edition of *Capital*, with the dedication: "Mr. Charles Darwin / On the part of his sincere admirer / [signed] Karl Marx / London 16 June 1873," after which Darwin wrote a courteous but noncommittal reply.[6]

This kind of scientism within Marxism, which flourished in the early twentieth century among socialists and then as the governing ideology of Stalin's Soviet Union, has been subjected to critique by independent Marxist thinkers, ever since Georg Lukács in the 1920s and Jean-Paul Sartre in the 1940s, who often see it as similar to positivism in the social sciences. These philosophers have criticized Engels's concept of dialectic as schematic and crudely materialist. These critiques of Engels were not connected to his *Origin of the Family*, however, except in the sense that Simone de Beauvoir was certainly relying on Sartrean categories—and her own independently arrived at existentialist concepts—when she criticized Engels in *The Second Sex*, as will be discussed below. But for Lukács and Sartre, the critique centered on Engels's writings on the dialectic proper.

In the case of Sartre, this meant a peremptory rejection of Engels tout court, and of Marx post-1844, for a lack of understanding of the subjective side of the dialectic, while praising the writings of the young Marx "in 1844, that is, until the unfortunate meeting with Engels."[7] Lukács criticizes the scientistic aspects of Engels's concept of dialectic: "Engels's deepest misunderstanding consists in his belief that the behavior of industry and scientific experiment constitutes praxis in the dialectical, philosophical sense. In fact, scientific experiment is contemplation at its purest."[8] He also writes that Engels "does not even mention the most vital

6 Margaret A. Fay, "Did Marx Offer to Dedicate Capital to Darwin?" *Journal of the History of Ideas* 39: 1 (1978), p. 134. See also Margaret A. Fay, "Marx and Darwin: A Literary Detective Story," *Monthly Review* 31:10 (1980), pp. 40–57.

7 Jean-Paul Sartre, "Materialism and Revolution," *Literary and Philosophical Essays*, trans. Annette Michelson (New York: Criterion, [1946] 1955), p. 233. Sartre's essay is most notable for its separation of the young Marx (good) from the later Marx (determinist), something that Louis Althusser later inverts, now against the young Marx.

8 Georg Lukács, *History and Class Consciousness: Studies in Marxist Dialectics*, trans. Rodney Livingstone, with a new introduction by Michael Löwy (London: Verso [1923] 2023), p. 132.

interaction, namely the dialectical relation between subject and object in the historical process, let alone give it the prominence it deserves."[9] Thus, for Lukács, Engels overestimated the importance of "scientific" historical "laws" while leaving out the subjective side of the dialectic, wherein human beings shape history just as they are shaped by it.

But attacking Engels on gender was a different matter. Eleanor Leacock, a Marxist feminist anthropologist close to the positions of Engels and Morgan, declared in the 1970s that Engels was the best of any Marxist on women, and that the reason "male Marxists, especially in France" criticized him so much was because they could not "take" Engels's forceful statements against sexism in *Origin of the Family*.[10] Leacock's anti-critique should not be dismissed lightly, however, as her response highlighted the fact that very few prominent male Marxists had ever written anything of substance on women or gender. In this sense, Engels's *Origin of the Family* forms an important milestone in Marxist thought, as it places women's oppression at the center of the whole structure of class society, from the ancient Greco-Roman world to capitalism. Engels also advocates the radical emancipation of women from their position in the family as much as from their exploitation in the workplace.

Engels's concomitant critique of modern industrial civilization in *Origin of the Family* also earned him a rare open criticism from within Stalinist orthodoxy, which claimed the heritage of Marx and Engels, albeit in an alienated, ideological form. The Stalinist critique of Engels occurred after the forced industrialization of the 1930s and during the drive for production that accompanied World War II. In "Teaching of Economics in the Soviet Union," an unsigned programmatic text published in the key journal *Pod Znamenem Marksizma* [Under the Banner of Marxism], these ideologues wrote:

> In the past the teaching of political economy was in error in its treatment of the *primitive communal system*. These errors consisted in this,

---

9   Ibid., p. 3.

10   Leacock made these remarks in response to my query about whether feminists needed to criticize Engels in light of Krader's edition of Marx's *Ethnological Notebooks*, which Dunayevskaya had begun to use as the basis for a new critique of Engels. Leacock did so in the question period after her presentation, "The Origins of Women's Oppression," part of the Engels Lecture Series at the New York School for Marxist Education, December 1978.

that, firstly, it violated the principle of historical materialism, according to which a definite form of production relations is determined by the character of the productive forces; and, secondly, it permitted an idealization of the primitive communal system in clear contradiction of historical reality. The basis of the erroneous interpretation of the development of the primitive communal order was the familiar remark of Engels in the introduction to *The Origin of the Family, Private Property and the State*, to the effect that in the period preceding civilization, the social structure was determined by the conditions of the production of material goods as well as by the conditions of the production of man himself, *i.e.*, by the forms of the family [MECW 26, pp. 131–2] . . . The above erroneous remark of Engels contradicts the many entirely unequivocal statements of Marx and Engels himself that the development of the productive forces is the basis of production relations.[11]

In short, in giving so much weight to forms of the family, Engels was "departing from the monistic view of history" by failing to reduce everything to the "development of the productive forces" and looking at gender as an independent force.[12] This is to Engels's credit, although he did so only partially in *Origin of the Family*, as against the more creative probings Marx himself carried out in his notes on Morgan. The fact that Stalinist ideologues attacked *Origin of the Family*, any more than that most Marxists have canonized it, should not, however, spare Engels from criticism.

Engels's key theses in *The Origin of the Family* include the notion of a relatively free, communal, and egalitarian prehistory of humanity, with a typical early human community consisting of democratic tribal federations. He bases this view almost completely on Morgan. According to Engels and Morgan, the preliterate human community is matrilineal and democratic, and sexual relations take the form of group marriage. On the position of women in these kinds of societies, Engels writes:

But communistic housekeeping implies the supremacy of women in the house; just as the exclusive recognition of the biological female

---

11   "Teaching of Economics in the Soviet Union," trans. Raya Dunayevskaya, *American Economic Review* 34: 3 (194), pp. 504–5.
12   Ibid., p. 505.

parent, because of the impossibility of determining the biological father with certainty, signifies high esteem for the women, i.e., the mothers. One of the most absurd notions taken over from the Enlightenment of the eighteenth century is that in the beginning of society woman was the slave of man. Among all savages and among all barbarians of the lower and middle stages, and to a certain extent of the upper stage as well, women occupied not only a free but also a highly respected position. (MECW 26: 158)

Engels develops this point in lengthy descriptions of preliterate and more contemporary examples of communist social relations in widely separated geographic areas and time spans—from the Pacific islands of his own time to North American Indigenous peoples at the time of European penetration, and to very early European peoples. It is hard not to feel an affinity between Engels's arguments here and Rousseau's concept of the "noble savage." As discussed in the previous chapter, Marx refrains from this kind of idealization of early communal societies. In addition, for Engels and Morgan, the history of different peoples moved through clearly defined and universal stages. The key dividing line was the advent of the stage of monogamous marriage under patriarchal domination. Engels regards this new stage as "the world historical defeat of the female sex" (MECW 26: 165). He continues:

The man seized the reins in the house also; the woman was degraded and reduced to servitude, the slave of his lust and a mere instrument for the production of children. Women's humiliating position, especially manifest among the Greeks of the Heroic and still more the Classical Age, has become gradually glossed over [beschönigt] and dissembled and, to an extent, clothed in a milder form, but by no means eliminated. (MECW 26: 165)

Engels's concept of a "world-historical defeat of the female sex" exhibits an undialectical dismissal of any kind of serious contradiction or resistance within this unbroken chain of patriarchal domination. A second problem is that it lumps together what Marx—and to an extent Engels— saw as different modes of production within class society—ancient, Asian, feudal, capitalist—stretching over, at a minimum, some 4,000 years of history. Third, Engels's formulation is imbued with a certain conceptual rigidity in how it divides this long period of patriarchy from what went before. This contrasts with how the mature Marx theorized modes of production, when he held in *Capital* that "epochs in the history of society are no more separated by strict and abstract lines of demarcation than are geological epochs" (CAP: 492).

For Engels, the birth of the patriarchal family and the subjugation of women occur at the same time as the birth of class society and of private property. Thus, although Engels espouses—and with utter sincerity—a radical rejection of sexism, he ties the oppression of women in too deterministic a fashion to the rise of class society and of private property. In such a framework, socialism could appear to automatically abolish sexism by destroying its material basis in class society and private property. This is problematic enough, in that it undercuts the need for an independent women's movement challenging sexism within capitalist society.

But Engels goes further, conceding certain changes amid capitalist modernity, but adding that sexism is not really a problem within the proletariat because it lacks a material foundation:

> But here all the foundations of classical monogamy are pushed aside. Here there is a complete absence of all property, for the safeguarding and bequeathing of which monogamy and male domination were created. Therefore, there is no incentive [*Antrieb*][13] whatever here to assert male domination. What is more, the means too are absent: bourgeois law, which protects this domination, exists only for the propertied classes and their dealings with the proletarians. It costs money, and therefore, owing to the worker's poverty, has no validity in his position vis-à-vis his wife. Moreover, since large-scale industry has moved the woman from the house to the labor market and the factory, and made her, often enough, the breadwinner of the family, the last remnants of male domination in the proletarian home have lost all foundation—except, perhaps, for a bit of that brutality toward women that became firmly rooted with the establishment of monogamy. (MECW 26: 179)

---

13   Could also be translated as "motive," "propulsion," or "impetus," but "incentive" maintains better the economistic flavor of the entire passage.

Here, Engels concedes that the situation of women workers may not be fully equal to that of male proletarians, passing over partner abuse with a brief phrase. But overall, proletarian women experience relative equality in relation to proletarian men under capitalism because the latter own no property! This is a "materialism" verging on caricature.

Engels's stages of history and society, drawn directly from Morgan, show the family changing from matrilineal to patriarchal and then to the modern semi-monogamous (for women but not in reality for men) family, just as the economic basis of society changes from hunting and gathering to agriculture and, finally, to industry. Socialism constitutes the last stage, which will free women from their oppression just as it will free the workers as a whole. Only at this point will women recover from their "world historical defeat" of thousands of years ago. Part of this would involve freeing women from subordination to forced monogamy, and here Engels compares marriage to slavery. Marriage, he writes, "often enough turns into the crassest prostitution," but even worse than that, as "the wife . . . differs from the ordinary courtesan only in that she does not hire out her body, like a wage worker, on piecework, but sells it into slavery once and for all" (MECW 26: 179).

At this point, Engels cites the French utopian socialist Charles Fourier. Engels was a great admirer of Fourier, as shown in a footnote at the end of *Origin of the Family*:

> I originally intended to place the brilliant criticism of civilization which is found scattered through the work of Charles Fourier beside that of Morgan and my own. Unfortunately, I have not the time. I will only observe that Fourier already regards monogamy and private property in land as the chief characteristics of civilization, that he calls civilization a war of the rich against the poor. (MECW 26: 276)

This probably has a relationship to Engels's overly positive treatment of the condition of women in the communal societies he examines in *Origin of the Family*. Here, it should also be noted that Marx did not share this high assessment of Fourier's notion of sexual liberation.[14]

---

14   For example, Marx refers acidly in *Capital* to Fourier's notions of sexual liberation—"phanerogamie"—in describing the sexual exploitation of teenage girls in rural work gangs (CAP: 852).

Conversano notes another problem with Morgan as well as Engels, from a different vantage point than the Stalinist critique. She writes of a reductionist tendency to view kinship and family forms as outcomes of "material progress of the means of subsistence" in a universalist stage theory that amounts to "a design superimposed on all peoples." "On the contrary," Conversano avers, "Marx emphasizes the active, primary role of family relationships as a driving force inside society," not only as a reflection of supposedly deeper social forces.[15] In this sense, Marx recognizes gender and family relations as structures operating with a degree of independence and autonomy from the economic "base."

In appropriating Morgan's findings about early and contemporary "primitive" peoples for Marxism, Engels argues convincingly against the supposed virtues and vaunted "progress" of modern capitalist civilization. This argument became more attractive in the era of imperialist conquests of Africa and Asia, and later, of destructive world wars and concentration camps in the twentieth century. However, the rigid stages Engels borrows from Morgan—and even amplifies—leave no room for any other path than the destruction of early communalism by class society and eventually capitalism. Only much later could a socialist transformation develop. Modern communism might keep something from the dim memory of early communalism, but that was all.

For Engels, the most important reason for writing *Origin of the Family*, it seemed, was to demonstrate that through most of its existence, the human species had practiced forms of communism. This proved the practicality of communism while also suggesting that it was our "natural" state. However, Engels's book makes no explicit connection to forms of agrarian or Indigenous communism that still existed at the time, or to modern capitalist colonialism and imperialism. In that sense, *Origin of the Family* was no more and no less than what the title suggested, an inquiry not into the varieties of contemporary human society, but into its distant origins.

The classic feminist response to Engels is found in Simone de Beauvoir's *The Second Sex*. In a chapter entitled "The View of Historical Materialism," she questions Engels's view of prehistory, seeing it as superficial. She writes: "The turning point of all history is the passage from the communal regime [*régime communitaire*] to that of private

---

15 Conversano, "Ethnological Notebooks," p. 238.

property, and it is in no wise indicated how this could have come about."[16] De Beauvoir chides Engels, not only for failing to explain adequately how private property emerged from communal social formations but also for how he links this development schematically to a putative "world historic defeat of the female sex," maintaining, contra Engels, that "it is impossible to *deduce* the oppression of women from the institution of private property."[17]

Far from attacking Marxism tout court, De Beauvoir acknowledges elsewhere in *The Second Sex* the profundity of Marx's 1844 theorization of the relationship of man to woman as the most fundamental one, underlying all other human relationships. She cites Marx at length in the book's penultimate paragraph:

> The direct, natural, necessary relationship of human being [*Mensch*] to human being is the *relationship of man [Mann] to woman [Weib]*. [. . .] The nature of this relationship determines to what point the human being itself is to be considered a species being, a human being; the relation of man to woman is the most natural relationship of human being to human being. [. . .] Therefore, in it is revealed the degree to which the *natural* behavior of the human being has become human or to what degree the human being has become its natural being, to what point its human nature has become its nature.[18]

De Beauvoir identifies strongly with this ringing statement of the young Marx: "The case could not be better stated. It is for man [the human being] to establish the era [*reigne*] of freedom."[19]

De Beauvoir also opposes notions of women's emancipation that are confined to the sphere of sexual freedom in a one-sided fashion. In this regard, she also offers a probing critique of Fourier. De Beauvoir writes that although Fourier championed non-coercive sexual relationships, he "confused the emancipation [*affranchissment*] of women with the

---

16   Simone de Beauvoir, *The Second Sex*, trans. H. M. Parshley (New York: Vintage, [1949] 1989), p. 53.

17   Ibid., p. 57.

18   Ibid., p. 731–2; see also Marx, "Economic and Philosophical Manuscripts," trans. Tom Bottomore, in Erich Fromm, *Marx's Concept of Man* (New York: Ungar, 1961), p. 126.

19   Beauvoir, *The Second Sex*, p. 732.

recovery of bodily freedom [*réhabilitation de la chair*]."[20] In this way, de Beauvoir concludes, Fourier minimized women's intellectual capacities and "considered woman not as a person but in her amorous functions."[21] This also may have been an implicit critique of Engels's reliance on Fourier. Equally important, de Beauvoir here offers insight into a long-standing effort on the part of Marx interpreters to view his long 1844 statement about women's emancipation as a measure of general human emancipation as a mere paraphrase of Fourier. Yet whereas Engels adopts much of Fourier's stance on sexuality, Marx does not do so, either in 1844 or in the 1880–81 notes on Morgan that inspired Engels to write *Origin of the Family*. Perhaps this problem is also related to Marx's vehement condemnation in 1844 of a "crude communism" that replaces woman's position as private property of the husband "with the community of women in which women become communal and common property," in a form of communism that would mean "universal prostitution" and that for this and other reasons, "negates the personality of the human being."[22] Such a crude communism, Marx adds, leaves women "as the spoils [*Raub*][23] and handmaiden of communal lust." Here, de Beauvoir, with a sharp feminist eye, has put her finger on an important issue.

In the late 1970s, Dunayevskaya put forth the first feminist critique of *Origin of the Family* that contrasted this work to Marx's own findings and methodology concerning communal social formations, their gender and kinship relations, and the subsequent development of class societies permeated with patriarchal gender and kinship relations. Taking issue with Leacock, Dunayevskaya notes that the Marxist-feminist anthropologist had failed to mention Marx's *Ethnological Notebooks* in her introduction to *Origin of the Family* and that in this way, "She perpetuated the myth that *The Origin of the Family* is a product of Marx as well as Engels."[24] Krader had been rather circumspect in portraying key

---

20   More literally, "rehabilitation of the flesh."

21   Beauvoir, *The Second Sex*, p. 113.

22   Marx, "Economic and Philosophical Manuscripts," p. 125.

23   *Raub* connotes the abduction and rape of women, or the turning of women into war "booty" in such circumstances. Marx, "Economic and Philosophical Manuscripts," p. 126.

24   Raya Dunayevskaya, "Marx's and Engels' Studies Contrasted: Relationship of Philosophy and Revolution to Women's Liberation," *Women's Liberation and the Dialectics of Revolution: Reaching for the Future* (New Jersey: Humanities Press, [1979] 1985), p. 206.

differences between Marx and Engels, to wit: "Marx was more critical than Morgan or Engels of hypothetical reconstructions of the past based upon organicist assumptions in regard to the workings of society" (EN: 53). But Dunayevskaya hits out hard at Engels, acknowledging only in passing some revolutionary qualities in *Origin of the Family*:

> It is true that it was great, in 1884, to stress the manner in which woman had always been oppressed since her "world historic defeat," how different it had been in "matriarchal" society, and how socialism would be the re-establishment of primitive communism on a higher scale . . . But the fact is that Engels's writing there is neither very dialectical nor comprehensive when it gets fixed on the family.[25]

How did that lack of a fully dialectical analysis manifest itself?

Dunayevskaya refers to what she terms the "two worst 'Engelsian-isms'" in *Origin of the Family*. The first of these is the concept of a "world historic defeat of the female sex," which as Dunayevskaya notes, "is no expression of Marx's." She holds that "Marx rejected biologism" in Morgan and Darwin, as against Engels's nearly uncritical appropriation of each of these thinkers into historical materialism. The second problematic "Engelsianism" lies in how the concept of a world historic defeat is developed in such a way that allows Marxists, insofar as women are concerned, "to conveniently put off freedom until the millennium." In the framework developed by Engels, women's oppression persists over millennia in undiluted and more or less unchanging form and can only be uprooted as part of "larger" struggles over class and property relations. In short, Engels makes a class/economic reductionist argument concerning both women's oppression and how it is to be overcome.[26]

More recently, the feminist scholar Melda Yaman, who has translated Dunayevskaya into Turkish, has carried out the most comprehensive critique to date of Engels on the "world-historical defeat," which she terms "one of the deepest divergences between *The Origin* and the *Ethnological Notebooks*."[27]

25   Raya Dunayevskaya, *Rosa Luxemburg, Women's Liberation, and Marx's Philosophy of Revolution*, second edition (Urbana: University of Illinois Press [1982] 1991), p. 106.

26   Ibid., p. 105.

27   Melda Yaman, "Origin of Engels' *The Origin*: A Reappraisal in the Light of *The Ethnological Notebooks of Marx*," *Marxism & Sciences* 1: 1 (2021), p. 122.

Similar to Lukács in his 1923 critique, Dunayevskaya also acknowledges Engels's "mechanical positivism."[28] In contrast to Lukács, however, she does so not in terms of Engels's confusion of natural science experimentation, which lacks a reference to the human subject, with dialectics. Rather, her critique targets the unilinear theory of stages of the family/kinship that Engels appropriated from Morgan, doing so uncritically rather than dialectically:

> As against Marx's multilinear view which kept Marx from attempting any blueprints for future generations, Engels's unilinear view led him to mechanical positivism. By no accident whatsoever, such one-dimensionality kept him from seeing either the communal form under "Oriental despotism" or the duality in "primitive communism" in Morgan's *Ancient Society*. No wonder, although Engels had accepted Marx's view of the Asiatic mode of production as fundamental enough to constitute a fourth form of human development, he had left it out altogether from *his* analysis of primitive communism in the first book he wrote as a "bequest" of Marx—*Origin of the Family*. By then Engels had confined Marx's revolutionary dialectics and historical materialism to hardly more than Morgan's "materialism."[29]

From this perspective, Engels's "mechanical positivism" is linked to his failure to view societies outside Western Europe as more than one-dimensional. Because of this, he misses the dualities and contradictions within both the "Asiatic" mode of production and much less technologically developed communal forms like those of the Iroquois of North America.

In the above discussion, I have attempted to untangle Marx from Engels on gender and kinship to help us view him on his own terms. With that in mind, let us turn again to Marx's 1879–82 notebooks, now with a focus on gender and kinship.

---

28 Dunayevskaya, *Rosa Luxemburg*, p. xxxvi.
29 Ibid.

Marx and Morgan on Gender Relations and Indigenous Communal Forms

Since Kovalevsky takes up gender and kinship hardly at all in his book on communal social formations, I will begin the discussion here with Marx's notes on Morgan, focusing first on Native American and other Indigenous societies where communal social formations exhibited a degree of women's social power that Marx, like Engels, found intriguing and important.

Marx begins his discussion of gender/kinship with Morgan's typology of different stages within hunter-gatherer societies ("savagery" in Morgan's terminology) and later semi-agrarian ones ("barbarism" in Morgan's terminology), here mapped onto successive forms of kinship. As Engels emphasizes, Morgan and Marx see a development from very egalitarian societies with low levels of technology to increasingly hierarchical ones.

To be sure, this assumption of communistic social relations as fundamental to early human existence stands in sharp contrast to many mainstream interpretations in popular culture, which continue to read back into the preliterate past the hierarchical forms of later class societies. An example of this is found in a recent journalistic article on DNA findings concerning the neolithic societies in Ireland that built Newgrange, a mound with a passage leading to an underground chamber constructed so precisely that the sun's rays shine onto what may have been an altar twice a year, at the winter and summer solstices. As a *New York Times* article intoned breathlessly in 2020:

> A team of Irish geneticists and archaeologists reported Wednesday that a man whose cremated remains were interred at the very heart of Newgrange was the product of a first-degree incestuous union, either between parent and child, or brother and sister. The finding, combined with other genetic and archaeological evidence, suggests that the people who built these mounds lived in a hierarchical society with a ruling elite that considered themselves so close to divine that, like the Egyptian pharaohs, they could break the ultimate taboos.[30]

---

30   James Gorman, "DNA of 'Irish Pharaoh' Sheds Light on Ancient Tomb Builders," *New York Times* (June 17, 2020, updated June 23).

The article offers no evidence as to why the mere existence of brother-sister or parent-child sexual unions—considered to be incestuous in most societies—is clear proof of a "pharaonic" social hierarchy, except that such unions also existed among the Egyptian pharaohs thousands of miles away during the same time period. The scholarly article on which the journalistic report is based refers to evidence that the general population at the time was not apparently involved in such sexual unions.[31] While it is likely that those buried inside Newgrange enjoyed some type of special status, the notion that they formed a "ruling elite" with "divine" pretensions, or that Irish society in this period even had such elites, is highly speculative.

We cannot know what Marx would have thought of such an interpretation of the social implications of such a DNA finding, but his remark in a June 8, 1862, letter to Engels on Darwin and "competition" suggests he might have been skeptical:

> It is remarkable how among beasts and plants Darwin recognizes his English society with its division of labor, competition, opening up of new markets, "inventions" and Malthusian "struggle for existence." It is Hobbes's "war of each against all" and reminds one of Hegel's *Phenomenology* where civil society figures as the "spiritual animal kingdom," whilst with Darwin the animal kingdom figures as civil society. (MECW 41: 381)

As discussed in the previous chapter, at this very general level, Engels and Marx are mostly in accord, with the caveat that Marx perceives some social forces reaching for hierarchy even inside the most egalitarian social forms, while Engels holds back on any criticism of Morgan's idealizations of early clan societies.

In a remark in his notes on Morgan, Marx holds that forms of the family "correspond above all [*verhält es sich* überhaupt] to political, religious, juridical, philosophical systems" (EN: 112). He seems to adopt Morgan's typology of egalitarian societies shifting toward more hierarchical ones in terms of gender relations and kinship patterns. However, as already discussed above and in the previous chapter, Marx does so

---

31   Lara Cassidy et al., "A Dynastic Elite in Monumental Neolithic Society," *Nature* 582 (June 18, 2020), p. 384.

without the kind of idealization of these preliterate societies as found in Engels and, to a lesser degree, Morgan. He also attempts to discern dualities and contradictions within these societies, finding incipient class relations within them.

Here is Marx's abbreviated quotation of Morgan's list of kinship forms, which the American anthropologist calls "family" forms:

1) *Consanguine family; intermarriage of brothers and sisters in a group;* . . .
2) *Punaluan family*; name derived from the *Hawaiian* relationship of *Punalua*. Founded upon the *intermarriage of several brothers to each other's wives in a group; and of several sisters to each other's husbands in a group.* "Brother" includes the first, second, third, and even more remote cousins, all considered as brothers; and "sister" includes first, 2nd, 3d, and even more remote female cousins, all sisters to each other. The *Turanian and Ganowanian systems of consanguinity* are grounded in this form of family. Both forms of the family belong to *period of savagery.*
3) The *Syndyasmian family* . . . Founded *upon the pairing of a male and a female* under the form of marriage, *but without an exclusive cohabitation*, is germ of the Monogamian family. Divorce or separation at the option of both husband and wife. *No particular system of consanguinity* was grounded in this family form.
4) *The Patriarchal family*; founded upon the marriage of one man to several women. In *Hebrew pastoral tribes* the *chiefs and principal men* practiced polygamy. Little influence on mankind for want of universality.
5) *Monogamian family; marriage of one man with one woman, with an exclusive cohabitation*; preeminently the *family of civilized society, essentially modern. An independent system of consanguinity* was grounded in this family form. (EN: 102; MG: 27–8)

Marx does not study consanguine brother-sister forms very much, except to note very briefly that they were displaced by punaluan kinship forms.

In Morgan's conceptualization of the punaluan form, society is organized into gender-based "classes" where groups of biological brothers and sisters marry each other. These are not social classes, in the sense of hierarchies based on property and power, but, rather, more egalitarian social divisions. On the transition from consanguine to punaluan kinship, Marx takes down a sentence from Morgan: "The organization into classes seems to have been directed to the single object of breaking up the intermarriage of brothers and sisters" (EN: 143; MG: 58).

Marx moves quickly to the transition to clan-based societies and to syndyasmian marriage systems, as described in anthropological accounts of Australian Aborigines. Here, Marx seems particularly interested in Morgan's notion that clan-based or "gentile" societies evolved out of and in opposition to the group marriages of the punaluan stage—with women and men as separate "classes"—that Morgan posits as dominant in earlier social formations. Within the more clan-based Australian societies, traces of these earlier forms can be found and also deduced: "Evident from internal considerations that the male and female classes older than the gentes, that, among the Kamilaroi, are in processes of overthrowing the classes," that is the social divisions based upon gender (EN: 139). As the clan-based social forms displace these older ones, new types of kinship and marriage are developing, as seen in this passage from Morgan that Marx paraphrases:

> Absolute prohibition for males or females to marry into their own gens. Descent in female line, which assigns children to the line of their mother. These features of archaic form of gens. But outside of this exists further and older division of people in 8 classes, 4 exclusively of males and 4 exclusively of females. It is accompanied with a regulation in respect to marriage and descent which (obstructs) the gens (shows that this organization later . . . Marriage is restricted to a portion of the males of one gens with a portion of the females of another gens, which in developed gentile organization members of each gens allowed to marry persons of the opposite sex in all the gentes except their own. (EN: 140; MG: 52)

Thus, features of the punaluan system persist into the clan or gentile stage. Both of these forms feature matrilineal forms of descent, which to Morgan and Marx suggests a high degree of gender equality and of female social power.

Marx's only other treatment of Australian Aborigines in his 1879–82 notebooks, albeit not on gender per se, occurs a year or so later in his notes on John Lubbock's 1870 work of popular science, The Origin of

Civilisation and the Primitive Condition of Man. In these passages he records from Lubbock, which are among Marx's very last writings, he ridicules in parenthetical expressions a British missionary's abstract religious idealism and sides with "the intelligent black":

> The *belief* in the *soul* (not identical with ghosts) *in an universal, independent and endless existence is confined* to the *highest* (?) races of mankind. The Reverend Lang in his "*The Aborigines of Australia*" had a friend, the which friend "tried long and patiently to make a very intelligent Australian *understand* (should say make him believe) his existence without a body, but the black never would keep his countenance . . . for a long time he could not believe ("he" is the intelligent black) that the "gentleman" (i.e. the Reverend Lang silly friend) *was serious*, and when he did realise it (that the gentleman was an ass in good earnest), the more serious the teacher was the more ludicrous the whole affair appeared to be." (245, 246) (Lubbock makes a fool of himself and does not realize how this has happened.) (EN: 349)

Marx does something similar with another passage in Lubbock, where the journalist generalizes in a racist and rather obtuse manner about matrilineal succession among "lower races":

> "Among many of the lower races *relationship through females is the prevalent custom*" thus "the curious (!) practice that *a man's heirs* [but they are therefore not the *man's heirs*; these civilized asses cannot let go of their own conventionalities] are not his own, but *his sister's children*." (EN: 340)

Marx carries out his most extensive discussion of these issues in his treatment of the Iroquois in his notes on Morgan on Native American societies, to which I now turn.

Marx singles out a number of passages concerning Iroquois gender practices, stressing the relative social power of women, as here in a long quote from one of Morgan's sources, an 1873 report from Asher Wright, a former missionary among the Seneca nation of the Iroquois Confederacy:

> *As to their families, when occupying the old long-houses . . .* some *one clan predominated, the women taking in husbands from the other clans;*

and *sometimes*, for a novelty, *some of their sons* bringing in their young wives until they felt brave enough to leave their mothers. *Usually, the female portion ruled the house . . . The stores were in common*; but woe to the luckless husband or lover who was too shiftless to do his share of the providing. No matter how many children, or whatever goods he might have in the house, he might at any time be ordered to pick up and budge, cannot attempt to disobey. The house would be too hot for him, . . . he must retreat to his own clan; or, as was often done, go and start a new matrimonial alliance in some other. *The women were the great power among the clans, as everywhere else.* They did not hesitate, when occasion required, *"to knock off the horns,"* as it was technically called, from the head of a chief, and send him back to the ranks of the warriors. *The original nomination of the chiefs also always rested with them.* (EN: 116; MG: 455)

Women thus ruled the household, including its material property, its "stores." But something more was suggested by the practice of "knocking off the horns" of chiefs, or of nominating them. These, too, were formidable forms of authority held by women, linked firmly to the matrilineal clan structure.

Marx also gives much attention to the matrilineal succession system found among the Iroquois and among some other Native American groups:

With almost all American Indian tribes *2 grades of chiefs, sachem* and *common chiefs; from these 2 primary grades all other grades* were varieties; *elected in each gens from among its members, a son* could not be elected to succeed his father, where *descent in the female line,* because he *belonged to a different gens.* (EN: 145; MG: 71)

The office of sachem or peace chief, he also records from Morgan, was *"older than the gens,* belongs likewise to *punaluan group* or even the *anterior horde"* (EN: 145; MG: 72). This process of election, which excluded patrilineal descent, was, as Marx again quotes Morgan, a "choice, by *free suffrage of both males and females of adult age"* (EN: 146).

Marx also examines Iroquois religious practices during their six annual festivals, pointing—in the following passage excerpted from Morgan—to gender equality and the lack of any kind of clerical hierarchy:

Each gens furnished a number of "*Keepers of the Faith*," male and female, charged with celebration each of the festivals; themselves conducted the ceremonies together with Sachems and Chiefs of the Tribes who, *ex officio*, "Keepers of the Faith." With no official head, none of the marks of a priesthood, their functions equal. The "*female keepers of the faith*" esp. charged with preparation of the feast, provided at all councils at the close of each day for all persons in attendance. The *dinner in common*. (EN: 149; MG: 82)

Perhaps Marx's underlining of the phrase "female keepers of the faith" at the point where Morgan discusses their food preparation duties, while presumably the men enjoyed the food and drink, may have been a way of noting for future reference that the gender equality described by Morgan might not have been as complete as the American anthropologist seemed to suggest.

Marx does something similar with Morgan's discussion of women's speaking and voting rights during meetings of the (male) "council of chiefs." These councils were conducted in public and with a wide level of participation not limited to chiefs, as he records from Morgan:

Called together under circumstances known to all, held in the midst of the people, open to their orators, it was certain to act under popular influence. *Council* (tribal) had to guard and protect the common interests of the tribe. Questions and exigencies arising through their incessant warfare with other tribes. As a general rule, the council open to any private individual desiring to address it on a public question. (EN: 162; MG: 117)

Women's participation was, however, subject to some restrictions. Women exercised somewhat limited speaking rights and were denied actual voting rights, since they did not serve as chiefs. Marx seems to emphasize these limitations in this excerpt from what follows immediately in Morgan's text: "The *women allowed to express their wishes and opinions through an orator of their own election. Decision* given by the Council" of Chiefs (EN: 162; MG: 117).

Marx makes the evolution from matrilineal to patrilineal forms of succession, especially in other Native American societies, a major theme in these notes, which he links to the development of greater hierarchy and of the accumulation of property. Marx notes that the Winnebago (actually Ho-Chunk) in what is today the upper-midwestern US changed over to patrilineal forms of descent even though their development of property was still very limited. Other peoples like the nearby Ojibwas, he notes, "had changed descent to the male line, the inheritance followed the rule which prevailed when descent was in the female line," thus passing through the mother's sisters, for example, "to the exclusion of her brothers" (EN: 130). He records from Morgan how the Shawnees of the Ohio Valley transitioned to patrilineal forms that allowed sons of chiefs to inherit their fathers' titles. They did so via changes in the ways clan members received their names, on which Marx remarks pungently: "*Innate casuistry of man* to *change things by changing names!* and to find loophole in order to break through the tradition from within the tradition, where *actual interest* gave powerful motive for this" (EN: 181).

However, many aspects of matrilineality and of other forms of women's social power persisted in a variety of settings among the Indigenous peoples of the Americas, even where considerable property had accumulated. Concerning the Laguna Pueblo of the US southwest, Marx records a first-hand report that Morgan cites:

Rev. Sam. Gorman, missionary with the Laguna Pueblo Indians, in address to the Historical Society of New Mexico says: "*The right of property* belongs to the female part of the family, and descends in that line from mother to daughter. *Their land is held in common*, but after a person cultivates a lot he has *personal claim to it*, which he *can sell to one of the community* . . . Their *women*, generally, *have control of the granary*, are more provident than *their Spanish neighbors* about the future. Ordinarily they try to have a year's provision on hand. It is only when *two years of scarcity* succeed each other, that Pueblos, *as a community*, suffer hunger." (EN: 132; MG: 536)

In recording this without comment, Marx seems to suggest that these Indigenous communal societies, which were producing pure use values rather than value in the capitalist sense, were considerably more protective of the community's welfare than their Spanish capitalist peers.

Even among the far more hierarchical and technologically developed Aztecs, some of these kinds of gender and kinship relations persisted, with matrilineal succession, women's property rights, and women's right to divorce. On this point, Marx quotes the Spanish observer Antonio de Herrera y Tordesillas as cited by Morgan, who notes concerning Aztec marriage, "*All that the bride brought* was kept in memory, that in cases they should be unmarried again, as was usual among them, the goods might be parted; *the man taking the daughters, and the wife the son, with liberty to marry again*" (EN: 117; MG: 456).

Greco-Roman Society

Shifting to Greece and Rome, Marx continues to annotate Morgan's book, noting the severe diminution of women's position, especially among the Greeks during the ascendancy of Athenian civilization. The shift to patrilineal descent was the key:

> The change of descent from the female line to the male injurious for the rights of women and mothers; her children transferred from her gens to the gens of her husband; she thus lost her agnatic rights, received no equivalent for this; before the change, the component [*Glieder*] of her own gens predominated in the household; this gave full force to the maternal bond and made women rather than men the center of the family. (EN: 120–1; MG: 473)

In the above paraphrase of Morgan, Marx removes Morgan's "in all probability" after "predominated," making women's authority under matrilineal forms more definitive.

He touches briefly upon gender relations in the earliest period of patriarchy but does not tarry long there, copying some text from Morgan to which he adds a parenthetical insertion about women's seclusion:

> Homeric Greeks: Monogamian family of a low type. The treatment of their female captives reflects the culture of the period with respect to women in general; *tent life of Achilles and Patroclus*; whatever of monogamy existed, was *through an enforced constraint upon wives* [some degree of seclusion]. (EN: 120; MG; 473)

Nor does he address same-sex relations in this "tent life," a topic Morgan avoids as well.

In terms of a later period, Marx treats gender relations at the height of Athenian power with as merciless a critique as that he made of Greek slavery, as discussed in the previous chapter:

> From beginning to end under the Greeks a principle of studied self-ishness among the males, tending to lessen the appreciation of women, *scarcely found among savages.* The usages of centuries stamped upon the minds of Grecian women a sense of their inferiority. [[But the relationship to the *goddesses on Olympus* shows remembering and reflection back to an earlier, freer and more powerful position for women. Juno craving for domination, the goddess of wisdom springs from the head of Zeus, etc.]] . . . The Greeks remained *barbarians* in their treatment of the female sex at the height of their civilization; their education superficial, intercourse with the opposite sex denied them, their inferiority inculcated as a principle upon them, until it *came to be accepted as a fact by the women themselves.* The wife not companion equal to her husband, *but in the relation of a daughter.* (EN: 121; see also MG: 474–5)

Two dialectical processes are operative in the above passage, mostly recorded or paraphrased from Morgan. First, Marx calls into question the contrast between "barbarian" and "civilized," with the Greeks in total contradiction to their democratic and humanistic norms with regard to women. Marx strengthens the stark character of this deep contradiction by removing the word "essentially" from Morgan's phrase "essentially barbarians in their treatment of the female sex." A few lines later in his notes, again paraphrasing Morgan, Marx refers to this as "*the seclusion of wives*; plan of life among the civilized Greeks—*a system of female confinement and constraint*" (EN: 121; see also MG: 477).

The second dialectic is Marx's alone, in the bracketed sentences he inserts above concerning the powerful goddess Juno/Hera and the even more powerful goddess of wisdom, Minerva/Athena, seen as evoking memories that likely still existed in the culture of "an earlier, freer and more powerful position for women." This differs from Morgan's one-dimensional presentation of women's subordinate position at the height of Athenian civilization, as Marx is here evoking countertendencies rooted in past egalitarian practices that, by implication, could also have welled up again as forms of revolt in this later period. Marx's dialectical presentation on this point differs even more sharply from Engels's notion of a relatively unbroken "world-historical defeat of the female sex," beginning with the rise of patriarchy hundreds of years earlier, in Homeric Greece and other locations.

Yaman specifies what is needed for a genuinely dialectical investigation:

> Those comments Marx added also reveal the dialectic in his reasoning. Marx did not take facts as they were, as they seem, but evaluated them together with their negation through their dialectical movement. For example, as the quotation above shows, where Morgan spoke of the freedom of the Iroquois women, he pointed out that women's rights were restricted by men. Likewise, where Morgan stated that the Greeks exhibited a principle of studied selfishness among the males, tending to lessen the appreciation of women, Marx referred to the situation of the goddesses on Olympus as the demonstration of the formerly free and more influential position of women.[32]

In fact, Engels did quote part of Marx's parenthetical remarks about the goddesses, but in such a way as to undercut Marx's dialectical point: "While as Marx observes, the position of the goddesses in mythology represents an earlier period, when women still occupied a freer and more respected place, in the Heroic Age we already find women degraded" (MECW26: 170).

Marx's passage has evoked some discussion, and it deserves more. The US feminist poet Adrienne Rich is probably referring to it when she writes: "Marx saw the resistance of women in every revolution, not simply how they were disempowered by the development of patriarchy and by European invasion and colonization."[33] Heather Brown delves into some of the implications concerning countertendencies:

> To begin with, both of these goddesses lived among men, rather than in seclusion, and played a significant role in society, albeit not always a positive one. More importantly, both maintained a great deal of

---

32 Yaman, "Origin of Engels' *The Origin*," p. 124.

33 Adrienne Rich, "Raya Dunayevskaya's Marx," *Raya Dunayevskaya's Intersectional Marxism: Race, Class, Gender and the Dialectics of Liberation*, ed. Kevin B. Anderson, Kieran Durkin, and Heather A. Brown (Cham: Palgrave Macmillan [1991] 2021), p. 99.

control over their sexuality, despite the limits imposed both by the primitive state of contraception and by the social forces at the time. Hera [Juno] was able to decide on her own that she would not raise her son Hephaestus, while Athena likely chose to remain a virgin, given the difficulties at that time of remaining in a position of authority while raising a family.[34]

Marx's dialectical turn here also speaks to efforts to recover for today feminist and LGBTQ practices in precolonial societies across the world.

As we have seen, Marx distances himself from Morgan's idyllic portrait of Iroquois gender relations. But here, with the Greeks, he is taking the opposite tack, pointing to countertrends to what Morgan portrays as an unrestricted patriarchy. The common thread here is Marx's dialectical sensitivity to social contradictions.

Similarly, in another remark from his notes on Morgan, Marx bends the text to make it involve the subjectivity of women as well as men in preliterate Greek society:

> The *Agora*—later institution than the council of chiefs [which earlier, as among the Iroquois, was so bound to the agora that the leaders of the people (also women) could *speak* there & the masses always present] had power to adopt or reject public measures submitted by the council. The agora—in Homer & in Greek Tragedians—has same characteristics which it afterward maintained in the ecclesia of the Athenians & the comitia curiata of the Romans. In heroic age, the *agora* a constant phenomenon among the Greek tribes [Ditto Germans in Upper Status of Barbarism]. Anyone could speak in Agora; in ancient times they usually made their decision by *show of hands*. (EN: 205; MG: 245–6)

Above, in the first bracketed passage that he adds, Marx is drawing on the Iroquois experience to suggest that in earlier, preliterate times, Greek and Roman women would have participated in the agora, a form of popular assembly. He also declines to record— although it appears in the

---

34   Heather A. Brown, *Marx on Gender and the Family* (Chicago: Haymarket, 2012), p. 161.

same passage—Morgan's condescending view that the Greek agora or "assembly of the people, with the right to accept or reject public measures, would evince an amount of progress and intelligence and knowledge beyond the Iroquois" (MG: 245). Finally, in a shorter bracketed insert, Marx extends the comparison to the popular assemblies of the ancient Germans. Overall, he is in search of a more general perspective on the relative gender equality of preliterate human cultures.

At this point, Marx adds another interpretation that bends Morgan's text. Concerning Euripides' *Orestes* and Aeschylus's *The Suppliants*, Morgan suggests that the chorus in Greek tragedies represented the popular assembly, thus indicating the long persistence of popular will in the culture. Morgan does so without, however, mentioning women. But Marx notes that another rendering of the title of Aeschylus's play is *The Suppliant Maidens*, who form part of its chorus, thus taking on a speaking role as a collectivity of women (EN: 205–06; MG: 246).[35] Marx's evocation of women's important role in this play, written in the fifth century BCE at the height of Athenian ascendancy under Pericles, seems to be another attempt on his part to suggest—in dialectical fashion—that earlier forms of more egalitarian gender relations endured in Greek culture all the way into a period of overwhelming patriarchal domination.

With the Romans, as with the communal form in general, the surviving evidence on early forms of women's power and authority is more limited. Marx does note, based upon Morgan's citation of the historians John Cramer and Luigi Lanzi concerning the Etruscans, whose empire dominated Rome in the archaic period: "As we see from their monuments, . . . admitted their *wives* to their feasts and banquets; they invariably *describe their parentage and family with reference to their mother,* and *not the father*" (EN: 235; MG: 348).

In the notes on Morgan, Marx also contrasts the relative autonomy and respect accorded Roman women at the height of Roman power as compared to their Greek, especially Athenian, counterparts:

Roman family: *Materfamilias* was mistress of the family; went into the streets freely without restraint by her husband, frequented with the

---

35 I owe a particular debt here to David Norman Smith for excavating this reference by Marx as part of his forthcoming meticulous annotated translation of Krader's edition of the *Ethnological Notebooks.*

men the theaters and festive banquets; in the house not confined to
particular apartments, nor excluded from the table of the men. Roman
females thus more personal dignity and independence than Greek; but
marriage gave them *in manum viri* [under the power of the husband];
was = daughter of the husband; he had the power of correction and of
life and death in case of adultery (with concurrence of the council of her
gens). (EN: 121; MG: 477–8)

This "more personal dignity and independence than Greek" meant a
greater degree of freedom and autonomy, albeit within a deeply patriarchal structure, where husbands had the legal power literally to execute
errant women in their families. The overall structure held women under
male tutelage, usually on the part of fathers and then husbands. Even
here though, as Marx mentions next, women developed greater rights
later, as those forms of marriage that involved placing women under the
domination [*manus*] of the husband receded. They "fell out *under the
Empire* when *free marriage* generally adopted, not placing the wife in
manus of the husband" (EN: 121; MG: 478). Here is a key area in which
Marx's notes differ markedly from Engels's notion of a "world-historical
defeat" for women, as some positive developments for women took
place from Greece to Rome, and within Rome as the Republic transformed to the Empire. Placing this in a broader context, Eleonora
Cappuccilli and Roberta Ferrari hold that Marx stresses, contra Engels,
"women's unwillingness to submit silently to male domination," as he
"emphasizes the moments of rupture that mark the development of
patriarchal social relations, up to the point where capital transfigures
them, assuming their hierarchical traits."[36]

Marx traces these developments in Roman kinship in far greater detail
in his 1879 notes on Lange's 1856 book, *Ancient Rome*. As discussed in
the previous chapter, the Lange notes appear to have been composed
before those on Morgan, but after Marx had gained a basic familiarity
with Morgan's arguments. Marx disputes Lange's attempts, like those
of the other historians whom he also criticizes, to place the family

---

36   Eleonora Cappuccilli and Roberta Ferrari, "The Feminine Ferment: Marx and
the Critique of Patriarchy," in *Global Marx: History and Critique of the Social Movement
in the World Market*, ed. Matteo Battistini, Eleonora Cappuccilli, and Maurizio Ricciardi
(Leiden: Brill Publishers, 2022), pp. 64–5.

ahead of the gens or clan in the historical development of Roman kinship practices. Inserting his own bracketed comment into a passage recorded from Lange, Marx writes, "The family gradually becomes gens [*in fact, this whole portrayal is wrong, insofar as the gens principle is fundamental*]." At another point, Marx remarks, "Lange falsifies this whole thing, because he makes the family (individual) prior to the gens."

This probably also represents a turning point for Marx, who was breaking with his own earlier conceptions about the origin of the family. As Musto recounts by quoting Henry Hyndman, a British socialist who knew Marx in this period but who became estranged from Marx after plagiarizing *Capital*: "As Hyndman recalled: 'When Lewis Henry Morgan proved to Marx's satisfaction in his Ancient Society that the gens and not the family was the social unit of the old tribal system and ancient society generally, Marx at once abandoned his previous positions.'"[37]

Nonetheless, Marx makes very detailed notes on Lange's description of the various types of Roman marriage and their evolution. The notes on Lange comprise over 20,000 words, much of them devoted to the evolution of the Roman family. Marx seems to take this material very seriously, despite what he sees as Lange's fundamental error in assuming the family as the original kernel of Roman kinship relations. It is likely that he sees Lange's descriptions as valid for the period from the Roman Republic onward, when patrilineal descent and patriarchy became firmly established. Marx records material on the unusual level of power held by the paterfamilias, for example: "*Paterfamilias* is *high king, high priest* and *owner* of the *family*." Such a family is more than a biological unit, at least for the upper classes, comprising an entire household that is a site not only of reproduction but also of production, as Marx records from Lange in the following:

> *Organization of the family: pater familias, mater familias, filii et filiae familias* [male head of the family, mother of the family, sons and daughters of the family], the *wives, sons, and unmarried daughters* of the *sons*, etc.; *family property (familial property)* [res familia (res familiaris)], partly *slaves (family* in the narrower sense), partly other

37   Marcello Musto, *The Last Years of Karl Marx, 1881–1883: An Intellectual Biography* (Stanford: Stanford University Press, 2020), pp. 26–7.

objects of value; mainly *livestock*; hence: *"family and property"* [hinc: *"familia pecuniaque"*].

All of this is covered by Roman family law, which, Lange emphasizes, forms the oldest Roman law.

Marx also records in detail Lange's descriptions of the enormous power over his wife held by the paterfamilias, who

> has authority over her person, exercises marital rights, can kill her [[later on *unconditionally* for adultery alone, otherwise only after a hearing in a court of relatives]]; *in the power of life and death* [in jus vitae necisque] the right of physical punishment is included; . . . she also likewise comes into the *patria potestas* of her father-in-law, for whom she is *in place of a granddaughter* [in neptis loco].

The first bracketed passages in the above is also from Lange, and Marx seems to be emphasizing here not only the harshness of Roman marital law but also the weakening over time of the husband's right to kill his wife. Something similar happened with the right of the paterfamilias to kill his son, as Marx also records from Lange concerning the late imperial period under Emperor Constantine (r. 306–37 CE), who "completely revoked the *right to kill* (he classified killing a child under the criminal law of parricide [*parricidium*])."

The practice of guardianship or tutelage also evolved in women's favor. Children and even adult women lacked full legal capacity, which meant that a woman not under the tutelage of her father or her husband needed a guardian. In the case of a widow, the guardian was traditionally drawn from her husband's male relatives. Over time, civil law intruded into these long-standing familial practices amid the increasing use of wills and testaments rather than customary division of estates. As Marx records from Lange, widows developed the right to have a say over the choice of their guardian and even became

> free to *choose a guardian* a limited number of times (*limited choice*) or as often as she wanted (*extended choice*) . . . *Concerning the chosen guardian* [tutores optivi] and *the entrusted one, Cicero pro Murena 12* says: Women were not in the potestas of the guardian any longer, rather guardians in the potestas of the women.

Obviously, these changes over time in the direction of greater rights for Roman women contradict Engels's notion of a "world historical defeat of the female sex."

As Brown, who has published the only detailed discussion to date of the Lange notes, concludes:

> Marx paid particular attention to how the conflict among patricians, plebeians, and other groups contributed to the weakening of the patriarchal Roman family as the main unit of society, and the concomitant rise in the power of the state. This generated positive effects on women's position in society, at least among the upper classes, since the men in the family and especially the *paterfamilias* lost some of their authority over their relatives, including women.[38]

However, as Brown also notes, and as Marx records in his notes on Lange, women's inheritance rights remained limited. Despite the changes in guardianship, even women of the upper classes failed to attain the right to make their own wills/testaments establishing the disposition of property they had inherited from their husbands or fathers.

Marx also records material on the Roman practice of adoption, widely practiced among the upper classes, who saw little difference between adopted and biological children. The most famous case was that of Octavian (later Augustus Caesar), who used his status as the adopted son of his biological great-uncle Julius Caesar to rally the army to him in the battle for succession with Mark Antony, and thus to become Rome's first emperor. As Marx records from Lange, but with his own parenthetical comment, "The adopted son assumes another name—*change of name* (also among savages [*Wilden*])." This name is that of the new family. Marx's parenthesis suggests he is comparing this to something taken up in the previous chapter, Morgan's discussion of name changes among the Iroquois, probably the "savages" to which he is referring.

In his notes on Morgan, Marx follows up this theme as he begins to define the term "family." To be sure, he is linking it to what he was discussing in the notes on Lange, but he is expanding the discussion to the economic level, to the rural patrician household, where slaves and other

---

38   Brown, *Marx on Gender and the Family*, p. 207.

subordinates not only maintained the dwelling and its aristocratic members but also worked the land as a large economic unit:

> *Family* modern appearance with Roman tribes; proved the meaning of *familia*, contains same element as *famulus* = *servant*. *Festus* says: "*Famuli* originally comes from the Oscian, according to which the *slave* is called *Famul*, whence the term for *family*." Thus in its primary meaning *family* unrelated to the married pair or their *children*, rather in relation *to the body of slaves and servants* who labored for its maintenance and were under the power of the *paterfamilias*. (EN: 119; MG: 469)

Thus, at its origin, the Latin word *famulus* is close to the Greek one for household, *oikos* (the root of the term "economics" as well), which was an agrarian economic unit with slaves and servants as well as what would today be called "family" members. Importantly, the word's initial meaning is "unrelated to the married pair and their children." Again, in the Morgan notes, Marx hones this to a point in a brief genealogical remark on the term "family":

> *Fourier* characterizes *epochs of civilization through monogamy and landed property*. The modern family contains in embryo not only *servitus* (slavery) but also *serfdom*, since from the outset in relation to *services for* agriculture. It contains within itself in *miniature* all of the antagonisms that later develop widely in society and its state. (EN: 120)

Here, Marx is stressing that the ancient Roman family was a microcosm of the society as a whole and its social "antagonisms." Given the genealogical form of his comment, he also puts forth the notion that these antagonisms carry over in latent form right up through the modern bourgeois family. Finally, his recourse to Fourier in the above, which is not explained, may have convinced Engels that Marx endorsed Fourier's positions. For his part, Engels not only quotes this passage from Marx's notes in *Origin of the Family* but also states at the end of *Origin*, as mentioned above, that he would have liked to have incorporated Fourier's "brilliant criticism of civilization" into his book, had time allowed (MECW 26: 276).

India and Ireland: Patriarchy and Resistance

Although Kovalevsky did not refer much to women in his notes on India, Marx finds material on gender and the family in other authors he takes up in his 1879–82 notebooks. In his notes on John Budd Phear's 1880 book, *The Aryan Village in India and Ceylon*, a study of contemporary rural Ceylon (Sri Lanka), he singles out a few issues concerning women. He records in his notes Phear's report that women "*do all the menial work of the household*, even when family of the better classes" (EN: 248). He also records material on women's exclusion from religious knowledge:

> *Thakurbari, chamber* where the figure of the family deity (*thakur*) resides and where its daily service and worship is performed. *Women* cannot themselves worship the family idol or any visible thakur, except the *clay figure of Shiva* made for every day worship. *The Shastras forbid to women* and *Sudras* all knowledge and use of sacred texts. (EN: 259)

These kinds of themes continue in the notes on Maine, made at a slightly later point, when Marx extensively annotates a chapter, "The Early History of the Settled Property of Married Women."

Marx begins by castigating Maine's ignorance concerning new research challenging the assumption that the patriarchal family was the oldest form of kinship: "The comfortable Maine is still not acquainted with *Mother Right* (Bachofen etc.), nor had he yet available *Morgan's* book to give it an 'elegant' thrashing" (EN: 323). This sentence also drips with hostility toward Maine as an establishment scholar with—in Marx's view—a condescending attitude toward truly original research. Marx then looks into married women's property under Hindu law in this long discussion, partly quoted from Maine. But he also mentions Thomas Strange's 1825 book, *Elements of Hindu Law*, which Maine does not cite, adding as well his own pungent remarks:

> The tendency of Indian legislation toward women, which until now has made the *Stridhan* ("settled property of married women") incapable of alienation by her husband, indeed this is pledged that the property of the married woman goes to the daughters or to the female

members of her family (cf. *Strange: Hindoo Law*) etc.—all this Maine does not rightly understand, he lacks any insight into the *gens* and thus the *original hereditary transmission* through *female*—not *male*—line of descent. The ass shows with which colored spectacles he sees when he says: "Among the Aryan" (the devil with this "Aryan" cant!) sub-races, the Hindoos *may be as confidently asserted as the Romans* to have had their society organized as a *collection of patriarchally governed families*. [From Niebuhr he could have already discovered that the *Roman family* was still enmeshed in the *gens* even after it had developed its own specific form, the patria potestas.] If, then, (a nice "If" only resting upon Maine's own "*confident assertion*") *then*, (this "then" Pecksniffian), *at any early period*, [Maine transports his "patriarchal" Roman family into the very beginning of things] the married woman had among the Hindoos her property *altogether enfranchised from her husband's control* ["enfranchised," that is to say, from Maine's "confident assertion"], it is not easy to give a reason why the *obligations of the family despotism* [a principal pet-doctrine of blockheaded John Bull to read in original "despotism"] were relaxed in this one particular. (323) (EN: 324; MN: 321–4, passim)

Here Marx is reading Maine, or, rather, in his view, seeing through Maine, to get at the notion that ancient Indian practices involved married women's separate property, something that was eroded as patriarchal family forms replaced gentile/clan kinship forms. And Strange was no radical, but, rather, an English judge in colonial Madras [Chennai] in the early nineteenth century. Marx also rejects Maine's Whig interpretation of history, one of progress from "despotism," instead viewing Indian society as having lost something important with the rise of the patriarchal family. Finally, his peremptory rejection of Maine's use of the term "Aryan" as a social and cultural category, rather than a merely linguistic one, shows Marx's distance from some of the more fanciful (and often racist) cultural history and anthropology of the era.

Marx next takes up how later Hindu law obfuscated this form of women's property with matrilineal succession, again referring directly to Strange's book to supplement Maine:

From the original sources given by Strange it can be seen that already in the *Mitakshara*, not to speak of later Hindu legal commentaries, the *authors* no longer understand the *Stridhana* and instead seek to construct a plausible but false rationale. A process similar to that of Roman lawyers in Cicero's time who did not understand old Roman legal practices and forms, already "archaic" by their time. Such a rationalization is, e.g., where *in Mitakshara* the *"fee"* for the fiancée is explained as "what is given her in her bridal procession, upon the final ceremony, when the marriage already contracted and solemnized, is about to be consummated, the bride having hitherto remained with her mother." (EN: 324)

Here, Marx notably generalizes this point by comparing it to the time of the Roman Republic, when the extant patriarchal law and jurisprudence could no longer grasp earlier, more gender-egalitarian legal practices, and thus presented a false explanation of some of their lingering effects. Marx then quotes Strange again before commenting at some length on his insights and limitations:

Strange continues: "The *fee* of a Hindu wife has moreover this anomaly attending it, that, upon her death, it descends in a *course of inheritance peculiar to herself.*" This "anomaly" is only a fragmentary survival, covering only a small part of the total property, of the older normal rule among primitives which was based on descent within the gens along the female line. It is frequently so with "anomalies" in the law. (In language, too, exceptions are frequently remnants of the older, more original.) The old norm appears relative to the modern situation as an anomaly, an incomprehensible exception. (EN: 324–5)

Here, Marx seems to believe that he is also seeing through Strange's account, to uncover "the older normal rule among primitives which was based on descent within the gens along the female line."

Returning to Maine, Marx again portrays him as trapped within dogmatic assumptions concerning an earlier strictly patriarchal family system that was modified over time in the direction of some rights for women. Thus, Maine resorts to a "cunning" explanation, which actually reveals, in Marx's eyes, his overall failure to grasp the reversals women experienced as Hindu law was consolidated:

The cunning Maine explains this matter as follows: Among the Aryan communities are found the earliest traces of the separate property of women in the widely diffused ancient institution known as *Bride-Price*. Part of this price, which was paid by the bridegroom either at the wedding or the day after it, went to the bride's father as compensation (!) *for the Patriarchal or Family authority which was transferred to the husband*, but another part went to the bride herself and was generally enjoyed by her separately and kept apart from her husband's property. It further appears that under a certain number of Aryan customs the *proprietary rights of other kinds which women slowly acquired* were assimilated to their rights in their portion of the *Bride-Price*, probably (!) as being the only existing type of women's property." (324) (EN: 325; MN: 324)

After this, though, Marx, in a rare concession to Maine, writes that the British jurist did grasp some of what was going on:

Concerning this Maine rightly says: "There are in fact clear indications of a sustained *general effort on the part of the Brahminical writers on mixed law and religion*, to limit the privileges of women which they seem to have found *recognized by older authorities*." (325) (EN: 325; MN: 324)

In fact, Maine's discussion of this issue is extremely brief, whereas Marx's recourse to Strange as well in these notes adds tremendous detail to Maine's account, while also challenging most of it.

Marx now moves to a critique of the institution of sati (suttee), or widow burning, usually construed as self-immolation, viewing it as part of the effort to rob women of their property. He again treats the subject in far greater detail than does Maine by referring to Strange's book for most of his notes on this issue:

The beastliness of the Brahmins reaches its height in the "*Suttee*" or *widow burning*. Strange considers this practice to be a "malus usus," not "law," since in the *Manu* and other high authorities there is no mention of it; these "as the condition on which the widow may aspire to Heaven" have simply required that she should, on the decease of her husband, live a life of seclusion, privation, and decency" . . . The Brahmins themselves clarify the matter ("*property designed for religious uses*") and the interest these fellows have in receiving the inheritance . . . Strange speaks explicitly of "designing Brahmins" and "interested relatives."[39] (EN: 325)

He adds more detail on the property accruing to the husband's relatives, again drawing from Strange:

> The matter is clear: the *suttee* is simply *religious murder*, in part to bring the inheritance into the hands of the (spiritual) Brahmins for the religious ceremonies for the deceased husband and in part through Brahmin legislation to transfer the inheritance of the widow to the closest in the gens, the nearer family of the *husband*. Hence the violence and infamies, usually on the part of the "connexions," to bring the widow to a flaming death. (EN: 326)

At this point, Marx also taxes Maine for his portrayal of the entire pre-modern period as despotic: "The English philistine Maine interprets the whole ancient primitive period as 'the despotism of groups over the members composing them'" (EN: 326; MN: 327). In this sense, Maine is a dogmatic English individualist with little sense of collective power or rights in a positive sense. Throughout, Marx also makes sharper critiques of religion and of male domination than those Maine puts forth.

He also avoids Maine's smug and ethnocentric condemnation of Indian civilization as some kind of outlier in terms of women's oppression, refraining, for example from recording this summary statement from Maine: "Now, it is true that in the legal institutions of the Hindoos . . . the despotism of the family group over the men and women composing it is maintained in greater completeness than among any similar civilization and culture" (MN: 327). Instead, Marx embarks upon a comparative, contextual analysis of sati, bringing in European forms of the acquisition of women's property by religious institutions:

> This ancient atrocity [sati] was revived in priestly heads and then naively attributed to its ancient origins. When Sir Maine says: "There can be no serious question that, in its ultimate result, the *disruption of the Roman Empire* was very unfavourable to the personal and

---

39 In keeping with the rough character of these notes, in this passage Marx uses quotation marks inconsistently.

proprietary liberty of women" (337), this damned thing needs to be taken with a grain of salt. He says: "The place of women under the *new system* (the barbarians) when fully organised (that is, through the development of the feudal system) was worse than it was under Roman law, and *would have been very greatly worse but for the efforts of the Church.*" (337) This is fatuous, considering that the Church suppressed (Roman) *divorce*, or made it as difficult as possible, and treated matrimony, although a sacrament, as a sin. In relation to "proprietary right" the wily church certainly had an interest in securing the rights of women (the opposite interest from the Brahmins!). (EN: 327; MN: 337)

As Brown notes, "Here, Marx bitterly criticizes the ancient Brahmins for their argument that this was a practice based upon religious tradition, and not an invention to circumvent women's property-rights without the use of direct force."[40] Much of the above passage from Marx's notes concerns the medieval Roman Catholic Church's championing of the rights of women, especially widows, to dispose of property in their wills, allowing them to give bequests to Church institutions rather than their male relatives. Marx makes a similar point in a remark regarding the early Middle Ages in Europe in his notes on Kovalevsky on India from about two years before this: "Other peoples too, for instance the Germano-Roman world (see Merovingians, Carolingians) the same hierarchy—*gift-giving to the priest* the first *form of the alienation of immovable property* preceding all others" (KOV: 367). The overall point is again dialectical. Hindu priests restricted women's property rights while the Roman Catholic Church "defended" them. However, these seeming opposites, when viewed as a totality, show at the same time the common goal of acquiring property from women on the part of male-dominated institutions.

As with his treatment of their Greek and Roman counterparts, Marx's considerations of Indian women in these notes are not limited to the delineation of various forms of objectification, oppression, and subordination. In his 1879 notes on Robert Sewell's *Analytical History of India* (1870), Marx also records material on women's subjectivity, on their resistance to British imperialism during the Sepoy Rebellion of 1857–59. He does so by focusing on Lakshmi Bai, Rani of Jhansi, a Maratha entity annexed in 1853 by the British:

---

40 Brown, *Marx on Gender and the Family*, p. 198.

Annexation of Jhansi (in Bundelkhand). The *Rajah of Jhansi*, originally tributary of the Peshwa, *recognized in 1832 as independent Rajah, died* without natural issue but *adopted son* living. Monsieur Dalhousie again refuses to recognize the latter; hence rage of the dispossessed *Rani*, later *the most prominent leader in the Sepoy mutiny*.[41]

This refers to Lakshmi Bai (1835–58), the Rani (Queen) of Jhansi, who was deprived of her kingdom when British governor-general James Dalhousie refused to acknowledge her and her husband's adopted son as heir to the throne. In one of the many legends that have grown up around her name, she is said to have died in the thick of battle dressed in a man's clothes while leading her army.

Marx records some material on what he evidently considers to have been the Rani Lakshmi Bai's heroic resistance, as one of the last holdouts as the uprising was finally suppressed by the British. The notes also refer more briefly to another woman rebel leader, the Begum of Oudh, concerning whom Sewell omits that much of her military force was composed of women, a fact of which Marx seems unaware as well:

> *Finishing stroke dealt to Insurrection*[42] by *Sir Hugh Rose's 2 months'* (May and June) campaign[43] in Central India.
>
> *January 1858,* Rose took *Rathgarh, in February, Sangur and Garrakota,* marches on *Jhansi* where the Rani had taken her stand.
>
> *April 1,* 1858 severe action against *Tantia Topi,* cousin of *Nana Sahib,* who advanced from *Kalpi* to protect *Jhansi*; Tantia defeated.
>
> *April 4: Jhansi taken*; the Rani and Tantia Topi escape, await the English at *Kalpi*; while marching thither . . .
>
> *June 2nd: young Sindhia* (English dog-man)[44] driven out of *Gwalior* by

---

41   Marx, *Notes on Indian History (664–1858)* [hereafter referred to in-text as MSW] (Moscow: Progress Publishers, n.d., c. 1960), pp. 145–6. Although I am referencing the sometimes imprecise early Moscow edition of these notes, I am actually quoting from the version transcribed by Norair Ter-Akopian, Georgi Bagaturia, and Jürgen Rojahn for MEGA IV/27, based upon the forthcoming all-English version of the latter, trans. and annotated by Ashley Passmore, Spencer Leonard, and me.

42   Marx's word; Sewell writes "rebellion." See Robert Sewell, *The Analytical History of India* [hereafter referred to directly in text as SW] (London: W. H. Allen & Company, 1870), p. 278.

43   Marx leaves aside Sewell's adjective, "splendid" (SW: 278).

44   Marx's parenthetical phrase; Sewell evokes instead his "utmost gallantry and fidelity to the English in these trying times" (SW: 279). They are referring to the young Ali Jah Jayaji Sindhia.

his troops after hard fighting, flees for his life to Agra. Rose marches on *Gwalior*; the Rani of Jhansi and *Tantia Topi* at head of the rebels give him—

June 19: battle at the Lashkar Hill. (before Gwalior); Rani killed, her army dispersed after much slaughter. *Gwalior in hands of the English.*

During July, August, and September, 1858: Sir Colin Campbell, Sir Hope Grant, and General Walpole engaged to hunt down the more prominent rebels and take *all forts* whose possession disputed; *the Begum made some final stands,* then fled *with Nana Sahib across the Rapti River* to the territories of the English dog man,[45] *Jang Bahadur of Nepal*; he allows the English to pursue the rebels into his country, thus the "last bands of desperadoes dispersed";[46] *Nana and the Begum flee into the hills,* while their followers lay down their arms.

Early 1859: Tantia Topi's hiding-place detected, he tried and executed.— *Nana Sahib* is "supposed" to have died in Nepal.[47] *Khan of Bareilly* was seized and shot; *Mammu Khan* of *Lucknow,* sentenced to life imprisonment; others transported or imprisoned for various terms; *bulk of the rebels -* their regiments disbanded—laid down the sword, *became Ryots.*[48] The *Begum of Oudh* lived at Kathmandu in *Nepal.*

Confiscation of the soil of Oudh, which *Canning declared to be the property of the English-Indian Government!*[49] (MSW: 155–6)

In this way, Marx bends to his own purposes the rather dry and pro-colonialist account of the young historian Sewell, who was also a minor colonial official.

In Marx's long notes on Ireland from Maine's book, there is only one important mention of gender, but it is a highly significant one, along a similar track to his notes on Hindu law, again showing his comparative bent:

---

45 "Dog man" is again Marx's phrase, here describing the pro-British ruler of Nepal.

46 Marx's irony quotes.

47 Marx's use of quotation marks suggests doubt about Nana Sahib's death.

48 Marx leaves aside Sewell's adverb, "humbly," in reference to their new status as peasants.

49 "English-Indian" is Marx's phrase, as is the exclamation point. For his part, Sewell writes of "guilty Oude [Oudh]" (SW: 280).

According to the *Ancient Irish Law* women had some power of *dealing with their own property without the consent of their husbands*, and this was one of the institutions *expressly declared by the [English blockheaded] Judges to be illegal at the beginning of the 17th century.* (EN: 323)

Marx quotes most of the above from Maine, deleting his qualifying language to make the first clause more affirmative, whereas Maine writes at this point: "The exact extent of the separate ownership which the ancient Irish law allowed to married women is still uncertain." (MN: 324). The bracketed phrase referring to the English judges as "blockheaded" is obviously Marx's. This issue was not new to Marx.

Gender under Modern Working Class and Indigenous Communism: The Paris Commune and Algeria

Marx's long analysis of the Paris Commune in *The Civil War in France* of 1871 contains some important references to women's leading role in what he saw as an attempt to create a form of modern communism. Since these reflections occur eight years before the 1879–82 notebooks I have been discussing, their relationship to the latter is unclear. Two things can be noted, however, in terms of their affinity: (1) *The Civil War in France* includes more discussion of women than is found in Marx's writings on the other major European revolution of his lifetime, in 1848; and (2) the Paris Commune actually used the word "commune" and reached toward a form of communism, whereas the 1848 revolutions were mainly democratic revolutions, with a small working-class and socialist element coming to the fore, most notably in Paris.

In *The Civil War in France*, Marx notably salutes the working-class women of Paris as key participants, contrasting them to the courtesans known as cocottes:

The *cocottes* had refound the scent of their protectors—the absconding men of family, religion, and, above all, of property. In their stead, the real women of Paris showed again at the surface—heroic, noble, and devoted, like the women of antiquity. Working, thinking, fighting, bleeding Paris—almost forgetful, in its incubation of a new society, of the Cannibals at its gates—radiant in the enthusiasm of its historic initiative! (MECW 22: 341)

He also refers to the great sacrifices on the part of women under the ensuing repression:

> The self-sacrificing heroism with which the population of Paris—men, women, and children—fought for eight days after the entrance of the Versaillese, reflects as much the grandeur of their cause, as the infernal deeds of the soldiery reflect the innate spirit of that civilization, indeed, the great problem of which is how to get rid of the heaps of corpses it made after the battle was over! (MECW 22: 348)

In addition, he notes how the counterrevolution demonized the Commune, singling out especially the women participants:

> The women of Paris joyfully give up their lives at the barricades and on the place of execution. What does this prove? Why, that the demon of the Commune has changed them into Megaera and Hecates! (MECW 22: 350)

Despite their brevity, these references to the women Communards seem to show a new sensibility on Marx's part with regard to women and revolution.

Eight years later, in his 1879 notes on Kovalevsky on Algeria, Marx underscores the fact that the fullest attempt by French colonialism to destroy the Indigenous communal social forms came in the aftermath of the Paris Commune of 1871. This took the form of new laws designed to hasten the break-up and privatization of the land of Algeria by the conservative National Assembly—derided as the "Assembly of Rurals" by the left. This same assembly, dominated by monarchists even though formally part of a republic, had voted for the bloody suppression of the Commune in 1871 and had enacted anti-worker and other repressive policies in an attempt to stamp out communism on French soil:

> 1873: Hence the first concern of the *Assembly* of Rurals *of 1873* was to reach for more effective measures for *stealing the land of the Arabs*.[50]

---

50 "Stealing the land" is Marx's phrase, sharpening Kovalevsky's "deprivation of land."

[[*The debates in this assembly of shame*[51] concerning the project "*On the Introduction of Private Property*" in Algeria seek to hide their gangsterism[52] under the cloak of so-called *eternally inalterable laws of political economy.* (224) In these *debates* the *"Rurals"* are all in accord concerning the purpose: *destruction of collective property.* The debate revolved only around the *method, how* to kill it off. (KOV: 410)[53]

In these 1879 notes on Algeria, Marx also singles out efforts by the French to break up the communal and clan social forms and the particular effects of this on gender relations. As the French colonial system privatized landholdings, undermining the clans, this "modernization" actually increased male, patriarchal domination within the Arab population, whereby "the *authority of the male heads of household* grew and received through law a recognized, *official, political character*" (KOV: 409). But even after this, the communal social forms persisted within these household economies. On this point, Marx records earlier a passage from Kovalevsky on the role of women in these household economies and their communal or at least elective structure:

The *household economy of the undivided family* is entirely in the hands of the *oldest woman by birth* (see the *Croats*)[54] *or to she who is the most competent manager,* in each case elected by all family members. Not infrequently, *women alternate* in this function. (KOV: 402)

To be sure, Marx leaves only implicit these connections of the Paris Commune to the Indigenous Algerian agrarian communes. And Marx's references to women and the family here are somewhat brief, whether

---

51   "Assembly of shame" is Marx's pejorative insertion, alluding to a common leftist slogan of the time, "Assemblée de ruraux, honte de la France [Assembly of Rurals, the Shame of France]." For emphasis, he puts extra space between the letters of the phrase "Assembly of shame."

52   Marx's word, again sharpening Kovalevsky's statement that the deputies were acting "for far from altruistic motives as understood by everybody."

53   This sentence and the previous one are formulated by Marx, sharpening Kovalevsky's language. In keeping with these notes' rough character, a parenthesis in this passage is not closed.

54   Marx's parenthetical insert. Here and below, he is comparing Algerian communal forms to the *zadruga,* a widely discussed form of communal family and communal property among the South Slavs of his own era.

among the Parisian working classes or in French-ruled Algeria. Nonetheless, given all his discussions of gender and kinship elsewhere in his
1879–82 notes, and given that he often sees older forms of gender
equality and of women's empowerment as persisting *sub rosa* even after
patriarchal domination is firmly in the saddle, it seems more than possible that Marx saw some type of renewal or rediscovery of women's
ancient powers and freedoms—developed as they were in so many premodern communistic societies—as connected, at least as a potentiality,
to the struggle for a modern communism that emerged in Paris in 1871.

These notes on Morgan and other scholars on communal forms that
sometimes include the democratic participation of all genders in a
classless society need also to be seen in another light, that of Marx
expanding and deepening his vision of communism. The conventional
interpretation by both Marxists and Marx scholars, as espoused by the
recent biographer Stedman Jones, is that these kinds of Marx writings
are simply dated, part of a Romantic "nineteenth-century phantasm."[55]
Tacking in the opposite direction, the Franco-Brazilian social theorist
Michael Löwy, writing in an article subtitled "Marx and Engels, Romantic Communists," views in a positive light the late Marx's "great attention
to the work of anthropologists and historians inspired by Romanticism
with regard to so-called 'primitive' communities."[56] Saito makes a similar
argument. He finds "a new idea of communism" in that period, not least
because of Marx's engagement with ecological issues in his notes on
natural science.[57] Saito concludes that, by the 1880s, "Marx's idea of
communism itself significantly changed" and he was able "to formulate
his vision of non-class society based on what he had learned through his
study of rural communes."[58]

---

55   Stedman Jones, *Karl Marx: Greatness and Illusion* (Cambridge, MA: Belknap
Press, 2016), p. 568.
56   Michael Löwy, "La Commune rurale russe: Marx et Engels, communistes roman-
tiques?" in Karl Marx et al., *Le Dernier Marx, Communisme en Devenir* (Paris: Eterotopia
France Rhizome, 2018), p. 9. See also Michael Löwy and Robert Sayre, *Romanticism
against the Tide of Modernity*, trans. by Catherine Porter (Durham: Duke University Press,
[1991] 2001) for a comprehensive treatment of Marxism, revolution, and Romanticism.
57   Kohei Saito, *Marx in the Anthropocene: Towards the Idea of a Degrowth Communism* (New York: Cambridge University Press, 2023), p. 190. Marx's notes on ecology,
which Saito first outlined in his important 2017 book, *Karl Marx's Ecosocialism*, fall
largely outside the scope of the present study.
58   Saito, *Marx in the Anthropocene*, p. 199.

Most of the present book is concerned with another, though often related issue: Marx's conceptualization of new forces of resistance and opposition to capitalism and colonialism, from Russian and Indian villagers to Irish peasants and immigrant workers, and to Algerian peasants and Latin American Indigenous and peasant communities. This is what Dunayevskaya is driving at when she writes, "And yet, Marx drew no such unbridgeable gulf between primitive and civilized as Engels had."[59] The two issues—that of a vision of communism and that of conceptualizing forces of resistance to capitalism in one's own time— are, of course, related, in the sense that any really fundamental resistance to capitalism needs to be imbued with some kind of emancipatory vision of a new society where human beings will really flourish. Keeping all this in mind, I will turn in the next chapter to the late Marx's multilinear concept of social development, and then, in chapter 4, to his late writings on colonialism and resistance.

---

59   Dunayevskaya, *Rosa Luxemburg*, p. 185.

3

Multilinear Concepts of Historical and Social Development

In recent decades, the term "multilinear" has taken on increasingly positive connotations in social thought, especially its left-wing and critical variants. In this discourse, Marx often comes under attack as a determinist and unilinear theorist whose dialectic fails to capture the full variety of human culture and historical development. Anthropologists David Graeber and David Wengrow imply as much in their comprehensive and original study of the origins of human society, which has done so much to open up discussion about the variety of the human past and how oppression and domination have been challenged at so many junctures. They target not only liberal thinkers who assume the state and capital as inevitable but also Marx. This is seen in the particular ways in which they oppose any idea of "the same grand evolutionary ladder" across the variety of human societies.[1] Instead, they lean toward a hyper-subjectivism wherein not only is there "no simple pattern" of human development, but "the only consistent phenomenon is the very fact of alteration."[2] To be sure, Graeber and Wengrow inject an element of structure when they acknowledge Marx's notion that human beings make "our own history, but not in conditions of their own choosing," which they paraphrase from the opening paragraphs of his 1852 book, *Eighteenth Brumaire of*

---

1   David Graeber and David Wengrow, *The Dawn of Everything: A New History of Humanity* (New York: Farrar, Strauss, and Giroux, 2021), p. 61.

2   Ibid., p. 115.

Louis Bonaparte (MECW 11, p. 206). Despite this cursory acknowledgment, they tend in the course of their study to ignore the objective factors Marx is here referencing, alongside various subjective ones. I refer especially to how, as Marx writes a few lines further on in the *Brumaire*, the existing social structure, above all the particular mode of production prevalent at the time, "weighs like a nightmare on the brain of the living" (MECW 11, p. 103). To Graeber and Wengrow, it is unclear if modes of production exist at all. As anarchists, they view the issue of power, of the political, as paramount, almost foundational, writing that the interaction of human beings with one another "is always, at root, political," a realm that they see as one of almost unconditioned choice.[3] In fact, though, at least for Graeber, as he acknowledges in an earlier work, there is an overall pattern that can be discerned across human societies and cultures. Human societies, Graeber argues, "follow . . . a cyclical pattern."[4] It is one thing to reject rigid stage theories, but is an ahistorical, even "cyclical" form of political subjectivism a better alternative?

The hyper-objectivism of a rigid series of successive historical modes of production, into which various societies around the world can be slotted, forms a sharp contrast to such hyper-subjectivism and political determinism but is equally problematic. The most prominent examples of this kind of hyper-objectivity are those linked to crude versions of Marxism. In such frameworks, some parts of the world were modern and bourgeois, while others were stuck in feudal or semi-feudal social relations. The latter were therefore backward in their social development and would first have to raise themselves to the bourgeois level before they could even think about going beyond it, to socialism or communism. In these locutions, Marxism and Cold War liberal theories of development were not in the near term that far apart, as both sought to modernize what they saw as the semi-feudal and feudal Global South along bourgeois lines, the one as an end in itself and the other as a stepping stone toward socialism or communism. To what extent did such interpretations reflect accurately Marx's own thinking?

To get at this question, it is necessary to separate two related but distinct issues: (1) Did Marx hold to a unilinear theory of historical

---

3 Ibid., p. 203.
4 David Graeber, *Debt: The First 5,000 Years*, expanded edition (New York: Melville House 2014), p. 212.

development from the earliest human societies to his own time, demarcated by clear and universally applicable historical stages, denoted at the most general level by the successive modes of production? (2) In his own time, did he see specific non-Western societies as subject to general laws of society and history, whereby they could not bypass key historical stages? For example, could a society skip the bourgeois phase, going directly into socialism or communism? In short, would a precapitalist class society, as in various Asian social systems, have to pass through bourgeois capitalism first, before even beginning to move toward socialism or communism?

The notion of Marx's adherence to the unilinear notion of bourgeois capitalism as a necessary stage on the road toward socialism for precapitalist or partially capitalist societies persists more than some academic Marxists would like to concede. As Peter Hudis notes:

> Sometimes referred to as the two-stage theory of revolution, the notion that socialism can be reached in a developing country only if it first endures an extended period of capitalist industrialization has been upheld by an array of political tendencies, from Social Democrats and liberals to Stalinists and independent socialists. Far from being a distant or outdated historical issue, the unilinear model of development continues to have a powerful hold on many thinkers and activists today. It is reflected in the South African Communist Party and ANC's imposition of a bourgeois-democratic stage upon South Africa, Evo Morales's notion that a "national-capitalist development" model based on resource extraction is the necessary prerequisite for any subsequent move toward socialism in Bolivia, and the Chinese government's embrace of the neoliberal market as what will supposedly one day deliver "genuine socialism" (or even communism!) to that land.[5]

This remains the case even as such unilinearism is being increasingly rejected by intellectual and academic schools of Marxism and critical theory.

---

5   Peter Hudis, "Beyond Unilinear Evolutionism," *Theory and Praxis: Reflections on the Colonization of Knowledge*, ed. Murzban Jal and Jyoti Bawane (New York: Routledge, 2020), p. 31.

Unilinear and Multilinear Theories of Historical Development

Within Marxism, the most rigid notion of the unilinear stage theory emerged during high Stalinism, but its imprint remains, even if in less rigid forms. A 1938 programmatic article, "Dialectical and Historical Materialism," which lists none other than Josef Stalin as author, states: "Five *main* types of relations of production are known to history: primitive communal, slave, feudal, capitalist and socialist."[6] This dogma reigned in the USSR, China, and other political systems and intellectual currents formed on the Stalinist model. Those who deviated from this by evoking an "Asiatic" mode of production based upon some of Marx's writings in the 1850s were marginalized, or worse. A prime issue in this controversy has been whether precapitalist class societies across the globe could generally be described as "feudal." This notion was not limited to Stalinists but has also been found in the perspectives of many other socialists as well as liberal social scientists and historians.

Let us begin by examining the various ways in which Marx himself conceptualizes, or at least lists, the principal modes of production across history. What does Marx mean by a mode of production? One interesting indication is found in a little-noticed remark in *Theories of Surplus Value*, part of the long "economic" manuscript of 1861–63 that also contains the main drafts of what was to become Vols. II and III of *Capital*. Here, Marx stresses that modes of production are large-scale developments that are not sharp breaks but rather overlap with their successors and predecessors: "Just as one should not think of sudden changes and sharply delineated periods in considering the succession of the different geological formations, so also in the case of the creation of the different economic formations of society" (MECW 33: 442). For my purposes here, the most important issue is the rarity of new economic formations or modes of production, their persistence over centuries if not millennia, and their objective character; that is, forming structures that shape human social action in definite ways and that cannot easily be transcended while these structures still exist in robust form.

----

6   Josef Stalin, "Dialectical and Historical Materialism" (1938), *Marxists Internet Archive*, marxists.org.

The *German Ideology* is the first text in which Marx and Engels discuss historical modes of production, including feudalism, at some length. This book-length manuscript was written in 1845–46, discarded, and then published for the first time in the late 1920s in the Soviet Union as part of the first MEGA. It was subsequently translated widely as a key Marxian text, with some like Louis Althusser seeing it as the first truly "Marxist" text, in which Marx supposedly broke away from the humanism and idealism of the *1844 Manuscripts*.[7]

In the *German Ideology*, Marx does not yet employ the term "modes of production," but refers instead to "forms of ownership [*Formen des Eigenthums*]" of property, which he discusses in relation to changes in the "division of labor [*Theilung der Arbeit*]":

> The various stages of development in the division of labor are just so many different forms of ownership, i.e., the existing stage in the division of labor also conditions [*bestimmt*][8] the relations of individuals to one another with reference to the material, instrument, and product of labor. (MECW 5: 32; MEGA2 I/5: 129)

Once again, it is notable that the property forms are not the most basic category. Rather, they are conditioned by the type of division of labor in a given society. Thus, slave labor gives us ancient Greco-Roman society and its forms of property, not the reverse. In the *1844 Manuscripts*, Marx theorizes a similar relation between alienated labor and private property: "Private property is therefore the product, the necessary result, of alienated labor."[9] In the *German Ideology*, Marx delineates three of these forms, akin to modes of production.

---

7   In recent decades, and especially with the publication of MEGA2 I/5 in 2017, the "classic" 1920s edition of the *German Ideology* has come into question for having created too smooth and coherent a text from various fragments. On this, see especially Terrell Carver and Daniel Blank, *Marx and Engels's "German Ideology" Manuscripts* (New York: Palgrave Macmillan, 2014). This controversy does not affect very much the status of the pages in which Marx and Engels discuss successive historical modes of production, widely considered their joint work. This is clear in MEGA2 I/5, which better separates the various manuscripts than the earlier edition. Since Marx was invariably the senior or final author of the texts they wrote together, as seen most notably in the *Communist Manifesto*, I will consider this part of the *German Ideology* to be basically Marx's own.

8   Could also be translated, as in MECW, as "determines."

9   Marx, "Economic and Philosophical Manuscripts," trans. Tom Bottomore, in Erich Fromm, *Marx's Concept of Man* (New York: Ungar, 1961), pp. 105–6.

The first of these is called tribal or clan property, but in relation to a certain division of labor and an overall set of production relations:

> The first form of ownership is tribal ownership [*Stammeigentum*]. It corresponds to the undeveloped stage of production, at which a people lives by hunting and fishing, by the rearing of beasts or, in the highest stage, agriculture. In the latter case it presupposes a great mass of uncultivated stretches of land. The division of labor is at this stage still very elementary and is confined to a further extension of the natural division of labor existing in the family. The social structure is, therefore, limited to an extension of the family; patriarchal family chieftains, below them the members of the tribe, finally slaves. The slavery latent in the family only develops gradually with the increase of population, the growth of needs [*Bedürfnisse*], and with the extension of external relations, both of war and of barter. (MECW 5: 32–33; MEGA2 I/5: 129–30)

This is similar to what Marx later calls "primitive communism" and to the classless clan societies he researches in his notes on Kovalevsky and Morgan during his last years, as discussed in chapters 1 and 2. One big difference here in the *German Ideology*—versus the late writings that are the focus of the present book—is that Marx is still assuming the patriarchal family as the earliest form of gender relations.

The second stage is that of ancient Greco-Roman society, grounded in slave labor on a massive scale. It grows out of the first form, with several tribes or clans uniting to form a state, and the development of private property out of the earlier communal property:

> The second form is the ancient communal and state ownership which proceeds especially from the union of several tribes into a *city* by agreement or by conquest, and which is still accompanied by slavery. Beside communal ownership we already find movable, and later also immovable, private property developing, but as an abnormal form subordinate to communal ownership. The citizens hold power over their laboring slaves only in their community, and on this account alone, therefore, they are bound to the form of communal ownership. It is the communal private property that compels the active citizens to remain in this spontaneously derived form of association over against

their slaves . . . The division of labor is already more developed. We already find the antagonism of town and country; later the antagonism between those states which represent town interests and those which represent country interests, and inside the towns themselves the antagonism between industry and maritime commerce. The class relation between citizens and slaves is now completely developed. (MECW 5: 33; MEGA2 I/5: 130)

Over time, this leads to the development of private property on a substantial scale, the concentration of that property into the hands of the few, and the formation of classes and class conflict, albeit in a manner different from modern capitalism:

With the development of private property, we find here for the first time the same conditions which we shall find again, only on a more extensive scale, with modern private property. On the one hand, the concentration of private property, which began very early in Rome . . . and proceeded very rapidly from the time of the civil wars and especially under the emperors; on the other hand, coupled with this, the transformation of the plebeian small peasantry into a proletariat, which, however, owing to its intermediate position between propertied citizens and slaves, never achieved an independent development. (MECW 5: 33; MEGA2 I/5: 130)

Thus, Roman class conflict has a substantially different basis than under modern capitalism, because of the key differences between the class position of slaves and the formally free proletariat.

Feudalism constitutes the third stage, which grows out of the demise of the Roman Empire, amid incursions from Germanic "barbarian" tribes. It has a rural basis and extends over a wider geographic area. And, instead of a subject class of slaves carrying out the essential material production, an enserfed peasantry has been formed as the key subordinate class:

From these conditions and the mode of organization of the conquest determined by them, feudal property developed under the influence of the Germanic military constitution. Like tribal and communal ownership, it is based again on a community; but the directly producing class standing over against it is not, as in the case of the ancient community, the slaves, but the enserfed small peasantry. As soon as feudalism is fully developed, there also arises antagonism to the towns. The hierarchical structure of landownership, and the armed bodies of retainers associated with it, gave the nobility power over the serfs. This feudal organization was, just as much as the ancient communal ownership, an association against a subjected producing class; but the form of association and the relation to the direct producers were different because of the different conditions of production. (MECW 5: 34; MEGA2 I/5: 133)

In the towns, corporativism develops through the guilds, who join together "against the organized robber-nobility" (MECW 5: 34; MEGA2 I/5: 133).

But at an overall level, feudalism was, compared to the Greco-Roman world, a less developed form of society, with "little division of labor":

Thus, the chief form of property during the feudal epoch consisted on the one hand of landed property with serf labour chained to it, and on the other of the labor of the individual with small capital commanding the labour of journeymen. The organization of both was determined by the restricted conditions of production—the small-scale and primitive cultivation of the land, and the craft type of industry. There was little division of labor in the heyday of feudalism. Each country bore in itself the antithesis of town and country; the division into estates was certainly strongly marked; but apart from the differentiation of princes, nobility, clergy and peasants in the country, and masters, journeymen, apprentices and soon also the rabble of casual laborers in the towns, no division of importance took place. In agriculture it was rendered difficult by the strip-system, beside which the cottage industry of the peasants themselves emerged. In industry there was no division of labor at all in the individual trades themselves, and very little between them . . . The grouping of larger territories into feudal kingdoms was a necessity for the landed nobility as for the towns. The organization of the ruling class, the nobility, had, therefore, everywhere a monarch at its head. (MECW 5: 34–5; MEGA2 I/5: 133–4)

I have quoted this discussion from the *German Ideology* at great length because it is the most detailed description anywhere in Marx's work of what he was later to call the historical modes of production. While he later discusses "Asiatic" modes of production in the *Grundrisse*, comparing them to the Greco-Roman ancient mode of production, he never returns at much length to feudalism.

What of the question of unilinear historical stages? In 1845–46, did Marx see these three stages—early stateless societies based upon tribe and family, Greco-Roman societies based upon slave labor, and feudalism based upon serfdom, and by implication, a fourth stage, bourgeois capitalism based upon wage labor—as universal, global stages? We cannot know. But we can say that at this point, there is nothing to exclude the possibility that these are intended to be universal stages rather than merely Western European ones. Lawrence Krader sees Marx's 1846 stages as unilinear and global, and therefore rather restricted: "The developmental concept is unilinear, the single historical sequence; once the tribal form is passed, it is that of ancient and medieval Europe."[10] It should also be noted that, as late as 1858, in an article of June 7 for the *Tribune*, Marx refers in passing to the zamindars of India as "feudal landholders" (MECW 15: 548). But, as discussed below, his later writings suggest he came to reject such labels for India and other societies outside Western Europe.

Following the deaths of Marx and Engels, Marxists developed schematic and teleological lists and conceptualizations of these stages, with feudalism becoming a catch-all for premodern and precolonial agrarian societies anywhere in the world. This gave us Ming China, Mughal India, Tsarist Russia, the Inca Empire, Japanese feudalism, and Western European feudalism, all lumped together in the category "feudal." Even a creative Marxist thinker like Leon Trotsky tries to force the "feudal" concept onto Tsarist Russia, here at variance with Marx's own approach, or that of Engels, something Trotsky does not even acknowledge: "The existence of feudal relations in Russia, denied by former historians, may be considered unconditionally established by later investigations. Furthermore, the fundamental elements of Russian feudalism were the same as in the West."[11]

---

10   Lawrence Krader, *The Asiatic Mode of Production* (Assen, Netherlands: Van Gorcum, 1975), p. 137.

11   Leon Trotsky, *History of the Russian Revolution*, Vol. I (London: Sphere Books, [1932] 1967), p. 22.

As for Marx, in his *Critique of Political Economy* (1859) he adds an "Asiatic" mode or production to the framework of the *German Ideology*, this time in a published work. He now writes, "In broad outline, the Asiatic, ancient, feudal, and modern bourgeois modes of production [*Produktionsweisen*] may be designated as progressive epochs [*progressive Epochen*] in the economic development of society" (MECW 29: 263; MEW 13: 9). He does not elaborate further on these four modes of production, but, pointing toward the future, he adds:

> The bourgeois relations of production [*Produktionsverhältnisse*] are the last antagonistic form of the social process of production—antagonistic not in the sense of individual antagonisms, but of an antagonism that emanates from the individual's social conditions of existence—but the productive forces developing within bourgeois society create also the material conditions for the solution of this antagonism. The prehistory of human society accordingly closes with this social formation [*Gesellschaftsformation*]. (MECW 29: 263–4; MEW 13: 9)

In this sense, Marx posits another mode of production, one that comes after what he calls prehistory and that exists just beyond bourgeois society. This would be communism. This generates the following list of modes of production or social epochs: precolonial agrarian Asian societies, ancient Greco-Roman society with its enslaved labor, medieval European feudalism with its enserfed labor, bourgeois capitalism with its formally free wage labor, and communism with what he was to call its freely associated labor. An early communal or clan-based stage is missing here, but surely not excluded. At a more explicit, analytical level, Marx is also conceptualizing the four modes of production he names—"Asiatic, ancient, feudal, and modern bourgeois"—as societies based upon class oppression and antagonism, all of them part of human "prehistory" in relation to the communism he envisions as the future.

What does Marx mean by *progressive Epochen*? There is some textual ambiguity here, since, just as in English, the German term "progressive" carries two major meanings. First, It could refer to progress in substantial or at least technological terms. Restricting ourselves to the four modes of production Marx mentions here—"Asiatic," ancient, feudal, and bourgeois—"Asiatic" would be the least developed in technological or other ways, ancient would be superior in these ways to "Asiatic," feudal to ancient, and bourgeois to feudal. This would mean actual progress was taking place all along, in more or less linear fashion.

Engels seems to have thought this way, even including the establishment of slavery as social "progress" over earlier forms of society. He makes such an argument, surely not one of his best, in *Anti-Dühring*, first published in 1878. This is how Engels conceptualizes the transition from clan or tribal communal societies to "Oriental despotism" and then to slavery:

> It is very easy to inveigh against slavery and similar things in general terms, and to give vent to high moral indignation at such infamies ... And when we examine these questions, we are compelled to say— however contradictory and heretical it may sound—that the introduction of slavery under the conditions prevailing at that time was a great step forward ... Where the ancient communities have continued to exist, they have for thousands of years formed the basis of the cruelest form of state, Oriental despotism, from India to Russia. It was only where these communities dissolved that the peoples made progress of themselves, and their next economic advance consisted in the increase and development of production by means of slave labor ... In the historical conditions of the ancient world, and particularly of Greece, the advance to a society based on class antagonisms could be accomplished only in the form of slavery. This was an advance even for the slaves; the prisoners of war, from whom the mass of the slaves was recruited, now at least saved their lives, instead of being killed as they had been before, or even roasted, as at a still earlier period. (MECW 25: 168–9)

With this notion of slavery as marking progress, Engels seems to bend the concept of *progressive Epochen* in the *Critique of Political Economy* in a direction that it is hard to see Marx countenancing, given his unstinting attacks on these early forms of slavery that I took up in chapters 1 and 2.

It is also jarring to think that Engels penned these lines one year after the publication of Morgan's *Ancient Society*, a work that sees pre-slavery societies like "ancient communities" in a diametrically opposite light. Once he read that work, however, Engels seems to have reversed course, now viewing early communal societies in *Origins of the Family* in rosy tones. Krader believes that Engels "put aside" many of his "earlier formulations" from *Anti-Dühring* after having read Morgan.[12] But Engels only alludes briefly to Morgan in an 1885 preface to *Anti-Dühring*, without revising its descriptions of early societies as the "progressiveness" of slavery. To Engels's credit, however, he in no way seeks to force all contemporary or recent non-capitalist class societies into the category of feudalism.

Going back to Marx's list of *progressive Epochen*, it is also hard to see the transition from the ancient to the feudal mode of production in Western Europe as progressive in technological or other substantive ways. One does not have to subscribe to a notion of the "Dark Ages" to note that in this period Western Europe fell far behind other centers of economic and scientific development, like the Middle East, India, and China.

Second, the term *progressive Epochen* could also carry a much less expansive meaning: successive simply in temporal terms. If this were the case, then the "Asiatic" mode of production, presumably growing out of the previous tribal/communal one, is simply earlier in terms of when it appears in history. It is succeeded by the ancient Greco-Roman mode of production, which is succeeded by feudalism, which is succeeded by bourgeois capitalism. Less of a substantive notion of progress is at issue in this reading of the term *progressive Epochen*. But this interpretation is still problematic because it places "Asiatic" modes of production as earlier, perhaps even more "primitive," than both the ancient Greco-Roman and the feudal ones. This raises questions because of the high economic and technological levels of development found in a number of precapitalist Asian societies, especially compared to those found under Western European feudalism.

In *Capital*, Vol. I, Marx alludes even more briefly to historical modes of production: "In the modes of production of ancient Asia, of antiquity in general, the transformation of the product into a commodity plays only a subordinate role."[13] In this brief passage, he mentions the "Asiatic"

12   Krader, *The Asiatic Mode of Production*, p. 278.

13   Marx, *Le Capital. Livre I. Sections I à IV*, traduction de J. Roy, préface de Louis Althusser (Paris: Éditions Flammarion, [1872–75] 1985), p. 74; MEGA2 I/7: 59. I am giving my own translation here from the French edition, which seems clearer than the English or German versions on this point. Since the French edition is not widely accessible, I will be giving double references, to the widely circulated Flammarion edition of 1985 (in which Vol. I has two parts, with separate page numbers for each part) and to MEGA2. As will be discussed below, the 1872–75 French edition is the last one Marx saw through to publication, even after the second German edition of 1872–73. The French

and what appears to be the ancient Greco-Roman mode of production in the context of stressing that most of their production was for use rather than centered on commodity production. These modes of production, here taken together, certainly had substantial circulation of goods and a degree of commodity production, as seen in the vast trading networks across the Mediterranean Sea or the Indian Ocean. Yet they still stand in contrast to the modern bourgeois mode of production, where commodity production is not simply an important sector, but the central one, one that completely dominates society. But at this juncture, Marx does not attempt to sketch any temporal trajectory from these earlier modes of production to capitalism. Feudalism, the successor mode of production to the ancient Greco-Roman one, at least in Western Europe—and which is also the immediate predecessor of capitalism—is not even mentioned.

Despite their fragmentary character, one thing that stands out in these two lists—from 1859 and 1867–75[14]—is the "Asiatic" mode of production, not mentioned in the *German Ideology*, let alone by Stalin in his list of modes of production. To Krader, Marx in these two lists conceptualizes the development of historical modes of production "as multilinear, and not unilinear, in various historical lines among different peoples."[15]

But there is also a difference between the two lists. By the time of *Capital*, the language about *progressive Epochen* disappears. The passage in no way suggests that Western Europe's "ancient" mode of production is "progressive" either temporally or substantively with respect to the "Asiatic" mode of production. Instead, we have two well-developed and wealthy class societies, as seen in the "Asiatic" and ancient Greco-Roman modes of production, both of which stand in contrast to modern

---

original reads: "Dans les modes de production de la vielle Asia, de l'antiquité en général, la transformation du produit en marchandise ne joue qu'un rôle subaltern." The standard English version, based upon Engels's fourth German edition of 1890, reads: "In the ancient Asiatic, Classical-antique, and other such modes of production, the transformation of the product into a commodity, and therefore men's existence as producers of commodities, plays a subordinate role" (CAP: 172).

14 As discussed below, in keeping with much recent scholarship, I regard the 1872–75 French edition as Marx's final word on the text of Vol. I; hence, I use the dates 1867–75 to cover all editions of Vol. I that Marx personally prepared for publication: the German editions of 1867 and 1872–73, and the French edition of 1872–75, which initially appeared in serial form.

15 Krader, *The Asiatic Mode of Production*, p. 157.

capitalist society. Since what Marx calls "Asiatic" modes of production go all the way back to ancient Persia, if not earlier, and persisted into his own time in China and elsewhere, it is hard to view them as an early part of a temporal list of successive forms of society.

Overall, Marx creates room for what seems to be the best and clearest version of these successive modes of production, on the road toward how he conceptualizes them in his last writings. He does so by simply mentioning "Asiatic" and ancient modes of production as forms that precede capitalism, without ordering the list. Below I have created the list of modes of production that seem to emerge at this point, 1867–75, and remain until his death, based also on Marx's discussions of various societies around the globe in his notebooks and elsewhere. Or rather, there are two lists:

First list, based upon the Mediterranean and Western Europe: (1) All parts of the world experience an era of tribal or clan-based communal social forms. This is the earliest mode of production, everywhere. (2) In the ancient Greco-Roman world, this gives way to a class system wherein a ruling aristocracy employs slave labor on a vast scale, creates private property in land, and also establishes legal frameworks that come the closest of any precapitalist social formation to modern capitalism. (3) Out of the ruins of Rome, feudalism arises in Western Europe, with an enserfed peasantry in an agrarian society with few large cities. (4) Capitalism emerges out of the collapse of feudalism, as a result of industrial, political, and scientific revolutions, a society based upon the exploitation of formally free wage labor and a modern, capitalist form of slavery. (5) Socialism or communism emerges out of the contradictions of capitalism.

Second list, based upon Russia, the Middle East, and the rest of Asia: (1) All parts of the world experience an era of tribal or clan-based communal social forms. This is the earliest mode of production, everywhere. (2) The "Asiatic" social forms consolidate themselves next, maintaining within some very hierarchical and exploitative class societies a degree of communal social organization and property at the ground level, that of the village. In most parts of the world, this persists well into the eighteenth century, and in some places like China and Russia, right up to Marx's own time. (3a) Bourgeois capitalism does not arise internally from the "Asiatic" modes of production, but is imposed via European colonialism and the world market capitalism establishes. (3b) Alternatively, socialist revolution in Western Europe helps these societies to skip to the socialist or communist mode of production, bypassing bourgeois capitalism. This gives us the following trajectory: communal to Asiatic class societies to bourgeois, or, skipping the bourgeois stage, to socialist society.[16]

Am I making too much here of some brief mentions by Marx of an "Asiatic" mode of production? Is not feudalism the category Marx usually uses when he takes up precapitalist societies, as it is the one that gives birth to capitalism, after first having blocked its development?

The answer is no. Moreover, an explicit, detailed analysis of feudalism is also lacking in Marx's work, beyond what appears early on in the *German Ideology*. True, there is a fairly substantial passage on feudalism in the fetishism section of *Capital*:

> Let us now transport ourselves from Robinson's island bathed in light to the European Middle Ages shrouded in darkness. Here, instead of the independent man, we find everyone dependent, serfs and lords, vassals and suzerains, laymen and clergy. Personal dependence here characterizes the social relations of production just as much as it does the other spheres of life organized on the basis of that production. But for the very reason that personal dependence forms the groundwork of society, *all social relations appear as relations between persons*. Therefore, there is no necessity for labor and its products to assume a fantastic form different from their reality. They take the shape, in the transactions of society, of services in kind and payments in kind. Here the particular and natural form of labor, and not, as in a society based on production of commodities, its general abstract form is the immediate social form of labor. Compulsory labor is just as properly measured by time, as commodity-producing labor; but every serf knows that what he expends in the service of his lord, *without recourse to Adam Smith*, is a definite quantity of his own personal labor power. The tithe to be rendered to the priest is more matter of fact than his blessing. No matter, then, what we may think of the parts played by

16   These lists are similar to the ones developed by Marian Sawer, *Marxism and the Question of the Asiatic Mode of Production* (The Hague: Martinus Nijhoff, 1977), pp. 105–6.

the different classes of people themselves in this society, the social relations between individuals in the performance of their labor, appear at all events as their own mutual personal relations, and are not disguised under the shape of social relations *between things*, the products of labor.[17]

Here, the stress is not on feudalism as a historical mode of production that occurs before or after others, but on the directly social labor prevalent under feudalism, which renders social relations transparent rather than fetishized or mystified. While there is not a whiff of idealization of a precapitalist society here, neither is feudalism portrayed as backward in quite the sense of 1845–46. In fact, the notion of this period as one of "darkness" is viewed ironically, in a send-up of the Enlightenment progressivism that formed part of the pathway to the alienated and fetishized world of capitalist production.

Aside from the above, Marx does not write very much more about feudalism, leaving us his treatment in the *German Ideology*, discussed above, as his most substantial conceptualization of this mode of production. As historian Alain Guerreau writes in the *Dictionnaire critique du marxisme*, "As a whole it cannot be repeated enough that Marx never gave precise indications of what he considered to be the principal articulations of the feudal mode of production."[18] Guerreau adds that while Marx gave some attention to "the conditions for the birth of capitalism" that developed within feudalism, he "never analyzed" the "specific dynamics of the feudal mode of production."[19] The same could be said of the early communal, the ancient Greco-Roman, and the Asian modes of production. However, in his last working years, 1869–82, Marx devoted much of his research to the structures and contradictions of these latter kinds of societies, while not concentrating very much on feudalism.

Thus, it would be doubly wrong to consider the early communal, the ancient Greco-Roman, and the Asian modes of production as somehow

---

17   Marx, *Le Capital, Livre I. Sections I à IV*, pp. 72–3; MEGA I/7: 58. I have italicized three clarifying passages, all added to the French edition but not taken up by Engels in creating the standard edition that is the basis for the English translation (CAP: 170).

18   Alain Guerreau, 1982. "Féodalisme," *Dictionnaire critique du marxisme*, ed. Georges Labica and Gérard Bensussan (Paris: Presses Universitaires de France, 1982), p. 462.

19   Ibid., p. 463.

peripheral to Marx's work, while making feudalism central to it. First, it would be wrong in terms of his theoretical work, in the sense that he never conceptualizes other than very briefly any of the precapitalist modes of production, even though in the *German Ideology* and in *Capital*, he does develop a few paragraphs that describe the outlines of feudalism. Second, it would be wrong in terms of the focus of Marx's empirical work, especially in his later years. When one considers the lengthy notes during the years 1879–82 on the early communal, the ancient Greco-Roman, and the Asian modes of production, it would be hard to deny that these kinds of societies—none of them either feudal or capitalist—were a major focus of his work. Moreover, I know of no comparable sets of notes of such length Marx devoted to Western European feudalism during his last years.[20]

Although one can find no lists of successive modes of production in Marx's 1879–82 notebooks, one can find numerous remarks attacking the authors he was reading for categorizing precolonial India or Algeria as feudal. In the notes on Morgan, the situation is different, as Morgan himself rejects the "feudal" notion as a description of precapitalist Mesoamerican societies like the Aztecs, and Marx evidently agrees. All this obviously calls into question the schematic Marxist notion of primitive, slave, feudal, and bourgeois modes of production succeeding one another. The categorization of societies like India as "feudal" seems to have originated not in Marx but in the assumptions of some of the academic historians and anthropologists he was reading in 1879–82 and to have entered Marxism after the deaths of Marx and Engels.

Late Marx: Explicit and Deepening Attacks on the "Feudal" Interpretation

It is clear that Marx's notion of the non-applicability of the concept of feudalism outside Western Europe became explicit and vehement in his last years. The fact that these late notebooks have not been widely published or discussed has allowed the notion of feudalism as a universal

---

20   Brief notes on Rudolph Sohm's history of Roman and Frankish law, found in the notebook containing those on Morgan, are the only exception of which I am aware. These have now been published in MEGAdigital IV/27.

category to persist even within some Marx scholarship, without sufficient awareness that such theorizations were alien to Marx's own perspective after 1858.

Rejection of the "feudal" interpretation for precapitalist societies outside Western Europe can be found in Marx's notes on Kovalevsky (1879), Morgan (1880–81), Phear (1880–81), and Maine (1881). At the beginning of his 1879 notes on Kovalevsky, those dealing with the pre-Columbian Americas, Marx records without comment a passage from Kovalevsky espousing a "feudal" interpretation of the Indigenous empires:

> These attempts originated with *the feudalization of the immovable property* that was beginning in *Mexico* and *Peru*, a process in which the main role, as everywhere, fell to the *elders (leaders) of the people* and *the members of the emerging aristocracy* . . . In addition to *crown estates*, all around the breadth of *Mexico, the Isthmus of Panama* and the *Federation of Peru feudal estates*, the foundation of which had been laid by the *leaders of the conquering tribe*. (KOVLM: 27–28)

His attitude changes a bit later in the Kovalevsky notes when he gets to India, a society with which he was much more familiar.

Two years later, Marx's attitude toward the "feudal" interpretation seems also to have changed with regard to the Americas, as seen in the Morgan notes. For example, as already mentioned in chapter 1, Marx seems to approve of the following passage he records from Morgan on how the Spanish colonists misunderstood completely the social structure of the Aztecs, reading it erroneously as a version of European feudalism:

> The *Spaniards* (writers) have left the land tenure of the southern tribes in inextricable confusion. In *unalienable common land* belonging to a *community of persons* they saw *feudal estate*, in chief the *feudal lord*, in people *his vassals*; they saw that land owned in common; not the *community as owners themselves*—the *gens* or *division of a gens*. (EN: 133; MG: 537)

Marx amplifies this point in another passage he records from Morgan:

> The *feudal conceptions of the Spaniards* and the *Indian relationships* . . . are all mixed up—but are separable. The Aztec "*Lord*" was the *Sachem*,

civil chief of a *body of consanguinei* of whom he is called "the *major parent.*" The lands belonged to that body (*gens*) in common; when the *chief* died, his place (according to Herrera) went; over to his son; what passed over in this case the *office of Sachem*, not the land, which *no one "possessed" in trust*; if he had no son "the lands were left to the nearest major parent," that is, *another person* was elected *Sachem*. (EN: 192; MG: 201)

In the above passage, Marx puts a point on Morgan's argument by presenting the material—almost all of it Morgan's words—in a different order that gives even greater emphasis to the critique of the "feudal" interpretation.

The issue of feudalism—or not—in the pre-Columbian Indigenous empires was not very widely discussed in Marx's 1879–82 notebooks, but this was not true of India. This is because, as mentioned above, Marx probably felt on surer footing challenging Kovalevsky and others on "feudalism" on the Indian Subcontinent, given his much deeper study of this region since the 1850s. It is here, as well, that Marx's attacks upon the feudal interpretation become the most pointed.

In an example of an attack on the "feudal" interpretation, Marx inserts a sharp bracketed critique of the Russian anthropologist, who sees the special tax imposed on land owned by non-Muslims as an example of feudalism:

The owners were transformed from free to dependent, and simultaneously with this, their property from allodial to feudal. (129) [[This last reference only has meaning with regard to the Muslims—who received *iqta* II or III, and *at the very most to the Hindus insofar as they had to pay money or goods to the benefice-holder rather than to the state treasury*. The payment of *kharaj* led property to become feudal just as little as does payment of the *land tax* makes French landed property become so. This whole passage from Kovalevsky just scribbled stupidly.]] (KOV: 373)

Only the *iqta* system, wherein Muslim rulers granted land to military chieftains in exchange for military and other forms of service, seems to Marx to exhibit some aspects of feudalism. He calls even this into question later though, in the following excerpt from Kovalevsky with the insertion of the phrase "so-called feudalization," thus highlighting the much more centralized political system of Mughal India as compared to that of European feudalism: "At the end of the [Mughal] Empire the *so-called feudalization* only in certain districts, in most of the others *communal and private property* in the hands of the indigenous owners and the management of state functions in the hands of *officials named by the central government*" (KOV: 384).

Marx makes his most substantial critique of the notion of the Mughal Empire as a form of feudalism in a section of Kovalevsky's book entitled "Process of Feudalization of Landed Property in India in the Epoch of Muslim Rule" (KOV: 374):

> Kovalevsky finds feudalism here in the Western European sense, because he finds the "benefice system," "*the awarding of offices in return for service*," [[this however is not just *feudal*, given the case of Rome]] and *commendatio* in India. *Among other things, Kovalevsky forgets serfdom, which* is an essential moment, and which is absent in India. [[With regard to the *individual role of protection* (cf. *Palgrave*) of not only the unfree, but also the free peasants—by the feudal lords (who play the role of *stewards*), in India this plays a limited role with the exception of waqf]] [[*poetry of the soil* (see Maurer), characteristic of Holy Roman-Germanic feudalism, is found as little in India as it is in Rome. Nowhere in India is the *soil* considered *noble*, as if it might somehow be non-transferable to commoners!]] (KOV: 383)

One factor above is what might be called the whole "spirit" of the Indian social system, which Marx sees as antithetical to feudalism. In something like a definition of feudalism, he singles out a reverence for the land, serfdom, and the vassal-suzerain relationship. At a more general level, as Conversano notes, in such remarks, "Marx criticizes the universalization of European feudalism for the historiography of non-European societies."[21] For his part, Krader maintains, "The application of the category feudalism to the oriental community . . . is an abstraction from history and an ethnocentrism" (EN: 32–33). Instead, Marx sees the ancient Indian communal structures as persisting under Muslim rule, not

---

21 Conversano, "Zur Kritik der Anthropologie: Marx' Theorie des Kapitals und Seine Ethnologischen Studien," *Marx-Engels Jahrbuch* 2 (2017/18), p. 34.

displaced by feudal ones, as in Western Europe. Their uprooting would come only with a new type of colonial rule under the British, who brought with them capitalist social relations.

A year or more later, in 1881, as he makes notes on Phear's study of the village system in another part of the Subcontinent, Sri Lanka (Ceylon), Marx rejects the feudal interpretation in much sharper language than that which he applied, even privately, to his "scientific friend" Kovalevsky: "This ass [*Esel*] Phear calls the constitution of the village feudal" (EN: 256). He also attacks one of Phear's sources for having "falsified the facts through phraseology borrowed from feudal Europe" (EN: 283).

Similarly, in his 1879 notes on Kovalevsky on precolonial Algeria, Marx also rejects the term "feudalism." At one point, he criticizes the notion of feudalism under Ottoman rule in a parenthetical remark in a passage he records from Kovalevsky:

> The Turks supported *military colonies* for protection against rebellion by the ever-ready *local militias* (which Kovalevsky christens "*feudal*" for the wrong reason, that the Indian jagirs—under different circumstances—were able to develop something similar.) (KOV: 403)

Probably since even Kovalevsky applied the term "feudalism" more cautiously to Algeria, Marx does not take issue with him as much on Algeria and feudalism.

In a very different context, precapitalist Ireland, Marx refrains from taking issue with Maine's use of the category feudalism, even though he quarrels with him on many other points, as discussed in chapter 1. Here, Marx seems simply to accept Maine's overview:

> In feudal society everybody has become the subordinate of somebody else higher than himself and yet exalted above him by no great distance. (153) According to Stubbs (*Constit. History*. I, 252) feudalism has "grown up from 2 great sources, the *Benefice* and the practice of *Commendation*. (154) *Commendation*, in particular, went on all over Western Europe. (EN: 297; MN: 153–4)

Thus, feudalism spread in Ireland as in Western Europe as a whole. As the Irish Marx scholars Eamonn Slater and Terrence McDonough argue,

Marx's view was that premodern British colonialism "begat a feudal economy that lasted into the nineteenth century."[22]

Even when he inserts a parenthetical question mark in a passage by Maine portraying the rise of feudalism in Ireland as a "natural" process, as below, Marx does not question that the result is in fact a form of feudalism:

> This *natural growth of feudalism* was not, as some eminent recent writers have supposed, entirely distinct from the process by which the authority of the Chief or Lord over the Tribe or Village was extended, but rather formed part of it. While the *unappropriated waste lands* were falling into his domain, the villagers or tribesmen were coming through *natural* (?) agencies under his personal power. (EN: 300; MN: 167)

These passages from the notes on Maine underline Marx's rejection of the category of feudalism for India and the pre-Columbian Americas. At the same time, he readily accepts it for Ireland, where feudalism arrived with the Norman conquest of the twelfth century.

In sum, in his late notes on Indigenous America, the Indian Subcontinent, and Algeria, Marx vehemently rejects the notion that these societies were feudal. At the same time, he accepts the category for a Western European country, Ireland. At the very least, this shows that Marx espouses a multilinear concept of historical change and development through successive modes of production, wherein the Marxist model of "primitive," feudal, and bourgeois capitalist modes of production succeeding one another is restricted to Western Europe. At the same time, Marx does not create a single theoretical category in his late writings for the social structures of these non-European or non-Western class societies, which included India, the Middle East, North Africa, and parts of Indigenous America. He does not, for example, repeat the term "Asiatic mode of production" after referring to it for the last time in the 1872–75 French edition of *Capital*. We cannot know whether he intended to create a new theory of historical modes of production in his future work, replacing the Western European–centered approach of the *German*

---

22   Eamonn Slater and Terrence McDonough, "Marx on Nineteenth-Century Colonial Ireland: Analysing Colonialism as a Dynamic Process," *Irish Historical Review* 36: 142 (2008), p. 171.

Ideology. But, as I will discuss in the rest of this chapter, he did theorize the possibilities for social change and revolution in his own time among some of the varying social structures he found across the globe, focusing, in particular, on the differences between village society in Russia and Western Europe.

A Second Type of Multilinearity: Limiting Capitalism to a Sliver of the World in the French Edition of *Capital*

Up to now, I have been discussing Marx's theory of history, often called historical materialism, in terms of precapitalist modes of production: communal/clan, "Asiatic," ancient, or feudal. In contrast, most inter-preters of Marx have ascribed to him a conception of precapitalist class societies as universally feudal, despite his own statements to the contrary.

The debate over unilinear versus multilinear approaches in Marx's work belongs more to his own time but impinges upon the interpreta-tion of some present-day societies. Put succinctly: Will all societies become capitalist? Is there, in other words, a single historical trajectory of economic and social development? Is there an alternative to capital-ism for societies that are not yet capitalist? Finally, is passing through capitalist modernization a prerequisite for moving toward a modern form of communism?

Marx addresses these issues at two levels. He first does so at a general level in two passages in *Capital*, Vol. I, added rather late in the day, in the French edition of 1872–75. He also considers two societies still periph-eral to capitalism in his own time, Russia and Ireland.

For years disparaged—even in France—as an inferior and simplified edition of *Capital*, Vol. I, compared to the German ones of 1867 and 1872–73, the French edition, completed only in 1875, has gained greater respect among scholars as a serious alternative version. It was the last version of his *magnum opus* that Marx himself brought to press. Moreo-ver, it contains substantial textual variants—many of them clearly intended for inclusion in any later edition, even a German one—that have still not made it into the English editions, all of which take the fourth German edition of 1890, established by Engels after Marx's death, as their basis. (The 2024 Princeton edition, published too late for consideration here, includes nothing from the French edition, except in an appendix.)

The place of the French edition has become a widely debated issue in recent years, in no small part because some discussion has led to serious criticisms of Engels as editor of *Capital*. Since my intellectual mentor Raya Dunayevskaya alerted me to this debate the early 1980s, I have been writing on this topic.[23] I have continued to discuss it in *Marx at the Margins* and since, criticizing Engels as editor of *Capital*. In 2022, the first book in any language focusing on the French edition appeared, under the editorship of the indefatigable Marcello Musto, to which I also contributed an essay.[24]

Discussion of the French edition as a key development in Marx's critique of political economy has centered on two sets of issues.[25] The first of these considers *Capital*, Vol. I, as a work in progress and views Marx's thought as evolving from 1867, when the first German edition appeared in Hamburg, through 1872–73 and the second German edition, and then through 1875, when the French edition finally appeared in full. (It was initially published in serial form, 1872–75.) In many important cases, Engels incorporated key changes Marx introduced into the French edition, most of them also in the 1872–73 German edition. One of the most notable of these is the creation of a separate section on commodity fetishism after 1867, duly incorporated by Engels in his 1890 fourth German edition, the one that has remained the standard for most translations of *Capital* ever since.

The second set of issues, and the most debated, concerns Engels's relative neglect of the French edition in his creation of the "final" text of Vol. 1 for his 1890 German edition, and his decisions concerning the third German edition of 1883, already close to publication at the time Marx's death that same year. In 1989, editors Rolf Hecker et al. produced, in MEGA2 II/8, two sets of notes from Marx indicating passages to be taken up from the French edition in subsequent German editions, not all of which Engels incorporated. Then, in 1991, Engels's fourth German edition appeared in

---

23   Kevin Anderson, "The 'Unknown' Marx's *Capital*, Vol. I: The French Edition of 1872–75, 100 Years Later," *Review of Radical Political Economics* 15: 4(1983), pp. 71–80.

24   Kevin Anderson, "Marx's French Edition of *Capital* as Unexplored Territory: From the Centralization of Capital to Societies Beyond Western Europe," in Marcello Musto (ed.), *Marx and* Le Capital (London: Routledge, 2022), pp. 41–59.

25   These two issues have sometimes been confused, as seen in William Outhwaite and Kenneth Smith, "Le Capital," *Review of Radical Political Economics* 52: 2 (2020), pp. 208–21.

MEGA2 II/10, with a sixty-page list of passages from the French edition that Engels had left out. This extensive list of alternate texts from the French edition in MEGA2 II/10 (pp. 732–83) seriously undermines those who have portrayed the French edition as more popularized than the German ones, and thus inferior. To take a prominent example, Louis Althusser pontificates that in the French edition, "Marx, who was uncertain of the theoretical capacities of his French readers, sometimes dangerously compromised the precision of the original conceptual expressions."[26]

Although attempts to dismiss the French edition have become less frequent since the publication of the list of alternate texts in MEGA2 II/10, no English, French, or even German edition of *Capital*, Vol. I has ever been published that gives readers ready access to these alternate texts, aside from the MEGA2 volumes, with their very high prices and entirely German apparatus and prefaces. The more popular 2017 edition produced by Thomas Kuczynski, a scholar educated in the former East Germany, is a version, soon to appear in English in a translation by Gregor Benton, that attempts to incorporate all the changes from the French edition that editor Kuczynski thinks Engels should have included. Although it does not let readers see all the textual variants for themselves, it is a remarkable achievement of rigorous scholarship.

I believe that the French edition should simply be translated in its entirety into English, German, and other languages, as is happening in Brazil with a new Portuguese translation. This is because editions like Kuczynski's and even MEGA2 are always incomplete, and readers will invariably keep finding new alternative texts if both the French edition

---

26 Louis Althusser, "Preface to *Capital* Volume One," *Lenin and Philosophy and Other Essays*, trans. Ben Brewster (New York: Monthly Review Press, [1969] 2001), p. 58. Althusser was not alone, certainly in France, where Lucien Sève and Jacques d'Hondt, important Marxist philosophers who clashed with Althusser, also shared these judgments, as shown respectively in David Smith, "Marx's Capital after the Paris Commune," pp. 11–40 and in Jean-Numa Ducange and Jean Quétier, "The Contradictory Reception of the French Edition of *Capital*," pp. 175–88, both in Musto's *Marx and* Le Capital. Two younger contributors to the debate, the Brazilian Marx scholar Rodrigo Pinho ("The Originality of the French Edition of *Capital*: An Historical Analysis," *International Marxist-Humanist*, September 3, 2021, pp. 1–45) and the Belgian political theorists Kenneth Hemmerechts and Nohemi Jocabeth Echeverria Vicente ("*Le Capital*: A Transnational, Family, and Personal Endeavor," in *Marx and* Le Capital, pp. 95–116) have provided detailed accounts of Marx's correspondence and his interactions with his French publisher that establish the importance Marx attached to the French edition and his disagreements over this issue with Engels.

and those based upon Engels's 1890 German edition can be read more easily side by side.

Two passages from the French edition, both of which I discussed in *Marx at the Margins*, will serve to demonstrate Marx's increasingly multilinear approach to social development during his lifetime. These passages show clearly that Marx, at least by the time of the French edition of *Capital*, no longer believes that all societies of his time were destined to industrialize in the capitalist manner, or at least not through what he called the "primitive accumulation of capital." In the *Communist Manifesto* of 1848, he and Engels imply that such a unilinear process is inevitable, as they write of China and other non-European societies being forcibly incorporated into the global capitalist system.

In one passage in the French edition, Marx makes a change to the 1867 preface, without indicating he is altering the original text. In an oft-cited sentence on the relationship of industrialized to non-industrialized societies, the standard English and German editions read: "The country that is more developed industrially only shows, *to the less developed*, the image of its own future" (CAP: 91, emphasis added).[27] Some have seized upon this sentence to brand Marx a "unilinear" and determinist thinker. Using this passage as evidence, Marx editor Teodor Shanin writes in a still influential work, *Late Marx and the Russian Road*, that the "main weakness" of *Capital* "was the optimistic and unilinear determinism usually built into it" (SHN: 4). But in the French edition, Marx adds a clause that changes the sentence's meaning in important ways: "The country that is more developed industrially only shows, *to those that follow it up the industrial ladder*, the image of its own future."[28] With this textual alteration, he has essentially *bracketed out* the vast parts of the world that in the 1870s were not yet beginning to industrialize. Thus, whatever "laws" and tendencies Marx elaborates in *Capital* would seem to apply only to societies where industrial capitalism either dominated the economy or was in the process of doing so: in short, at that time only Western Europe and North America. This is not a unilinear perspective, but its opposite.

---

27 In the original German, this reads: "Das industriell entwickeltere Land zeigt dem minder entwickelten nur das Bild der eignen Zukunft" (MEGA2 II/10: 8; MEW 23: 12).

28 In the original French, this reads: "Le pays le plus développé industriellement ne fait que montrer a ceux qui le suivent sur l'échelle industrielle l'image de leur propre avenir" (Marx, *Le Capital. Livre I. Sections V à VIII*, p. 36; MEGA2 II/7, p. 12). This change is noted neither in MEGA2 II/7 nor MEGA2 II/10. I thank Kohei Saito for helping me to improve the translation of this crucial sentence over the one I used in *Marx at the Margins*.

With a few exceptions, this passage has not received as much discussion as it deserves, partly because it was not included in MEGA2 II/10's long list of changes that Engels omitted from the French edition. I first took it up four decades ago;[29] it gained more attention after I returned to it in *Marx at the Margins*, especially after MEGA2 researcher Claudia Reichel called its coming to light "an important development in Marxist research."[30] More recently, the German political theorist Kolja Lindner, who has usually hewn to a Marx-as-Eurocentrist[31] position, singled out this passage as an instance of Marx moving away from the "pseudo-universalist conception of development" found in the 1867 formulation.[32]

In the last part of the book, "Primitive Accumulation of Capital," Marx makes a second, similar amendment in the French edition. Unlike the revision to the 1867 preface, this altered passage has been known, at least to specialist scholars, for over a century, even though Engels did not include it.[33] After describing the brutal process of primitive or original accumulation of capital, in which the English peasantry is driven out of subsistence farming to become formally free proletarians living in precarious circumstances, Marx writes:

> The expropriation of the agricultural producer, of the peasant, from the soil, is the basis of the whole process. The history of this expropriation assumes different aspects in different countries, and runs through its various phases in different orders of succession, and at

---

29   Kevin Anderson, "Review of Teodor Shanin, ed., *Late Marx and the Russian Road*," *Review of Radical Political Economics* 17 (1985), pp. 259–61.

30   Claudia Reichel, "Marx zu den Rändern," *Marx-Engels Jahrbuch 2010* (Berlin: Akademie Verlag, 2011), p. 196.

31   This view is associated most often with the critique of Marx in Edward Said, *Orientalism* (New York: Pantheon, 1978). In his *Marxism, Orientalism, Cosmopolitanism* (Chicago: Haymarket, 2015), Gilbert Achcar offers an especially subtle and nuanced response to Said.

32   Kolja Lindner, "Le dernier Marx au-delà du marxisme," *Le Dernier Marx* (Paris: Éditions de l'Asymétrie, 2019), p. 12.

33   Already in the *Grundrisse,* the Italian Marx scholar Lucia Pradella holds, Marx is "limiting the validity of his own analysis of the transition to capitalism to Western Europe" when he writes: "Thus, England in this respect the model country for the other continental countries." This is a bit imprecise, since "continental" could include Russia, a country excluded by the formulations under discussion here from the French edition of *Capital* that were written some fifteen years later. See Lucia Pradella, *Globalisation and the Critique of Political Economy: New Insights from Marx's Writings* (New York: Routledge, 2015), p. 133; Karl Marx, *Grundrisse,* trans. Martin Nicolaus (New York: Pelican, 1973), p. 277.

different historical epochs. *Only in England, which we therefore take as our example, has it the classic form.* (CAP: 876, emphasis added)[34]

These sentences conclude chapter 26, "The Secret of Primitive Accumulation," in which Marx introduces the overall theoretical framework of primitive accumulation. In this brief chapter, Marx mentions only European examples, specifically the transition from feudalism to capitalism. Nonetheless, it could have been read as a global and unilinear process of capitalist development, with England exhibiting the "classic form" of this process. Given the implicitly unilinear language of the *Communist Manifesto*, this was how many read and still read this passage, if not the whole of *Capital*.

In the French edition, Marx extends and reworks this passage considerably, expressly limiting his analysis to Western Europe. Although he subsequently refers more than once to the following passage from the French edition, it has yet to make it into any of the standard English editions of *Capital*, save the forthcoming translation (in the *Historical Materialism* Book Series) of Kuczynski's edition:

> But the basis of this whole development is the expropriation of the cultivators. *So far, it has been carried out in a radical manner only in England: therefore, this country will necessarily play the leading role in our sketch. But all the countries of Western Europe are going through the same development*, although in accordance with the particular environment it changes its local color, or confines itself to a narrower sphere, or shows a less pronounced character, or follows a different order of succession. (emphasis added)[35]

---

34   In the original German, this reads: "Die Expropriation des ländlichen Produzenten, des Bauern, von Grund und Boden bildet die Grundlage des Ganzen Processes. Ihre Geschichte nimmt in verschiedenen Ländern veschiedene Färbung an und durchläuft die veschiedenen Phasen in verschiedener Reihenfolge und in verschiedenen Geschichtsepochen. Nur in England, das wir daher als Beispiel nehmen, besitzt sie klassische Form" (MEGA2 II/10: 644; MEW 23:744).

35   In the original French, this reads: "Mais la base de toute cette évolution, c'est l'expropriation des cultivateurs. Elle ne s'est encore accomplie d'une manière radical qu'en Angleterre: ce pays jouera donc nécessairement le premier rôle dans notre esquisse. Mais tous les autres pays de l'Europe occidentale parcourent le même mouvement, bien que selon le milieu il change de couleur locale, ou se resserre dans un cercle plus étroit, ou présente un caractère moins fortement prononcé, ou suivre un ordre de succession

This alteration makes clear that Marx's narrative of primitive accumulation is meant as a description of Western European development, nothing more, and hardly a global grand narrative.[36]

While Engels may not have noticed my first "multilinear" example, the altered sentence in the 1867 preface, by failing to include the above passage he seems to have violated Marx's explicit instructions. For, in an outline Marx made in the fall of 1882 for a new German edition, he writes that this passage was "to be translated from the French edition" (MEGA2 II/8:17).[37] Engels's omission here may well have been deliberate, since, in his 1883 preface, he indicates that he has consulted "notes left by the author" in preparing the third German edition (CAP: 110). This decision may have been rooted in Engels's early skepticism about the French edition in correspondence with Marx in 1873, after reading some drafts of Joseph Roy's translation.[38]

It is important to note that the changes in the French edition discussed above do not alter *Capital's* overall focus on Western Europe. In this regard, Jean-Numa Ducange reminds us that "despite everything colonization is not at the heart of *Capital*, Vol. I."[39] This is true enough, although one could say the same about commodity fetishism, now a core issue due to its greater relevance to subsequent generations as capitalism became ever more impersonal and technocratic. In this sense, it is

---

différent" (Marx, *Le Capital. Livre I. Sections V à VIII*, p. 169; MEGA2 II/7: 634, also listed as a textual alteration omitted in the standard German edition established by Engels in MEGA2 II/10: 778).

36 Not everyone agrees. For example, the German Marx scholar Michael Krätke, writing in the Musto collection, accepts as factual the main points made above, yet writes inexplicably that all this textual alteration "does not make a big difference at all" ("An Unfinished Project: Marx's Last Words on *Capital*," in *Marx and* Le Capital, p. 163. This may be related to the fact that Krätke does not give any attention to Eurocentrism, colonialism, or even Russia in his essay on the French edition.

37 I would like to thank Rolf Hecker for pointing this out and for also showing me Marx's handwritten notes—private conversation, Moscow, May 29, 1998.

38 In what is largely a defense of Engels versus his critics on the French edition, in their "Le Capital," Outhwaite and Smith point out with some justice—in contrast to my interpretation in *Marx at the Margins*—that Engels's disparagement at this point of the French edition seems to concern Roy's translation, not the final version of the French edition as considerably altered by Marx. Be that as it may, in the case of this passage from the part on primitive accumulation, Engels seems to have made a decision, and a bad one, concerning the utilization of the French text as brought to press by Marx.

39 Jean-Numa Ducange, "The French Edition of *Capital* and the Question of Colonialism," in *Marx and* Le Capital, p. 67.

possible to reinterpret Marx according to later developments and contemporary concerns, and, when one does so today, numerous parts of the book show just such a focus, whether an important passage on race, class, slavery in the US in the "Working Day" chapter, the pages on slavery and colonialism under "primitive accumulation," or in the long section on British colonial exploitation of Ireland, the latter updated for the French edition. Ducange adds: "The fact remains that if a real turning point on the colonial question is to be identified, it seems to come later, really in the very last Marx."[40] This too may be true, but the altered passages in the French edition discussed above arguably allow us already to discern where Marx was going by the early 1870s, and to do so not on the basis of notebooks, drafts, or prefaces, but via his greatest book, *Capital*.

Marx refers to the second of the altered passages from the French edition discussed above not once but twice in correspondence with Russians in his last years, although it is not clear if Engels ever saw this correspondence. I turn to this correspondence now, since it concerns Marx's attitude toward whether Russia, a non-Western society, albeit not a colonized one, was destined, in unilinear fashion, to go through a process of primitive accumulation as already experienced in Britain and other Western European countries. In the next chapter, I will take up Marx's consideration in his 1879–82 notebooks of outright colonialism and the resistance to it.

More on Marx's Second Concept of Multilinearity: Skipping Stages on the Way Toward Revolution

The late Marx's multilinear perspective on social development and revolution can be seen in his correspondence with Russian intellectuals in his last years. It can also be found in his writings on Ireland in 1869–70.

I will take up the Irish example first. Here, it is a question of the directionality of revolutionary events. In the *Communist Manifesto* of 1848, Marx and Engels see Western Europe, especially industrialized Britain, as the lead nation that was drawing all others into the world market, setting up the preconditions for global revolution by establishing

---

40   Ibid.

capitalism, a modern working class, and the ensuing class conflict. Whether this is simply an abstract model or an actual description of how they saw events unfolding is, of course, open to question. But what cannot be found in the *Manifesto* is any notion of revolutionary events flowing from less technologically developed to more developed parts of the world. This kind of directionality applies to Britain's relationship to Ireland, where capitalism was beginning to encroach but which still exhibited many aspects of feudalism, especially in the countryside. Thus, as British capitalism developed, so would the class struggle and the prospects for a proletarian revolution. That would create conditions for revolutionary change in less developed areas like Ireland.

By 1869, Marx writes that he has reversed his position on the directionality of revolution, previously thought to be moving from Britain to Ireland. On December 10, as the Fenian movement against British colonialism came to a boil in both Ireland and Britain, Marx writes to Engels in Manchester:

> It is in the direct and absolute interests of the English working class to get rid of their present connection to Ireland. This is my deepest conviction [*vollste Überzeugung*], and for reasons that, in part, I cannot share with the English workers themselves. For a long time, I believed it would be possible to overthrow the Irish regime by English working class ascendancy. I always took this viewpoint in the *New York Tribune*. Deeper study has now convinced me of the opposite. The working class will get nowhere [*nie was ausrichten*] before it has got rid of Ireland. The lever must be applied in Ireland. This is why the Irish question is so important for the social movement in general. (MECW 43: 398)

This letter is the clearest direct evidence of a change of position on Marx's part on the directionality of revolution in Europe.

Marx writes that his new position is the "opposite" of his previous one. Moreover, this is not a public declaration, where he might be holding back due to political or rhetorical considerations, but a private communication to his closest comrade. Marx writes that he is speaking more openly than he can to the "English workers," with whom he is working very closely in the First International. In his reversal of position, he now sees Ireland as the "lever" that would pry open the possibility of a working-class revolution in Britain itself, rather than, as before, conceptualizing the revolution as starting in industrialized Britain and moving to Ireland. I will discuss the full ramifications of this new concept of Ireland as the "lever" of a wider European uprising in chapter 6, but here I want to stress simply Marx's explicit reversal of position on the directionality of revolution.

Two of Marx's letters to Russian intellectuals in his last years also illustrate the increasing multilinearity of his overall theoretical perspective, not only on revolution but also on the direction of economic and social development more generally. These letters, from 1877 and 1881, address the question of whether Marx is predicting that agrarian Russia is destined to experience something akin to the primitive accumulation of capital, as outlined in the last part of *Capital*. He sees this as a cruel and brutal process, marked by "conquest, enslavement, robbery, murder, in short, force" (CAP: 874). During the period of primitive accumulation, beginning in the sixteenth century, the English peasants lost their customary small landholdings to a new set of aristocrats, who claimed this land as unrestricted private property. A system of use-value production rooted in subsistence agriculture under feudalism began to be replaced by capitalist agriculture based upon commodity production, leaving thousands of former peasants dispossessed of their means of production—land, draft animals, and tools—and sometimes reduced to outright starvation. Severed from their feudal obligations, the former peasants were faced with formal freedom under a system of wage labor. Both opponents and supporters of Marx, who gained a large audience in Russia after *Capital* was translated into Russian in 1872, seemed to agree that Marx saw things this way. His opponents often thought he was wrong about the inevitability of this process as far as Russia was concerned, whereas his supporters seemed to think it was a necessary evil on the road toward progress.

This issue is at the heart of the letter the Russian revolutionary Vera Zasulich sent Marx on February 16, 1881. Writing in French, the preferred language of the Russian intelligentsia, Zasulich recounts a debate raging among Russian intellectuals about the fate of the communal social form found across Russia's villages. She writes that some see this form of Indigenous, agrarian communism as a source of future positive development that could allow Russia to bypass the primitive accumulation of capital and develop "in a socialist direction . . . gradually organizing production and distribution on a collectivist basis" (SHN: 98; MEGA2 I/25: 823).[41] Others, followers of "scientific socialism" who call themselves "Marxists [*Marcsistes*],"[42] Zasulich writes, believe that "the commune is destined to perish," presumably in the process of primitive accumulation of capital and that, had Marx discussed Russia in *Capital*, "he would have said so" (SHN: 99; MEGA2 I/25: 823).[43] In the terms I am using here, these were multilinear and unilinear perspectives.

Marx writes several lengthy drafts and then sends a much shorter letter of response to Zasulich on March 8, 1881. In one of the drafts, he denies any connection to the unilinear-minded Russian "Marxists" mentioned by Zasulich, also implying disagreement with them: "The Russian 'Marxists' of which you speak are completely unknown to me. As far as I am aware, the Russians with whom I do have personal links hold altogether opposite views" (SHN: 101; MEGA2 I/25: 232).

In the actual response sent to Zasulich, Marx separates himself from the "Marxists" in Russia mentioned by Zasulich, but without saying so directly. He cites the French edition of *Capital*, different from the 1867 one that formed the basis for the existing Russian translation of 1872, as the latter could help settle the debate about his views on the future of the Russian village commune. In so doing, Marx writes, also in French:

> In analyzing the genesis of capitalist production, I say: "Underneath the appearance [*au fond*] of the capitalist system is therefore the separation of the producer from the means of production . . . the basis of this whole development is the expropriation of the cultivators. *So far, it has been carried out in a radical manner only in England . . . But all the countries of Western Europe are going through the same development*" (*Capital*, French edition, p. 315). The "historical inevitability [*fatalité*]" of this course is therefore *explicitly* restricted to the *countries of Western Europe*. (SHN: 124; MEGA2 I/25: 241)[44]

---

41   See also Marx, *Oeuvres, Économie* II, ed. Maximilien Rubel (Paris: Éditions Gallimard, 1968), p. 1515. The reason for these multiple citations is that while the French original appears in MEGA2, it includes only about two thirds of Zasulich's letter to Marx (running about five hundred words total), while a full version of the French original appears in Rubel's edition.

42   The term "Marxist(e)" was not used widely until after Marx's death.

43   See also Marx, *Oeuvres, Économie* II, p. 1556.

44   For the relevant passage in *Capital*, see also see also Marx, *Le Capital. Livre I. Sections V à VIII*, pp. 168, 169; MEGA2 II/7: 634.

The phrase "historical inevitability" is Marx's own, but it conveys the spirit of Zasulich's language. The passage cited is the very one discussed earlier in this chapter as one of the important changes indicating a multilinear perspective that Marx introduces into the French edition.

In his reply to Zasulich, he also adds some very brief comments on the prospects of the Russian village commune:

> The analysis given in *Capital* therefore provides no reasons for or against the vitality of the rural commune, but the special study I have made of it, in which I used original source material, has convinced me that the commune is the basis [*point d'appui*] for Russia's social regeneration, but in order for it to function as such, the harmful influences assailing it on all sides have to be eliminated, and then the normal conditions for its spontaneous development assured. (SHN: 124; MEGA2 I/25: 241–2)

Here he implies that a socialist future can emerge from the village communes if the influences bearing down on them from capitalist encroachment can somehow be overcome. The drafts of his letter detail this point more, as docs the preface he and Engels wrote about nine months later for the 1882 Russian edition of the *Communist Manifesto*, but the latter will be detailed in the next two chapters.

For the purposes of the present discussion, the key point is Marx's distinguishing of Western Europe from the rest of the world. It is the place where the process of "primitive accumulation" applies or would do so at least in the near future. As a component of this, his theorization of Russia is open to a different trajectory of future development. Thus, he espouses a clearly multilinear perspective when comparing Russia to Western Europe at this juncture in 1881, when Russia had not even begun to industrialize and still had a vital system of communal social forms in its villages. Moreover, he seems to see these long-standing communal social forms as a possible basis for a socialist transformation of Russia as a whole.

Marx makes this point at a more general level in another letter, written for the Russian intellectual journal *Otechestvennye Zapiski* [Notes of the Fatherland] and addressed to a critic of *Capital*. The letter was not sent, apparently due to warnings from Kovalevsky that doing so might endanger the journal and its contributors based in Russia. Dated sometime in

1877 and composed in French, it also limits the theory of primitive accumulation to Western Europe: "The chapter on primitive accumulation claims no more than to trace the path by which, in Western Europe, the capitalist economic order emerged from the entrails of the feudal economic order" (SHN: 135; MEGA2 I/25: 115). To support this point, here Marx also cites the above-mentioned passage from the French edition of *Capital*.

In addition, he alludes briefly to Russia's communal social forms in the villages as a possible basis for a non-capitalist pathway of development, stating the point negatively in a warning about capitalist encroachments: "I have come to the conclusion that if Russia continues along the pathway she has followed since 1861, she will lose the finest chance ever offered by history to a people and undergo all the fateful vicissitudes of the capitalist regime" (SHN: 135; MEGA2 I/25: 115).

After this, Marx discusses unilinear determinism at a more general level. He denies forcefully that he holds a unilinear perspective on Russia's future development, especially one rooted in a philosophy of history generalizable to the whole world on the basis of the history of capitalism in Western Europe:

Now what application to Russia can my critic make of this historical sketch? Only this: If Russia is tending to become a capitalist nation after the example of the Western European countries, and during the last years she has been taking a lot of trouble in this direction—she will not succeed without having first transformed a good part of her peasants into proletarians; and after that, once taken to the bosom of the capitalist regime, she will experience its pitiless laws like other profane peoples. That is all. But that is not enough for my critic. He feels himself obliged to metamorphose my historical sketch of the genesis of capitalism in Western Europe into an historico-philosophic theory of the general path [*marche générale*] fatally imposed upon all peoples, whatever the historical circumstances in which they find themselves, in order that they may ultimately arrive at this economic formation which will ensure, together with the greatest expansion of the productive powers of social labor, the most complete development of each individual producer. But I beg his pardon. (He is both honoring and shaming me too much.) (SHN: 136; MEGA2 I/25: 116)

Here, Marx is denying that he has created a general social theory of human development, "an historico-philosophical theory of the general path [*marche générale*] fatally imposed upon all peoples, whatever the historical circumstances in which they find themselves." Had he done so, he would have repeated the very ahistorical procedures he criticizes in the British political economists, even the greatest ones, who assume market and even capitalist relations in the precapitalist past, thus universalizing these relations in a manner Marx vehemently contests. This letter contains the most explicit denial of unilinearism that I have found anywhere in Marx's writings.

He concludes this 1877 letter with a further contrast, not between contemporary Russia and Western Europe, but between the latter to ancient Rome:

> At various points in *Capital*, I have alluded to the fate that befell the plebeians of ancient Rome. They were originally free peasants, each tilling his own plot on his own behalf. In the course of Roman history, they were expropriated. The same movement that divorced them from their means of production and subsistence involved the formation not only of large, landed property but also of big money capitals. Thus, one fine morning there were, on the one side, free men stripped of everything but their labor-power, and on the other, in order to exploit their labor, owners of all the acquired wealth. What happened? The Roman proletarians became, not wage-laborers, but an idle "mob" more abject than those who used to be called *poor whites* of the southern United States; and what unfolded [*se déploya*] alongside them was not a capitalist but a slave mode of production. (SHN: 136; MEGA2 I/25: 116–17)

Thus, Rome had a dispossessed peasantry that became an urban proletariat, a concentration of wealth in both landed property and money capital, and yet it did not develop a capitalist but an agrarian slavery-based mode of production. There is also an interesting allusion to the "poor whites" of the US South and their false consciousness, which worked against the possibility of class solidarity with Black slaves and freed people. Marx compares this to the lack of solidarity on the part of Roman proletarians toward the enslaved population, both of them part of the working people. I will discuss this more in chapter 5, but here I want to limit myself to the notion that for Marx, history is not unilinear, as shown by the fact that Rome did not become capitalist, despite some important parallels to the process of primitive accumulation.

Marx concludes the 1877 letter with another denial that he has created a general theory of historical development in a unilinear manner:

> Thus, events of striking similarity, taking place in different historical contexts, led to totally disparate results. By studying each of these developments separately, one may easily discover the key to this phenomenon, but this will never be attained with the master key [*avec le passe-partout*]⁴⁵ of a general historico-philosophical theory, whose supreme virtue consists in being suprahistorical. (SHN: 136; MEGA2 I/25: 117)

Again, there is the rejection of "a general historico-philosophical theory" that would explain both capitalist and non-capitalist societies in uni-linear fashion.

This is probably not, however, a rejection on Marx's part of patterns in history, let alone of specific modes of production, a type of perspective one finds in Graeber and Wengrow, as discussed above. Conversano argues persuasively on this point:

> The reference to historical circumstances, along with the use of histor-ical analogies in an anti-evolutionist and anti-determinist way, reveal Marx's effort not to abandon his historical and materialistic dialectics in the name of absolute relativism, but to repeatedly re-assess it in order to keep up with history and the heterogeneity of the real.⁴⁶

Thus, by the late 1870s, Marx has moved away from some earlier, more unilinear expressions, though without ever giving up on the idea of historical progress, of the advancement of the working class and of humanity in all its variety. As Löwy argues perceptively: "In Marx, there is another 'dialectic of progress': critical, non-teleological, and open."⁴⁷

---

45   Could also convey the notion of a master frame or framework.

46   Emanuela Conversano, "Marx, Hegel, and the Orient. World History and His-torical Milieus," *Philosophica* 54 (2019), p. 77.

47   Michael Löwy, "La dialectique du progrès et l'enjeu actuel des mouvements sociaux," *Congrès Marx International. Cent ans de marxisme. Bilan critique et perspectives* (Paris: Presses Universitaires de France, 1996), p. 199.

It should be underlined that, in this 1877 letter, Marx is contrasting not one but two societies to modern Western capitalism: contemporary Russia and ancient Rome. As discussed in previous chapters, in his last years Marx devotes considerable attention to India under the impact of British colonialism while making extensive notes on ancient Rome as well. Thus, in his last years, he is concentrating in his research on three large agrarian societies: Rome, Russia, and India, analyzing their social dynamics. This will be explored more in a chapter 5.

4

Colonialism and Resistance

In the last period of his life, Marx turned more than ever against colonialism, having moved decisively away from the more equivocal stance of his earlier years. This change was brewing for a long time, and it amounts to what the Franco-Lebanese Marxist sociologist Gilbert Achcar calls a "reversal of perspective" concerning "the idea of colonialism as a factor of economic progress," something Marx held to in the *Communist Manifesto* and the 1853 *Tribune* writings on India.[1] Equally important, in the years 1869–82 he engaged with several societies shaped by colonialism. He studied Latin America, Algeria, and India intensively in relationship to European conquest and occupation. Moreover, in the case of Ireland, he not only studied that society under the impact of British rule but also engaged directly with its anti-colonial resistance movement through his participation in the First International.

Spanish Colonialism in the Caribbean and Latin America

Marx's considerations of Spanish colonialism in the Caribbean and Latin America emerge mainly through his 1879 notes on Kovalevsky's *Communal Landownership*. Unlike Morgan, who adopts a stance of "scientific"

---

1 Gilbert Achcar, "Colonialisme/Impérialisme/Orientalism," *Histoire Globale des Socialismes*, ed. Jean-Numa Ducange et al. (Paris: Presses Universitaires de France, 2021), p. 114. English translation: "Socialism and Colonialism," *Historical Materialism* blog (June 13, 2023), p. 8.

objectivity, Kovalevsky shows a clear opposition to colonialism. The following passage in Marx's notes, which mixes quotes from Kovalevsky with Marx's summary, treats Spanish colonialism mercilessly:

> The original Spanish policy of extermination of the redmen [Rothäute].[2] (47) After pillage of the gold etc. that they found, the [Amer]indians are condemned to work in the mines. (48) With the decline of the value of gold and silver, the Spanish turn to agriculture, make the [Amer]indians into slaves in order to cultivate land for them. (1.c.) Through Garcia de Loyosa, the father confessor of Charles V, the colonists hammered out a decree that makes the [Amer]indians into hereditary slaves of the Spanish emigrants; the ukase of Madrid proclaimed 1525. (KOVLM: 29)

Marx goes on to incorporate descriptions of extreme brutality that Kovalevsky quotes from the sixteenth-century Italian traveler Girolamo Benzoni:

> Benzoni, who describes the hunt for redmen, says, among other things: "All the natives hunted [[seized]] for slavery are branded with a red-hot iron. Then the captains take a share of them for themselves and distribute the remaining ones to the soldiers; these gamble for them among themselves (play with each other for them) or sell them to the Spanish colonists. The merchants, who have purchased these commodities in exchange for wine, flour, sugar, and other objects of primary necessity, take them to those parts of the Spanish colonies with the greatest demand for them. During the period of transport a number of these unfortunates caput as a result of the lack of water and the bad air in the hold, which is the result of the merchants packing all the slaves together in the bottom of the ship, not leaving them enough room to sit or to breathe." (KOVLM: 30)

The term "caput" above is Marx's amplification of Benzoni's "perish."

This early period of extreme brutality and outright enslavement of the Indigenous population is succeeded by a system of serfdom, after

---

2 Could also be translated as "redskins." The German term did not carry the same racist, negative charge.

protests by Spanish clerics, most notably by Bartolomé de Las Casas. Marx treats this debate with his usual irony toward the clergy, referring to a "fuss" put up by them in a passage that is otherwise mostly quoted from Kovalevsky:

> Hence the *fuss* [Poltern] *on the part of the monks of the Order of St. Jacob* against the enslavement of the [Amer]indians. *Hence, 1531,* bull from *Pope Paul III* declaring [Amer]indians "human beings" and therefore "free from slavery." The *Royal Council for the West Indies,* established 1524, half of which consisted of the heads of the highest clergy, declared itself for the freedom of the [Amer]indians. *Charles V* (Law of May 21, 1542) accordingly prohibited that: "no person, whether engaged in war or not, can take, apprehend, occupy, sell, exchange any Indian as a slave, nor possess him as such"; likewise, the *Law of October 26, 1546,* prohibits the sale of [Amer]indians into slavery etc. (53) Resistance by the Spanish colonists against this law. (1.c.) Fight with the latter dogs by *Las Casas, Don Juan Zumaraga* and other Catholic bishops. (54) Hence the *Negro slave trade* as "surrogate" for the gentlemen colonists. (1.c.) (KOVLM: 30)

Marx adds to the above passage his own appellation, "dogs," for the Spanish colonists. More importantly, he here incorporates Kovalevsky's conclusion that these humanitarian debates and reforms had a most deleterious effect almost immediately, the development of the African slave trade on a vast scale.

However, neither Kovalevsky nor Marx pursues the point on the mass enslavement of Africans, which was especially significant in the Caribbean and Brazil. Instead, following Kovalevsky's narrative, Marx concentrates on a single issue regarding Spanish colonialism in South America and Mexico, the persistence of Indigenous communal social forms in the face of the destructive impact Spanish policies and actions. After the abolition of slavery for the Indigenous population, the Spanish state set up in the 1550s a system of *encomiendas.* In this new system, Indigenous communities gained collective ownership of land, albeit under the supervision of Spanish overlords, termed *encomenderos,* who could demand tribute and labor. The position of *encomendero* soon became hereditary, thus solidifying his power. The position of clan elder or *cacique* among the Indigenous population, which predated colonialism, also became hereditary. These *caciques* administered local affairs, including the oversight of tribute in kind and in labor services. Over time, the Spanish *encomenderos* gained the right to remove *caciques* from office in villages that fell into arrears. On this point, Marx records the following from Kovalevsky: "The right to intervene in the internal affairs of the American tribes had as result: *weakening of the communal system* and even its overthrow" (KOVLM: 32).

At a formal level, the Spanish monarchy passed laws and established procedures for the protection of the population against abuse. But, as Marx observes in a pungent passage in his notes, this amounted to a sham:

> Furthermore the *"Royal Council of the Indies,"* established by Charles V and Philip II, was to make special regulations for the enforcement of laws in the various parts of the West Indies and the American continent, was among other things, to watch over the enforcement of the laws for the protection of the indigenous people, to punish those who injured them. (58, 59) The *colonists, against whom the laws were passed, were* made into *the executors of the very laws* countering them! *Worthy this of the statesmen Carlos I (Charles V.) and Philip II!* The oversight over these scoundrels (the "encomenderos") again entrusted to the *Spanish officials* (*Viceroys, governors,* and protectors of the [Amer]indians.) (KOVLM: 32)

In the above, everything except for the first sentence is in Marx's own words, substituting for Kovalevsky's more circumspect language.

Marx records further from Kovalevsky that, as taxes in kind and labor increased, Indigenous people fled the villages and a significant number committed suicide. Even the right to appeal led to further degradation of the material conditions of the villagers, as they had to bear the high salaries and expenses of the Spanish officials sent to investigate, which itself could bankrupt them. Over time, the population was reduced to something like serfdom, as seen in one of Kovalevsky's citations from Mexican jurist Alonso de Zurita that Marx records, amending the text to add his own term, "horror," to describe this process:

> Despite all the horror [*Greuel*] of the encomienda system as denounced to the *Spanish government*, it expanded not only into the new

provinces (such as *Chile*) but also: *through the system of hereditary transfer of the encomiendas along the lines of descent and collateral lines of the first encomenderos, which transformed the* [Amer]*indians, once and for all, into a serf-like dependency.* (KOVLM: 35)

As this developed further, the Indigenous communal forms that survived early Spanish colonialism began to crumble, as described in these passages Marx records from Kovalevsky:

The *system of hereditary serfdom* carried out the policy further—the *systematic extermination of the* [Amer]*indian population and the theft*—by the colonists—*of the communal lands that belonged to them since ancient times* (this under the pretext they were "wasteland"); the *center of the communal associations, the clan (consanguineal) principle, was thus ultimately eliminated* (kinship principle), which was their life principle as long as *their* transition to *purely rural* (village) *communes* was not yet fully completed. (68). This dissolution of consanguinity (real or fictitious) led in some locations to the formation of *small-scale landed property out of the earlier communal allotments*; this in turn *passed little by little into the hands of capital-owning Europeans*—under the pressure of taxes from the encomenderos and *the system first permitted by the Spanish of lending money at interest*—Zurita says: *"under the indigenous leaders the* [Amer]*indians did not know usury."* (KOVLM: 36)

Marx's parenthetical phrase about possibly fictitious consanguinity marks a point of difference with Kovalevsky's biologism.

Under the impact of capitalist social relations, the tendency was toward atomization. One way this happened was through interference in the clan structures on the part of the *encomenderos*. Some of this was overt, like imposing their own *caciques* on communities, while others were more subtle, carried out by encouraging intercommunal conflict, as seen in a passage from Marx's notes that is mainly quoting Kovalevsky:

The leadership's clan character *was destroyed* from the moment that the encomenderos obtained the right to replace *with their own creatures* those caciques [[elder, leader]] who annoyed them. In addition, the *encomenderos' policy of solidifying* their *power* was based *on the one*

hand on the creation and exploitation of conflict between the [Amer]
indians and their leaders and ditto between the *various* [Amer]*indian*
villages and tribes themselves. (KOVLM: 36)

Conflicts often took the form of expensive legal proceedings that drained
the Indigenous communities economically. The overall tendency was
toward individual small-scale property ownership, as in this passage
Marx records from Kovalevsky, while adding his own expression about
"private property owners": "Tied to the decline of the clan character of
the whole obshchina, is its dissolution in many places into a merely rural
obshchina, in which individuals detached from one another strive to
become *private property owners*" (KOVLM: 37).

This was certainly the main tendency. At the same time, Marx in his
notes underlines in dialectical fashion some countervailing factors. In
this vein, he takes up at some length—but makes more pointed in his
notes—Kovalevsky's analysis concerning the persistence of Indigenous
communal forms in the face of all these pressures. Where Kovalevsky
tends to see the persistence of communal social relations as recessive,
Marx tends to see a glass that is half full rather than half empty. He
begins by recording and slightly amplifying Kovalevsky's account of the
persistence of communal forms:

By the middle of the 16th century (the time of Zurita's report) *the rural
obshchina had already ceased to exist in many parts of Mexico and Peru.*
Still, it was not completely extirpated. In the *legislation of Carlos II* it
exists: "All the goods that the body, and collection of Indians [*cuerpo,
y coleccion de Indios*] of each town are to enter into the communal
coffers, from which the necessary amount is to be spent for the
common good of all, taking care to conserve and augment it."
(KOVLM: 37)

In this context, "body [*cuerpo*]" refers to communal holdings, and "collection [*coleccion*]" to what they hold as separate individuals. Marx is
highlighting the former.

But, as Marx also emphasizes, communal social forms persisted for
hundreds of years, right up to his own period. Here he records Kovalevsky's extract from an 1858 study of Mexico by German writer and
theologian Christian Sartorius:

"The Natives," says Sartorius, "often live in communal associations, whether in the villages or in the cities, in neighborhoods. One peculiarity of the Indians is the solidity of their communal associations. The older members do not allow the younger ones to emigrate to other villages. The majority of the Indian villages own *land and capital communally* and do not want it divided. Only the *dwellings (farmsteads) with the surrounding gardens regarded as private property of the citizens*. The *farmland and hayfields* constitute the property of each village and are cultivated by the individual citizens without payment of any ground rent. *One portion of this is cultivated in common: the income from it serves to cover communal expenses*." (KOVLM: 37–8)

The way Marx reports this startling piece of evidence suggests that he is viewing the stubborn persistence of these social formations as something very significant to the entire region of Latin America.

This is borne out by the concluding sentence of Marx's notes on Latin America, where he again bends Kovalevsky's text toward the notion of the persistence of communal social forms across the region:

The survival—in large measure—of the rural commune is due on one hand to the [Amer]indians' *preference for this form of property in land*, as the one best corresponding to their level of culture; on the other hand, the *lack of colonial legislation* [[in contrast to the English East Indies]] *of regulations* that *would give the members of the clans the possibility* of selling the allotments belonging to them. (KOVLM: 38)

Most of the above is an extract from Kovalevsky's book, but with two significant additions by Marx. First, he adds the phrase "in large measure" at the beginning of the sentence, countering the Russian anthropologist's unilinear notion that the commune has practically disappeared and only a few traces remain. Second, Marx's bracketed insert, "in contrast to the English East Indies," sharpens the differences Kovalevsky is already drawing between Spanish and British colonialism.

Some broader issues are at stake here. Marx seems to be emphasizing the fact that, while the Spanish allowed capitalist social relations to penetrate the villages of Latin America, they did not actively promote this in the way that British colonial law did in India. In this case, the older, less fully capitalist Spanish colonialism did not undermine the precapitalist and precolonial communal social forms as thoroughly as did its British counterpart, which hit in full force only after the industrial revolution in the metropole.

India: Local Resistance Slows British Ascendancy

Marx made voluminous research notes on the Indian Subcontinent during his last years. This is seen in his notes on the chapters devoted to India in Kovalevsky's *Communal Landownership* (25,000 words), in those on Robert Sewell's *Analytical History of India* (41,000 words), and in those on John Phear's study of village life in Sri Lanka (20,000 words), as well as more briefly in other places, for a total of over 86,000 words. The Indian Subcontinent was, therefore, by far the area of the world to which Marx gave the most attention in his 1879–82 notes on non-Western and precapitalist societies and gender. The Kovalevsky and Sewell notes range through the whole of Indian history up to Marx's own time, but I will be concentrating on the period of British colonial inroads and then outright rule.

Over a century ago, Rosa Luxemburg described—with withering revolutionary critique and passion—British colonialism's cold indifference toward human social life and utter concentration on extracting value during its rule over India, arguing that its negative effects on the population surpassed even those of notoriously brutal conquerors like the Mongol Timur, who infamously massacred the population of Delhi in 1398 after the city's rulers refused to submit:

> Finally, the specifically capitalist method of colonization finds expression in the following striking circumstance. The British were the first conquerors of India to show a gross indifference toward the works of civilization that formed its public utilities and economic infrastructure. Arabs, Afghans and Mongols alike had initiated and maintained magnificent works of canalization, they provided the country a network of roads, built bridges across rivers and sunk wells. Timur, or Tamerlane . . . oversaw the allocation of resources for the cultivation of the soil, irrigation, security on the roads, and the provision of food and shelter for the travelers . . . "The Company that ruled India until 1858 (the East India Company—R. L.) did not make one spring

accessible, did not sink a single well, nor build a bridge for the benefit of the Indians."[3]

The quoted sentence at the end of the above passage is from Kovalevsky's book on communal land tenure, which Luxemburg also studied.

The key event here is the 1793 "Cornwallis Settlement," which moved toward the privatization of the village land of India, severely undermining the old communal structures discussed in chapter 1. In a certain sense, this was inevitable, given the growing power of capital, especially British capital, and the weakening of the Indian state during the last years of the Mughal Empire. Whereas Marx's 1853 writings present the establishment of British rule as the product of large economic forces, in these notes on India in his last years he seems to be stressing their contingent and unfinished character.

One of the larger themes in Marx's 1879–82 notes on colonialism in India revolves around how local forces exhausted themselves in conflict, paving the way for the British to move in far more easily. As recounted in his notes on Sewell's book on Indian history, the waning Mughal Empire allowed the British East India Company an important foothold in Kolkata in the northeast during the eighteenth century. But the British were still some distance from becoming the most important contenders to replace the Mughal Empire, for two other regional forces also sought the domination of India, both still far stronger than the East India Company. These were the Marathas and the Afghan forces of Ahmad Shah Durrani. The Hindu Maratha clan chiefs had for decades been winning victories over the Mughals and succeeded in carving out a large territory that constituted a sort of Maratha empire. But in the 1750s, they came up against the stronger army of Durrani, who had just reinvigorated the Afghan state and carried out raids into the rich agricultural lands of the Punjab, also attacking Delhi. The Marathas and Durrani's Afghan forces met in a major battle at Panipat near Delhi, where the Marathas suffered a severe defeat, as Marx records in these passages drawn from Sewell's book:

---

3   Rosa Luxemburg, *Accumulation of Capital: A Contribution to the Economic Theory of Imperialism. The Complete Works of Rosa Luxemburg*, Vol. II: *Economic Writings 2*, trans. Nicholas Gray, ed. by Peter Hudis and Paul Le Blanc (New York: Verso, 2015), p. 270.

January 6, 1761: 3rd Battle of Panipat: On this day the Maratha leaders inform *Sadashiv Bhao* that he must *offer battle* at once or the Marathas would disperse. [[Until then, the two armies confronting each other in fortified camps, constantly harassing each other and cutting off supplies; the Marathas suffering severely from starvation and disease.]] Sadashiv marched out; *furious battle*; near victory of the Maratha side, when Ahmad Shah Durrani orders *his own center* to charge and at the same time has his left flank by-pass the Marathas' right flank and attack it. This movement decisive. The Marathas fled in disorder, their army almost annihilated, left (it appears) some 200,000 dead on battlefield, the remnants of their troops back over the Narbada. (MSW: 51–2)

As Marx suggests in a further passage in his notes, this defeat shattered those Indian and regional forces that might have been able to mount the most serious challenge the British:

Ahmad Shah's own army so shattered in the contest that without reaping the fruits of his victory retires to the Punjab.
Delhi deserted; no one there to govern it; the governments all around shattered; *Marathas never recovered from the blow.*
State of the Country after this battle at Panipat: Mogul Empire gone; the *nominal Emperor, Ali Gauhar*, wandering in *Bihar.*—The *Peshwa* of the Marathas, *Balaji Rao*, [died] of grief; his power divided among the 4 great chieftains: the "*Gaekwad*" in *Gujarat*; the *Rajah of Nagpur* (Bhonsle), *Holkar*, and *Sindhia*. (MSW: 52)

There seems to be a note of poignancy here in Marx's notes, a sense of respect and even mourning for the "shattered" state of the major Indian and Afghan political forces. This left the country open to the advance of British colonialism.

While the Marathas may have been shattered as a force capable of ruling India in place of the Mughals, they had not disappeared from the scene and were not decisively defeated by the British until the early nineteenth century, something Marx also covers in his notes. But in terms of Marx's own perceptions of India, the more important point is that by time of these 1879 notes, he sees British colonial conquest as a process filled with contingencies. Thus he describes, again quoting

Sewell, the post-1761 situation as one in which "The *English* already then probably greatest power in India" (MSW: 52). But he clearly sees this is a contingent development, with the strong implication that events could have turned out differently, even after 1761. As Marx recounts in his notes, with the Maratha resurgence, a large portion of the Indian people had mounted a movement for self-determination, one that almost overthrew the Mughal Empire and was only done in by a force invading from outside India, that of the Afghan Durrani. That closed off a serious possibility of self-renewal on the part of the Indian people, thus opening the way for British ascendancy.

Marx continues to record in great detail Sewell's accounts of Maratha resistance, now against the British as well. He notes that the British dug the first real defenses around Kolkata in 1742, what Sewell calls "the celebrated: '*Maratha Ditch*.'" As Marx also records from Sewell, in 1775 the First Maratha War in the Mumbai (Bombay) area blocked the British from much in the way of territorial acquisition. A second episode of this conflict in 1779 was equally unsuccessful for the British, resulting in their "giving up every acquisition made during the last 5 years," as Marx incorporates into his notes from Sewell. The next phase of this war, also in 1779, results in a stalemate. As the nineteenth century dawns, the very divided Marathas constitute the only real rivals of the British, as Marx records from Sewell:

> *Beginning of the Century*: *besides the English*, only one great power, that of the Marathas; these divided in 5 principal parties, mostly at loggerheads with each other. 1) *Peshwa, nominal supreme chief of the Marathas, Baji Rao*, reigning at *Poona*; the *smaller states, not listed here*, half independent, half owing feudal submission to the Peshwa as their hereditary sovereign; 2) *Daulat Rao Sindhia*, strongest of the Maratha families, at *Gwalior* and in possession of Delhi, etc.; 3) *Jaswant Rao Holkar*, at *Indore*, mortal enemy of Sindhia; 4) Raghuji Bhonsle, Rajah of Nagpur, willing to fight anybody for a consideration; 5) Fateh Singh, Gaekwad of Gujarat, who seldom joins in Maratha politics. (MSW: 121)

Thus, Maratha power is attenuated by internal rivalries and divisions.

A few years later, in 1803, the second or Great Maratha War with the British begins. This results in the eventual defeat of the Marathas two years later. In 1817, a more decisive defeat by a very large British force of 120,000 extinguishes much of Maratha power on the Subcontinent. As Marx records from Sewell, "End of the sovereignty of the Maratha State, begun in 1666 with Shivaji" (MSW: 106–07).

India: Rural Communes Persist in the Face of British Privatization of Land Tenure

For Marx, a second important turning point in terms of India coming under colonial domination took place not at the military and political levels but at the economic level. This resulted from Governor General Charles Cornwallis's exploitative "permanent settlement" of 1793, which radically restructured land tenure and property relations, seriously undermining long-standing communal social formations in the country-side. Cornwallis was one of the main British commanders defeated in the American Revolution but was then dispatched to India to uphold colonialism there. This British move in India essentially privatized land tenure across India at one swoop. Years earlier, the Mughals had established a class of *zamindars*, hereditary tax collectors, who obtained revenue from the *ryots* or peasants and transferred it to the state, keeping a portion for themselves. Under Mughal rule, the office of *zamindar* was a relatively lowly position as a local tax collector. But under the Cornwallis Final Settlement, they became landowners with the right to evict peasants for nonpayment of rent. As Marx records from Sewell,

> 1793: *Lord Cornwallis* gives up the Commission and suddenly, without warning, *passed* a motion in the Council, which at once assumed the force of law, that the Zamindars were to be henceforth considered *as possessing all* they claimed . . . *as hereditary owners of all the soil* of the district, *paying annually—not their quota of public taxes which they collected for the government—*but a *sort* of tribute into the treasury! *Mr. Shore*, later *Sir John Shore*, scoundrel Cornwallis's *successor in office* spoke strenuously in Council *against the wholesale destruction* of Indian traditions; and when he saw that the majority of the Council resolved (only to *rid themselves* of the burden of constant legislation and of perpetual disputes concerning the status of the Hindus), to declare the zamindars the owners of the land, he suggested *decennial*

settlements. But Council declared for *permanency.* The *"Board of Commissioners"* applauded their resolution and passed the *1793* Bill for the *"permanent establishment of the Zamindars of India as hereditary landowners"* under the Premiership of Pitt; this decision promulgated at *Calcutta in March 1793* to the joy of the surprised zamindars! (MSW: 385)[4]

These are Sewell's words, but in the first sentence Marx highlights the word "claimed" and adds an exclamation point at the end, also adding the appellation "scoundrel" for Cornwallis a bit further down. The phrase at the end, "to the joy of the surprised zamindars," is also Marx's. Additionally, it is notable that he adds to the above a reference to Prime Minister William Pitt, who supported conceding independence to the United States but virulently opposed the French Revolution and advocated an unrestricted "free market" as part of a "reform" program for India.

It was that ideology that legitimated what Marx regards as a crime against the people of India, as the British in his view had no right to destroy the social fabric of society:

This measure as *illegal* as sudden and unexpected; because the English were supposed to be legislating for the Hindus as a race and as *far as possible administering to them their own laws.* The English Government passed at the same time several laws, *giving the ryots remedies in the civil court against the Zamindars, and protecting them from increase of rent.* These *nugatory, dead-letters* considering the state of the country; because the *ryots were so absolutely* at the mercy of their landlords that they seldom dared to raise a finger in self-defense . . . *1793:* Thus through *Cornwallis and Pitt artificial expropriation of the inhabitants of the land* of Bengal. (MSW: 385–6)

In the above passage from Sewell, Marx again adds Pitt's name, emphasizing that these changes were not simply the work of local administrator Cornwallis. At a more general level, he is singling out how the parts of

---

4   In this part of his notes on Kovalevsky, Marx places text from Sewell on the permanent settlement. Thus, he seems to have stopped reading Kovalevsky for a bit and picked up Sewell's book for greater historical and political detail than Kovalevsky was providing.

the law said to protect the peasants are not enforceable due to the class structure.

Resuming his excerpt notes from Kovalevsky, Marx records text on the larger social consequences of this ultra-liberal form of colonialism, including a brief reference to the 1867 famine, which claimed as many as six million lives:

> Results of the "settlement" [[cf. Report of the parliament. Commission on Famine in Bengal and Orissa. 1867. Part I]] Most immediate consequence of this theft of the "communal and private landed property" of the peasants: whole series of local peasant uprisings against the "landlords" given to them, which led in some localities to expulsion of the zamindars and the East India Company Co. stepped into their place as owners. (KOV: 387)

It is important to note from the above that even peasant rebellions only increased British domination in the short term.

As his notes from Kovalevsky continue, Marx emphasizes the consolidation of landed property by "urban capitalists":

> in other places impoverishment of the zamindars and forced or voluntary sale of their estates to pay for their arrears in taxes and private debts. Hence the greater part of the lands of the province were transferred quickly over to the hands of a few urban capitalists, for those who had capital freely at their disposal and who liked to invest in land. (KOV: 387)

At this point, Marx adds his own quotation from a colonial report to supplement Kovalevsky, highlighting the phrase "monied men":

> See Return: East India (Bengal and Orissa Famine (1866) 1867 Part I, Report of the Commissioners etc., ¶48, p. 222: "As usually happens under our system, there has been from the first a large transfer by sale of zamindaree rights, and the purchasers have been [[in Orissa]] almost universally monied men of the older-settled and richer province of Bengal, with whom the purchase of landed rights is the favourite form of investment." (KOV: 387)[5]

---

5   In keeping with the rough character of these notes, Marx does not close all the parentheses here.

Resuming his excepts from Kovalevsky, Marx records material on the emergence of a new class of absentee landlords operating on a capitalist basis, but he stresses, through an inserted parenthetical phrase about usurers, that this is far from a fully developed capitalism:

> They *remained* as *before in the cities*, that is to say away from any contact with the rural population; usually passed along their estates in *separate parcels* with *short-term leases* to the most well-to-do members of the rural population, often also to *small urban capitalists* (alias petty usurers) *Since the first land survey*, only a small number of *old zamindar families* are left over; without the necessary circulating capital, let alone fixed capital for agriculture; *rivalries* with the *leaseholders* in the art of making the *insignificant amounts of money available to peasants through loans at usurer's rates*. (KOV: 387)

At a general, comparative historical level, Marx in these excerpts also stresses that the British allowed Indian agriculture to stagnate.

The following passage Marx records from Kovalevsky draws a sharp contrast, as Luxemburg was to do, between their policies and even those of the Mughals, whom he calls Mongols:

> Hence nothing was done for *agriculture* (except by the tillers of the soil) (p. 163, 164). *Compare* to what *the Mongols* etc. did for irrigation etc. in comparison to the English). (*Note*, p. 164) [[See: *Count Warren: De l'état moral de la population indigène* etc.]] *Cornwallis* did absolutely nothing for the security of the peasants . . .]]. (KOV: 387)

It should be noted that Marx's parenthetical remark in the above excerpt credits the agency of the peasants themselves, something Kovalevsky does not do. More generally, the disarray of the agricultural sector is seen by Marx as an example of gross irresponsibility on the part of the British. Is this not similar to how in the *Communist Manifesto* he and Engels view British capital in its home country as "unfit to rule" (MECW 6: 495) because it cannot offer its subordinate class, the workers, any real economic security?

In the *Manifesto*, Marx and Engels find a countervailing force in Europe in the revolt of the working class. Likewise, in these 1879 notes, Marx stresses in dialectical terms not only the dissolution of India's communal social forms but also their resilience in the face of wrenching challenges. He quotes from an anonymous 1864 article in the *Calcutta Review*, which describes the persistence of communal social forms in the Madras [Chennai] region, in today's state of Tamil Nadu:

> *No private property* here in the strict sense of the term—*if so it would be possible for its possessors to sell!* All of these peasants indeed just "tax-units and whole provinces *simply resources that churn out a particular quantum of tax revenue*." (168) With this system, the government is not dealing with the total number of communal possessors in this or that village, but instead with the hereditary tillers of individual parcels, whose rights cease if taxes not paid promptly. Nevertheless *among these atoms certain relationships endure*, from a distance reminiscent of the earlier landowning communal villages. *Forests and meadows* are still indivisible property of all members, or rather families; *arable soil and pastures* still serve for *communal grazing* after they have been *harvested* and *cut down*. (KOV: 388)

The phrase "if so it would be possible for its possessors to sell" is Marx's remark, stressing that these are not yet fully capitalist social relations. More importantly, he adds to an excerpt from Kovalevsky his own very significant remark, "Nevertheless *among these atoms certain relationships endure*." Amplifying this point, Marx takes down a passage from Kovalevsky on even stronger communal relationships that persist in spite of the policies instituted by Cornwallis and Pitt: "In spite of this system there are in some parts of the Madras Presidency—located in the northern areas and along the river banks and populated by the *Tamil* and *Telugu tribes*—*traces* of the *communal associations* that existed until recently" (KOV: 388–9).

As Kovalevsky emphasizes and Marx records, British policies did severely undermine these communal forms. However, Marx also emphasizes, again in dialectical fashion, Kovalevsky's data on resistance, something to which Kovalevsky himself does not give as much emphasis: "This *transformation of the earlier communal owners into precarious cultivators of government land* did not occur without protest" (KOV: 389). Indeed, the British also recognized the danger of the communal social forms posed to their rule, as in this excerpt Marx records from Kovalevsky:

Thus a whole *series of rural communes,* with lands covering tens *of square miles,* continued in *various regions of Bundelkhand* up until their subjugation by the English. These were considered *politically and economically* "injurious." Often consisting of *some thousands of people,* bound together *through common descent* and *communal ownership of property,* these associations appeared on the one hand to be dangerous adversaries of the English government in case of a *possible rebellion,* and on the other hand as an obstacle in the *business* of *promptly covering the shortfall* on the way to *the public auction of the holdings of insolvent taxpayers.* (KOV: 392)

The reference above to "possible rebellion" arising from these communal structures could not have been more pointed. Moreover, Bundelkhand included several rebellious Maratha entities, among them Jhansi, on which more below. All this is at the core of Marx's new dialectical analysis of India and other places in his last years: the resistance of "rural communes" to colonialism and class rule.

In similar fashion, amid these excerpts from Kovalevsky, Marx adds a sentence targeting Maine, who undermined the communal forms by force of law while speaking of their decline as the product of economic forces:

The English officials of India and the publicists they supported, like *Sir Henry Maine,* etc., interpret the decline of communal property in Punjab—despite the tender loving care bestowed by the English upon the archaic form—as the simple outcome of *economic progress,* while they themselves are the *main* (active) *contributors* to this—to their own danger. (KOV: 394)

Here, again, the British were undermining the rural communes because they posed a danger of rebellion, as in the previous passage cited.

But there is something more here, perhaps of greater importance. Marx seems to be suggesting that it is not so much the ancient communal forms in their precolonial versions that are the loci of resistance. Rather, the key dialectical juncture occurs after the substantial penetration of British colonialism, after these communal forms were disrupted by aspects of capitalist social relations imposed by the British. One can surmise that he is suggesting that such a process is bringing about new types of thinking and organization that can form the basis of a new type of subjectivity. This is why the very success of the British in disrupting and undermining the communal forms does not produce stability, but instead, new forms of subjectivity and resistance. It is in this sense that the colonial successes Maine extolls are in fact, as Marx writes, a "danger" for that colonial domination, and therefore for global capitalism because of the social tensions they were setting in motion.

Outright Revolt: The Sepoy Uprising in India

A third major area of concentration for Marx in his studies of British colonialism in India in his last years is the Sepoy Uprising of 1857–59, an insurrection on the part of rank-and-file soldiers in the British-led sepoy regiments used to enforce colonial rule. Marx covers the uprising in great detail, including, as discussed in chapter 2, the important participation of women in anti-British resistance. Here, some Maratha leaders were also very prominent, as will be discussed below.

The sepoys were an Indian armed force recruited and led by British officers as an instrument of colonial rule. Here, Marx relies on Sewell's chronological account, as the Sepoy Uprising is not taken up at all by Kovalevsky. Marx seems to see the uprising as a dialectical contradiction emerging out of the very success of the British in expanding their rule in India, in their subjugation of Burma, and in a brief conflict with Iran. One particularly problematic aspect of this was British moves into the Kingdom of Oudh in northern India in 1856, which Marx denounced at the time in the *New York Tribune*. Referring to Oudh and these other British successes, Marx remarks, now in his notes on Kovalevsky, "*In answer to this swagger, the Sepoy Revolution (1857–1859)*" (KOV: 146).

The conquest of Oudh actually weakened Britain's sepoy forces, as newly incorporated and restive soldiers from Oudh comprised a large percentage of their 300,000 members across India. This is seen in the passage below from Sewell that Marx incorporates into his notes:

> For some years *Sepoy army* very disorganized; *40,000 soldiers from Oudh in it*, bound together by caste and nationality; one common pulse in army: insult to a regiment by its superiors felt as grievance by all the rest; officers powerless; laxity of discipline; *open acts of mutiny frequent,*

suppressed with more or less difficulty; *downright refusal of the Bengal army to cross the sea for the attack of Rangoon*, necessitating the *substitution of Sikh regiments* (1852). [[All this since *annexation of Punjab* (1849), became worse *since Annexation of Oudh* (1856)]] (MSW: 150)

The last, bracketed sentence in the above is Marx's addition to Sewell, who leaves out resentment over the conquest of Punjab and Oudh, except in the sense of regional ties binding many of the sepoys together. Instead, Sewell stresses only grievances resulting from attempts to deploy the sepoys outside their home areas, over the sea to Rangoon, Burma. Also, in this as in many other passages Marx incorporates, he eliminates positive or laudatory descriptions of the British.

Marx's notes then recount the well-known fact that cartridges for bullets greased with fat attributed to pigs and cows managed to outrage the religious sentiments of both Muslim and Hindu sepoys. In an insert, Marx blames right-wing prime minister Lord Palmerston for this situation. At another point he writes in French of *émeutes* [uprisings], versus Sewell's pejorative "open acts of violence" (MSW: 148, SW: 265). Marx's notes recount the uprising's success in Delhi, the old Mughal capital, leaving aside Sewell's ascription of "cruelty and violence" to the sepoys:

> *At Meerut* (northeast of Delhi) *11th and 20th Native Infantry* attack the English, shot their officers, fired the town, slay all English ladies and children, *went off to Delhi. At Delhi*: in night *some of the mutineers* gallop into Delhi, *Sepoys* there rise (*54th, 74th, 38th Native Infantry*); *English commissioner, chaplain, officers murdered*; 9 English officers defend the magazine, blow it up (2 perish); the other *Englishmen in the city,* flee to jungles, most killed by natives or severe weather; some *arrived* safely at *Meerut*, now deserted of troops. But *Delhi in the hands of insurgents.* (MSW: 148, SW: 266)

This was April 24, 1857.

By May 25, as Marx records in his notes, describing the British and their local allies like the Maratha leader Sindhia (Scindia) with pejoratives, the rebels took over most of northern India:

> *Rebellion spread throughout Hindustan*; in *20 different places simultaneously Sepoy risings and murder of the English*; chief scenes: *Agra,*

Bareilly, Moradabad. Sindhia loyal to the "English dogs," not so his *"troopers"; Rajah of Patiala*—for shame!—sends large body of soldiers in aid of the English! *At Mainpuri* (North-West Provinces), one young lieutenant, swine: *De Kantzow* saves treasury and fort. (MSW: 149)

This is the high point of the uprising, and it takes the British a while to counterattack effectively.

Marx also records material on the Kanpur (Cawnpore) massacre of British prisoners, an event that outraged British public opinion and was used to justify the brutal repression of the uprising. In excerpting Sewell, Marx leaves aside the British colonial historian's characterization of these events as "untold horrors," or his opining that "the horrors that revealed themselves are almost without parallel in history," let alone his description of the sepoys as "fiendish" or "treacherous demons" (SW: 268, 270):

> *June 26*, 1857: *Nana Sahib* offers safe retreat for all Europeans, if *Kanpur* delivered up; *June 27* (Wheeler having accepted) 400 of the survivors allowed to embark in boats and proceed down the Ganges; Nana opens fire on them from both sides; 1 boat escaped, attacked lower down, done in, of the whole garrison only 4 men escape. A *boat*, which had stuck fast on a sandbank, filled with *women and children*, seized, marched to Kanpur, there shut up closely as prisoners; *14 days later* (*in July*), more English prisoners dragged there by the revolted Sepoy from *Fatehgarh* (military station) 3 miles from *Farrukhabad*) . . . *July 16: Havelock's army on the outskirts of Kanpur*; defeats the Indians, but was too late *to enter the citadel; in the night: Nana butchers all English prisoners, officers, ladies, children*; then blew up the magazine and *abandoned the town.* (MSW: 150–1)

Marx also gives attention to the brutality of British repression in September 1857, once they retake Delhi.

There, the aging heir of the Mughal emperors, Bahadur Shah Zafar, had become a rallying point for the rebels. Marx records text from Sewell on the imprisonment by British forces of the eighty-one-year-old Bahadur Shah and of his wife, as well as their summary execution of the next generation of Mughal princes:

Delhi captured, after 6 days actual fight, under *General Wilson*. (cf. further pp. 272, 273). *Hodson* at the head of his body horse *in palace*, seizes *old king and queen* (*Zeenat Mahal*), (thrown in prison), while Hodson *with his own hand kills* (by shot) *the prince*. (MSW: 150–1)

In excerpting Sewell here, Marx leaves aside his justification of this massacre: "No quarter was given, and terrible was the slaughter of the rebels by the avenging comrades of those who had been murdered at Kanpur" (SW: 273). Marx adds the following in his notes concerning the punishment handed out to Bahadur Shah in January 1858: "*King of Delhi* before court-martial under Dawes, etc.; as 'felon' (representative of the Mogul dynasty, dating from 1526!) sentenced to death; this commuted to *transportation for life; to Rangoon. Conveyed at end of the year.*" In this passage, Marx places irony quotes around the term "felon" (MSW: 154, SW: 275).

As the British counterattack began to succeed, insurgents put up stiff resistance and were met by brutal repression, especially around Kanpur, site of the massacre of British civilians: "*December 6, 1857, victorious battle by Colin Campbell at Kanpur*; the rebels flee, leave the city deserted, are pursued and severely cut up by *Sir Hope Grant*" (MSW: 151). Sewell provides no specifics on Indian casualties.

Lucknow, the British administrative capital, was not recaptured until March 1858. On this, Marx records a passage from Sewell about British forces' "'looting' of the city, *where treasures of oriental art stored up*" (MSW: 152). On this point, Sewell, who in his later career became an archaeologist of South India, seems genuinely outraged over the destruction of Indian cultural artifacts, as can be seen when he is quoted more fully than Marx does in his notes:

The taking of all these palaces was followed by extraordinary scenes of plunder and destruction on the part of the British soldiers. The greatest treasures of oriental art were stored up here in profusion, and were "looted" with reckless prodigality. (SW: 277)

Sewell's interest in the preservation of the lives of the Indian people was much weaker, however.

As Marx records from Sewell's account, the rebels were able to keep fighting in 1858–59, even in retreat. As mentioned in chapter 2, two

prominent women leaders were at the forefront at the end. Rebels, Marx
records from Sewell, continued to fight under "*the standards of the
Begum*, the Prince of Delhi and Nana Sahib," as well as those of "the Rani
and Tantia Topi" (MSW: 152–3). This refers to (1) Harzat Mahal, the
Begum of Oudh ("Begum" is a Muslim/Urdu title referring to a woman of
high rank), the kingdom recently annexed by the British, as mentioned
above; (2) the by now imprisoned Bahadur Shah, the "Prince of Delhi";
(3) Nana Sahib, the ruler of Bithur, a city near Kanpur, and a key Maratha
leader who had massacred the British at Kanpur; (4) Tantia Topi, another
key Maratha leader allied to Nana Sahib, his cousin; and (5) Lakshmi Bai,
the Rani or queen of Jhansi, another Maratha state recently taken over
by the British. The first two were Muslims and the last three Hindus and
Marathas, a kind of Hindu-Muslim unity not always seen. Of these key
leaders, only Harzat Mahal, the Begum of Oudh, is certain to have survived the repression, making it across the border into Nepal. Nana Sahib
made it to Nepal as well, where, as Marx records from Sewell, he is
"'supposed' to have died" (MSW: 154). Marx places irony quotes around
the Sewell's "supposed," indicating doubt about his death coming so
soon, right after the suppression of the Uprising. Lakshmi Bai, the Rani
of Jhansi, died in battle, while Tantia Topi was captured and executed,
and, as recounted above, Bahadur Shah was deported to British-ruled
Burma. As to the rank-and-file rebels, Marx records this from Sewell,
who gives them little attention, "*bulk of the rebels*—their regiments disbanded—laid down the sword, *became Ryots*," that is, peasants (MSW: 154).
But he leaves aside Sewell's dehumanizing adverb, "humbly" (SW: 280).

At this point, East India Company rule was replaced by direct colonial
rule by the British state. One consequence of this change was even more
direct plunder of the land and treasure of India: "*Confiscation of the soil
of Oudh*, which [Governor General] *Canning declared to be the property
of the English-Indian Government!*" (MSW: 154). Marx adds an exclamation point to this sentence from Sewell. Here, Marx is emphasizing the
capitalist character of British imperialism, penetrating down the very
land and soil to confiscate it and turn in the direction of capitalist property relations. On the imposition of British state rule for the indirect one
of the East India Company, Marx concludes his notes with this passage
from Sewell, substituting his own bitterly ironical "'great' Victoria" for
Sewell's "England": "*August 2, 1858, Lord Stanley's India Bill passes*, and
thereby *end of the East India Co.* India a province of the empire of the

'great' Victoria!" (MSW: 154). As discussed above, Marx seems to have admired the Maratha rebels, both at this juncture and during their earlier struggles against the Mughals.

Overall, Marx's 1879 notes on India, whether from Sewell or Kovalevsky, sources he was evidently reading at the same time, ring with poignancy as he ruminates about an ancient civilization denied its potential and being slowly subjected to British colonial rule. Three implicit counterfactuals are at least implied: What if the Marathas had prevailed in the eighteenth century against the Mughals and the Afghans under Durrani, and united the country at the time British power was growing? What if the 1857–59 Sepoy Uprising, in many cases led by Maratha chiefs, had succeeded? These two questions stem especially from his reading of Sewell. And at a deeply social rather than a political level, another question arises: What if India had been able to preserve more of its communal social forms, its Indigenous communistic social relations in the villages? This question stems from Marx's reading of Kovalevsky.

Up until his death, Marx continues to engage British colonial exploitation of India and the possibility of another uprising, as seen in a letter of February 19, 1881, to Danielson:

In *India* serious complications, if not a general outbreak, is in store for the British government. What the English take from them annually in the form of rent, dividends for railways useless to the Hindus; pensions for military and civil service men, for Afghanistan and other wars, etc., etc.—what they take from them *without any equivalent* and quite apart from what they appropriate to themselves annually *within* India, speaking only of the *value of the commodities* the Indians have gratuitously and annually to *send over* to England—it amounts to *more than the total sum of income of the sixty millions of agricultural and industrial laborers of India!* This is a bleeding process, with a vengeance! The famine years are pressing each other and in dimensions till now not yet suspected in Europe! There is an actual conspiracy going on wherein Hindus and Muslims cooperate; the British government is aware that something is "brewing," but this shallow people (I mean the governmental men), stultified by their own parliamentary ways of talking and thinking, do not even desire to see clear, to realize the whole extent of the imminent danger! To delude others and by

deluding them to delude yourself—this is: *parliamentary wisdom* in a
nutshell! *Tant mieux!* (MECW 46: 63–4)

In predicting another Indian uprising in this letter, Marx does not
mention communal social forms as possible loci of revolt, but he will
introduce the Russian village commune a few months later, when he and
Engels write a new preface to a new Russian edition of the *Communist
Manifesto*, which appears early in 1882. I discuss this in chapter 6, but
let's first turn to another society, Algeria, and its anti-colonial resistance,
this time against the French state.

French Colonialism in Algeria: The Struggle Between Capitalist and Communal Social Relations

In his 1879 notes on Kovalevsky on Algeria, Marx concentrates on
French attempts to destroy that country's long-standing communal social
forms, also portraying French colonialism as an unmitigated disaster for
the populace. As mentioned in chapter 1, Ottoman rule in the period
preceding the French conquest introduces some aspects of private property in land, which begin to undermine the older communal structures.
Next comes a more modern colonial project originating in France, an
industrializing capitalist power. Although France is not at the level of
Britain in terms of industrial development, its dominant classes have had
a wider experience of revolution throughout the nineteenth century, as
seen especially in the 1848 revolution and the anti-capitalist Paris Commune of 1871. This political and historical experience gives them a
certain political sophistication, making them extremely sensitive to the
threat of any form of communism, even the technologically less developed agrarian communism of the Algerians. This is seen when, beginning
in the 1830s, France invades Algeria, occupies it after years of violent
repression, and establishes a form of setter colonialism. In the account
Marx draws from Kovalevsky, French imperialism attempts to eradicate
the local communal structures, to tear up Algerian society by its roots
and to reconstitute it.

While the theme of Algerian Indigenous communism as dangerous
not only for the colony but also for metropolitan France comes through
only intermittently, it is an extremely important one. It is illustrated in

the following excerpt Marx incorporates from Kovalevsky, who quotes from French parliamentary debates from the year 1873, only two years after the Paris Commune:

> *Establishment of private property in land* (in the eyes of the French bourgeois) necessary condition for every forward step in political and social spheres. Continuing *maintenance of communal property* is dangerous, both for the colony and the metropolis, "*as a form that supports communistic tendencies in people's minds*" (*Debates of the National Assembly.* 1873); the dividing up of the *clan holdings* is encouraged, even required, first as a means *to weaken subjugated tribes that are always ready to leap into revolt,* second as *only path toward further transfer of landed property* from the hands of the natives to those of the colonists. (KOV: 405)

In the above excerpt, Marx adds the parenthetical phrase "in the eyes of the French bourgeois," clarifying the policy's relationship to a typical member of the principal dominant French class and replacing Kovalevsky's less class-based explanations that remain at the level of ideological prejudice and political power: that free market prejudices motivated French officials, and that they simply wanted to dominate and control the population and saw the breakup of clan property as removing a locus of resistance. Thus, Marx's frames the "French bourgeois" as part of a dominant group, focusing on its overall ideology and interests.

Another key notion in the above, though not drawn out by Marx at this juncture, is that communal social forms are "dangerous, both for the colony and the metropolis." This danger to metropolitan France is not only material but also ideological, for, as stated in the National Assembly in Paris, continuation of the Indigenous communal forms in Algeria "*supports communistic tendencies in people's minds*" in Paris and elsewhere. One could think, for example, of French exoticist images of the Global South later in Paul Gaugin's paintings of Polynesia, which offered, in however romanticized a form, images of an alternative to industrial capitalist civilization. One could also recall that some of the Paris Communards, like the anarchist Louise Michel, were deported to the French colony of New Caledonia, where they formed alliances with the Indigenous population. This did not happen often with those French prisoners deported to Algeria, who too often became part of the racist colonial apparatus by obtaining and holding stolen land, but that could not have been known at the time by members of the French dominant classes.

While the above passage stresses the period soon after the Paris Commune, Marx also records right after it a passage that highlights that some of this was a long-term French policy, going back to the initial conquest in the 1830s:

> The same policies were pursued by the French among all the *regimes* that overthrew one another from 1830 to to-day. (211) *Means* sometimes change; *goal* always the same: *annihilation of indigenous collective property into object of unconstrained purchase and sale* and thereby easing its *ultimate transfer into the hands of the French colonists.* (KOV: 405)

This suggests a view of the basic continuity of the French state from the "bourgeois" monarchy of Louis Philippe that emerged from the 1830 revolution, through the liberal republic briefly established by the 1848 revolution, through the Bonapartist dictatorship (1851–70), and finally, the initially very elitist Third Republic that developed out of the collapse of the Bonapartist regime, and which defeated and brutally repressed its revolutionary alternative, the Paris Commune.

Inside Algeria, as Marx records from Kovalevsky, the French government twisted a provision in Muslim law that gave Muslim clerics ultimate ownership of the land. Since the French saw themselves as successors to the old rulers, this allowed them to "declare the greatest part of the conquered territory to be (French) government property" (KOV: 406). But, as Kovalevsky and Marx note, this is a legal fiction, since under Muslim law the imams only had the right to levy a capitation or head tax on the subject population. The French applied this fiction from the 1830s onward, however, as in the following passage Marx incorporates from Kovalevsky:

> Louis Philippe—as the successor of the imam, or rather of the subjugated deys, of course, grasps not only the *domanial property*, but also all of the land not currently being tilled, including the *communal* pastures, *forests* and—*uncultivated land.* (212) [[Europeans recognize foreign/non-European laws when they deem them "profitable"—as here with Muslim law—not only do they do so—immediately!—they

"misunderstand" it only to their profit, as in this case.]] The French predatory frenzy understands something immediately: If the regime is and was the original owner of the whole country, then recognition of the claims of Arab and Kabyle clans to any or all pieces of territory is unnecessary unless they can prove their title with *written documents*. (KOV: 406)

In the above quotation, the bracketed sentence and most of the one that follows are Marx's own, sharpening Kovalevsky's critique and focusing the passage more on the economic dimensions of imperialism. In this way, much Algerian land was essentially stolen, as both Marx and Kovalevsky emphasize.

Moreover, the land was stolen in the service of a settler colonialism that was markedly different from the type of colonialism the British established in India, because, here in Algeria, large portions of the peasantry were completely dispossessed outright, and very quickly. Other peasants were converted into temporary tenants, removable far more easily than before French colonialism established itself, in such instances more similar to the situation in India. Marx records a passage on this from Kovalevsky:

In this manner: on the one hand, the *earlier communal owners* reduced to the *position of temporary holders of government land*; and on the other, *violent theft of considerable portions of the property owned by the clans* and *thereupon the transplantation of European colonists*. In this sense the *decrees of 8 Sept. 1830, 10 June 1831* etc. Hence the *system of cantonments*: based on a *division of the clan land into 2 parts*, one of which was left with the members of the clan, the other retained *by the government* for the purpose settling European colonists upon it. (KOV: 406)

In incorporating the above passage into his notes, Marx leaves aside Kovalevsky's purely culturalist explanation that, as with the English in Bengal, it was a lack of cultural understanding rather than the economic imperatives of a capitalist imperialism that created the problem; that is, the French could not conceive of land not owned by a single individual.

However, as Marx records further from Kovalevsky, this system of cantonments, of dividing the Arab clans, ran up against the power of long-standing communal beliefs and practices, plus counter-swindling of the French by the Arabs, who would sell the same piece of land to French buyers multiple times:

> Moreover: The *Arabs* succeeded in the majority of cases in buying back *all of those lands and districts that had been sold or taken away*, whether by the *European colonists* or by the *regime itself*. Thus the *system of cantonments* ended in a brilliant fiasco. Precisely with this experiment their noses were thrust against the reality of a still completely vital *communal and clan-based landownership*. It would not do to ignore this any longer; they had to take up active measures for its dissolution. (KOV: 407)

The phrase "precisely with this experiment their noses were thrust against the reality" is Marx's expression, strengthening Kovalevsky's point about the durability of communal social forms.

This impasse persisted for three decades, into the 1860s, whereupon the Bonapartist regime enacted a new series of laws to individualize and privatize clan property holdings, with the intention of decisively breaking up these communal social forms. Marx records on this point Kovalevsky's description of an 1863 law:

> This was the purpose of the *Senate Bill of April 22, 1863*; which legally recognized the *property ownership rights of the clans in relation to the districts they occupied*, but any *collective property* was to be divided *not only among families*, but also *among their members . . . Article II of the Senate Bill of 1863* indicates that in the near future through an *imperial decree*: 1) *boundaries of the district* belonging to each of the clans *to be fixed*; 2) the *division of all of the clan's holdings among individual families*, except for those that are unsuitable for agriculture and which therefore remain *undivided property of the families*, 3) *establishment of private property* by means of *dividing the lands belonging to families* wherever such measures are recognized as appropriate. (KOV: 407–8)

In the above, the phrase "but any *collective property* was to be divided," which places Kovalevsky's findings into a more general, theoretical framework, is Marx's addition.

Marx records lengthy passages from Kovalevsky on how these new laws served to divide up the clans, while also, as discussed in chapter 2, increasing male patriarchal power within individual families. Below, Marx quotes Kovalevsky, who is quoting Eugène Robe, a prominent colonial jurist:

> After the clan elder has lost his earlier *character as patriarch* and is transformed into the position of a *Muslim official,* caid, the *authority of the male heads of household* grew and received through law a recognized, *official, political character*; the process of the *splitting of the clan* (into the numerically smallest groups of consanguineal relatives) began back at that time on its own and gradually advanced unnoticed . . . the *sense of consanguinity* (linking different families) gradually diminished; *the individual branches separated themselves off from the common lineage;* the closest relatives formed special settlements (villages); *each tent* became a center of particular interests, the center of its own *consanguineal group,* which had its own special needs, and special, relatively narrow and egoistic goals. Thus *the clan ceased to be the broad, all-embracing family* and became *an agglomeration of all settlements,* spread out over the clan's lands, a kind of *confederation of tents,* a confederation with much more restricted official and political character than before. (KOV: 409)

However, this too had its limits.

For the communal form persisted stubbornly at more local levels, as seen in a further passage that Marx records from Kovalevsky:

> It went quite differently with *their other task*: the *introduction of private property within the boundaries of the clan.* (220) According to *Title V, Article 26 of the Regulations* this was supposed to happen taking into account various rights of *historical customary law,* hence only *after figuring these out* beforehand. Nothing came of it; the whole thing given up by Badinguet. (KOV: 409)

"Badinguet" was a derisive nickname for Napoleon III. However, the liberal French Third Republic was to try this again after he was deposed in 1870, partly in reaction to the Paris Commune of 1871, as we have seen.

With these market-oriented liberals, as Marx records from Kovalevsky, the arguments revolve around the ideology of "the so-called eternally inalterable laws of political economy":

> 1873: Hence the first concern of the *Assembly* of Rurals *of 1873* was to reach for more effective measures for *stealing the land of the Arabs*. [[*The debates in this assembly of shame* concerning the project "*On the Introduction of Private Property*" in Algeria seek to hide their gangsterism under the cloak of so-called *eternally inalterable laws of political economy*. (224) In these *debates* the *"Rurals"* are all in accord concerning the purpose: *destruction of collective property*. The debate revolved only around the *method, how* to kill it off. For example, Deputy *Clapier* wants to do it in the manner prescribed by the *Senate Agreement of 1863*, according to which private property is first only introduced into those *communes* whose *portion of landed property* has *already been excluded from the land of the clan*; the Commission of "Rurals," whose president and general secretary *Warnier*, proposes to begin instead with the *end* of this *operation*, i.e. *with the identification of each individual share of every member of the commune, and to do this simultaneously in all 700 clans as well.*]] (KOV: 410)

In the above, Marx makes Kovalevsky's language more explicit at several junctures: (1) his phrase "stealing the land" sharpens Kovalevsky's rendering of this as "deprivation" of land; and (2) he adds the word "gangsterism" to describe the French parliamentarians.

At a more analytical level, he adds to Kovalevsky's text these two sentences: "In these *debates* the *'Rurals'* are all in accord concerning the purpose: *destruction of collective property*. The debate revolved only around the *method, how* to kill it off" (KOV: 410). Thus, the fight is between two social formations: a rapidly expanding French capitalism and the long-standing communal social forms of the Algerian peasants.

Most importantly, in this complex and revealing passage quoted above, Marx is also linking the situation of Algerian communal social forms to the 1871 Paris Commune. "Assembly of Rurals of 1873" is Marx's formulation, slightly reworking Kovalevsky's title for this assembly. This was the French left's derogatory term for the very conservative National Assembly, dominated by rural conservatives, that met at Versailles rather than Paris during the period of the 1871 Paris Commune.

It ordered the Commune's forcible suppression, which included numerous summary executions, as well as mass deportations. "Assembly of
shame" is also Marx's pejorative insertion, alluding to a common leftist
slogan of the time, "Assemblée de ruraux, honte de la France [Assembly
of Rurals, the Shame of France]."

Marx duly notes that Deputy Alexandre Clapier is more moderate in
his proposals to privatize Algerian landholdings and that he opposes
total alienability of land, which would open society to usury on a massive
scale. Marx adds this passage to Kovalevsky's account, generalizing
about the fate of peasants as capitalist relations take hold amid rural
communalism:

> As if this were not everywhere—in countries with non-capitalist mode
> of production—the *most shameless exploitation of the rural population*
> *by petty usurers* and by *neighboring landholders with ready access to*
> *capital?* Consider *India.* Consider *Russia.* (KOV: 410)

This is what begins to change under French capitalist colonialism, versus
all previous dominant classes, as in the following passage Marx annotates from Kovalevsky, noting parenthetically that this takes the form of
family property rather than the even more egalitarian forms found
among peoples like the Iroquois:

> Under the Muslim government, the peasant could at least not be *expro-*
> *priated of his land* by usurer-speculators. No *borrowing against*
> *(mortgaging) of land* was acceptable to it, because it recognized that
> *communal property* (respectively *undivided* family property) was
> *indivisible* and *inalienable.* (KOV: 410)

This precapitalist system was uprooted and destroyed, with terrible
consequences for the peasants.

For as Marx also records from Kovalevsky, inserting a comparison to
Russia, the new system gives

> priority to the person loaning money ahead of other creditors; he gets
> paid *before they do from the proceeds of the movable or immovable*
> *property of the debtor.* Thus here too a relative field of action opens up
> for the *usurer* (!) as in *Russia* etc. (226). The *Senate Agreement of 1863*

Article 6 first [to have] recognized the *right of unrestricted sale* of the landed property of private persons, i.e. the so-called *mulk* areas, *as well as of the tracts of land partitioned off for a whole subdivision of the clan*; this made possible the *sale and mortgaging of the communal lands* which immediately served the *usurers* and *the speculators buying up land*. The realm of their "enterprise" broadened out through the *"Rurals'" Law of 1873*, which accordingly established *private property in* land; every Arab can now freely dispose of his plot of land, separated off as private property; result will be *expropriation of land and soil of the indigenous population by European colonists and speculators*. But this is also the *conscious purpose of the "law" of 1873*. (KOV: 411)

In this way, the Algerian communal forms are severely undermined.

And, as Marx also records from Kovalevsky, this sets up a settler colonial society, while also undercutting the possibility of an uprising against the new system:

The *expropriation* of the Arabs was intended by law: 1) in order to furnish the French colonists with the greatest possible land; 2) by *tearing the Arabs away from their natural connection to the soil* and thus to crush the remaining power of the already disintegrating *clan associations*, and thereby any *danger of rebellion*. (KOV: 412)

In this sense, French colonial rule combines the economic with the political in new ways.

As in his notes on Latin America and India taken up in the present chapter, Marx is stressing, in dialectical fashion, not only the destruction of the communal social forms but also their persistence, sometimes in indirect form, a social fact that contributes to the possibility of revolt. And, in the India notes in particular, he suggests that the instability created by British destruction of communal social formations, the displacement of millions of people, lays the ground not only for capitalist social relations but also for a revolt against them. In the Algeria notes, he also hints at something else, parallels between French colonialism's drive to extirpate Indigenous communal forms at the very same time that, back home, the unrepresentative Versailles parliament of "Rurals," which the left regards as illegitimate because it shuts out from representation the working people of Paris, is repressing a modern communal form, that established by the Paris Communards in 1871. In fact, as Marx records in these notes, it was only after the French state suppressed the Paris Commune that it attempted the complete suppression of communal social forms in Algeria. This unites, at least in principle, two major forms of suffering and exploitation, and of anti-systemic resistance as well.

These 1879–82 notes do not form a theory of colonialism and resistance, but they surely offer many indications of the evolution of Marx's thought in that direction.

5

Rome, India, and Russia:
Three Agrarian Societies in Flux

In his last years, Marx examines intensively three major agrarian societies, ancient Rome, India, and Russia, all of them undergoing wrenching
social changes. Because I have treated India and Russia at some length in
previous chapters, discussion of his writings on these societies related to
the themes of the present chapter will be brief. I will need to outline more
comprehensively his overall view of Rome, however, given the relative
brevity with which it has been treated up to now.

As recorded in the late Marx's notebooks and discussed in some of his
other writings, Rome underwent shifts from a clan society, to a republic,
and then an empire, and from a smallholder to a large-scale, slave-based,
agrarian system, including extensive urbanization, aspects of a money
economy, and a legal system that stood above kinship relations. Extreme
class polarization and occasional but significant popular uprisings
ensued but were ultimately contained, allowing the system to persist in
relatively stable form for several hundred years. India experienced long-
term changes in its communal villages under Hindu and then Muslim
rulers, and significant resistance to the latter, especially toward the end
of the Mughal Empire. Then came the undermining of these communal
forms under British colonialism, which sparked another period of
massive resistance. Russia saw its communal villages transformed by
capitalist encroachments, at a time when revolutionary intellectuals were
seeking to overthrow the absolute monarchy through armed attacks and
by appealing to the peasantry. Of these three investigations by Marx,

only the one on Russia is fairly widely known, because of the 1882 preface to the Russian edition of the *Communist Manifesto*, Marx's last published text, as well as the subsequent publication of the drafts of the 1881 letter to Vera Zasulich. These texts discuss communal social forms in the Russian villages and their relationship to global revolution. The writings on India and ancient Rome are harder to assess because they comprise entirely notes rather than publications or even draft manuscripts. Still, I believe that it is possible to discern many of Marx's areas of interest from his notes on Rome and India, and to discuss the apparent direction of his thinking based on these notebooks, as I have done in previous chapters.

Rome: Class Structure, Class Tensions

I will begin this chapter with Marx's notes on ancient Rome, which he seems to have begun writing in the fall of 1879, the time when he was also studying Kovalevsky's book on communal social forms in the Americas, India, and Algeria, and Sewell's chronological account of Indian history. As mentioned in the introduction to this study, these notes on Rome are interspersed with those on India, in the same large notebook, apparently from fall 1879. He makes other notes on Rome a bit later, in 1880–81, from Morgan's *Ancient Society*. The following tables indicate the various notes on specific authors related to Rome.

Notebook B156/140 (begun around 1879)

Page Nos. in Marx's Handwritten Notebook	Text Marx Annotated
8–11	Karl Bücher's book on slave and plebeian uprisings in Rome
12–16	Ludwig Friedländer's book on Roman culture
17–24	Rudolf von Jhering's book on Roman law
117–40	Ludwig Lange's book on the social and gender history of Rome

Notebook B162/146 (December 1880- Spring 1881)

Page Nos. in Marx's Handwritten Notebook	Text Marx Annotated
4–101	Henry Lewis Morgan's book on clan societies and gender relations among the Iroquois, the Aztecs, and the ancient Greeks and Romans

I will not treat these notebooks one by one but, rather, chronologically and thematically, starting with Marx's investigations of early Roman society through the Empire before its decline in the latter part of the fourth century CE.

As discussed in chapters 1 and 2, Marx studied early Roman communal and kinship forms in a clan-based society and how these evolved into a male-dominated class society with a well-developed legal system, private property in land, and the primacy of slave labor in economic production. In his notes on Morgan, Marx focuses on the rise of a patrilineal and patriarchal aristocracy, the patrician order, from within the ancient clan/gentile society, recording the following:

> The distinction of patricians conferred upon their children and lineal descendants in perpetuity created at once an aristocracy of rank in center of the Roman social system where it became firmly intrenched; this aristocratic element now for the first time planted in gentilism (clan society). (EN: 227; Morgan 1877: 313)

As Morgan underlines and Marx records, property is a crucial motor of this transformation, especially with the accumulation of landed property in the hands of the patricians:

> Gentes remain for a long time in the empire, *as a pedigree and a lineage.* The element of property, which has controlled society *during* the *comparatively short period of civilization*, gave mankind *despotism, imperialism, monarchy, privileged classes* and finally *representative democracy.* (EN: 233; MG: 340–2)

While Marx probably appreciates the above passage, it is all but certain that he would reject the notion that "representative democracy" flowed out of rather than stood opposed to, in many ways, the reign of property.

According to a mixture of legend and historical records among the Romans, from early on, two wings of an aristocratic upper class emerged. Formally and legally, they were "orders," or what in the English-language Weberian discourse are usually called "status groups [*Stände*]." At the highest level of the aristocracy stood landowning patrician military chieftains claiming descent from the original Roman clans, who could serve in the Senate, the highest political body under the Republic. Next came the slightly lower-ranked aristocratic class of equestrians or knights, who may have initially owned merely a horse and armor—still a substantial marker of wealth—rather than any substantial amount of land. As Roman territory and wealth grew, equestrians took part not only in military affairs but also in commerce and in tax farming in conquered territories. For their part, patricians commanded the army, had the exclusive right to serve in the Senate (which according to Morgan evolved out of a clan-based council of chiefs), controlled the large, landed estates, and, while forbidden to engage in commerce as an activity beneath their status, were able to pursue moneylending on a large scale.

As discussed in Marx's sources and his notes, three other large social classes also appeared, by legend as early as the end of the sixth century BCE: plebeians, clients, and slaves, the latter completely excluded from recognition, except as bare human beings, and even then, only partially. To an extent, these groups fit the usual Marxian definition of social classes because they had different relationships to the principal means of production: land, tools, and draft animals. One of these lower class/status groups, the plebeians, gained more political rights over time. Economically, they could sometimes amass large property holdings that could allow them to mount higher in the class and even status hierarchy over the generations, often by intermarriage with aristocrats.

Early on, according to Marx's sources, both plebeians and clients—and of course slaves—were excluded from political participation, whether in the forms of voting or of holding office, but the plebeians enjoyed personal freedom and were able to accumulate social honor by serving in the army at the lower levels. The plebeians were not members of the ancient clans, but nonetheless members of the community, most of them without much in the way of property. The client class has an obscurer origin but seems to have been formed initially from conquered or subordinated peoples, or the portion thereof that was not directly sold into slavery. This afforded to the clientele the preservation of their family units, their communities, and other forms of personal autonomy. Clients also evolved from foreign guests allowed to reside on Roman territory for trading or other purposes, as well as from manumitted slaves. All varieties of clients received physical and legal protection from their upper class "patrons" in return for loyalty and service. Their liberty thus came with many limitations, as against the fuller freedom enjoyed by the plebeians. Slaves, in contrast to clients, were unable to keep their family and community ties, and they could be sold as individuals and taken great distances from their families of origin. They often labored under severe physical constraints, which at their most extreme included being chained and whipped, as in agricultural or galley slavery. They were also subjected to sexual slavery of various kinds.

In adopting the above distinctions between clients and plebeians, Marx differs somewhat with Morgan, who writes, "the clients were part of the plebeian body" (MG: 326). In stating this, Morgan was disagreeing with Niebuhr, but on this point, Marx seems to side with the German classicist, writing laconically in his own notes, "*Niebuhr* denies that *clients part of the plebeian* body," without even mentioning Morgan's criticism of Niebuhr (EN: 230; MG: 326).

In sum, the five main social classes/status groups were: (1) patrician landowners and senators; (2) equestrians engaged in commerce, also part of the aristocracy; (3) plebeian citizens lacking much in the way of status honor; (4) non-citizen clients obligated to show deference toward their aristocratic patrons; and, finally, (5) non-citizen slaves with virtually no rights.

As Morgan and Marx see it, the patricians emerged from the chiefs of the original clans that came together to found the city of Rome. As Rome expanded, they acquired vast landholdings and large numbers of slaves who worked their land. As to the plebeians, Marx seems to follow Morgan and other authorities in concluding that by the mid-sixth century BCE, on the eve of the Republic, the plebeians became citizens, albeit without the possibility of holding political office or military command. Plebeians received limited representation, however, via the Tribunes, aristocrats whom they elected and who could veto Senate legislation. Among the plebeians, the proletarians, those without any real property, constituted the poorest element.

One issue that comes to the fore in Marx's notes is the growth of class polarization over time. This is seen in his notes on Rudolf von Jhering's 1852–65 *Geist des römischen Rechts auf den verschiedenen Stufen seiner Entwicklung* (Spirit of Roman law in the various stages of its development), never translated into English. In annotating this celebrated social history that moves away from earlier more textual and idealist interpretations, Marx focuses on the causes of this class polarization. He records the following passage on how constant warfare during the Republic drained the plebeians of their land and other property:

1) *Uneven distribution of the pressures of war* on the *economic situation* of the well to do and the poorer classes. As soon as the poor man had to go to war, his fields remained untilled, the fields of the rich were worked by slaves. In the early period wars, *raids when there was nothing to do in the fields*. In the same way, as they gained importance, theater of war more distant, duration of the campaigns longer, reaction of this upon *agriculture*. And here decisive whether the possessor tilled *his fields or slaves* worked for him (243).

Thus, early Roman warfare was conducted during slack times for farm work. But ever longer and more distant military campaigns drove the plebeian soldiers into economic ruin, as their fields lay untilled, whereas the patricians could maintain their position through slave labor. By leaving aside from his notes Jhering's evocation of a somewhat mitigating factor, military pay, Marx gives slightly more stress to economic polarization than does Jhering.

As Marx records, again from Jhering, other factors leading to greater economic inequality were crop failure and other disruptions of agricultural production, which plebeian farmers could not withstand as easily as their aristocratic counterparts:

The small farmer in great difficulty; forced during bad harvests and times of war to borrow money at high interest; in a good year *price dropped* so much that he could not overcome the disadvantage; his *debt* then growing with new bad year or year of war. The *high interest* itself an effect of the helpless situation that the farmer found himself in as against large, landed property and capital. (246) Therefore problems for the self-sustaining farmer, even cultivation at standstill due to war (l.c.).

And as mentioned above, the patrician/senatorial class, while forbidden to take part in commerce, was allowed to loan money at usurious interest rates. All these processes—warfare, crop failure, and indebtedness—impoverished the plebeians and increased the relative and absolute holdings of the patricians.

As Marx records from Jhering, the Licinio-Sextian Laws of 367 BCE limited the size of landholdings, which should have benefited the plebeians, but this was circumvented by patricians' listing their property in the name of relatives. So too with a provision of the law of the Twelve Tables (legendary date 451 BCE) that limited interest to 8.33 percent, circumvented by recourse to compound interest. Thus, these and other measures to preserve plebeian property and lessen economic inequality largely failed.

As Marx records in his notes on Ludwig Friedländer's 1871 book, *Roman Life and Manners under the Early Empire*, the pattern of senators engaging in usurious loans persisted after the demise of the Republic, albeit in altered form, targeting the provinces rather than poorer Roman citizens:

> *According to law*, senators could invest their capital only *in landed property* or moneylending. *Pliny epistolae* [Letters] "Indeed, I invested almost everything (all my wealth) in land: I lend some of it at interest though: there will be no trouble borrowing." (p. 181) On the usurers, cf. Tacitus Annales VI. 16. [[In 32 AD as a monetary crisis forced the government to intervene, the whole Senate upset, since no senator was free of guilt from usurious money transactions.]] (These usurers driven mainly into *the provinces*; in this manner *Seneca* had required high interest from the Britons for a loan of 40 million sesterces; calling it in suddenly and forcefully cause of the *revolt of the province* in *60 AD*.)

Marx has recorded the above with some deletions, in a way that emphasizes, more than does Friedländer, how Seneca, the Stoic philosopher and adviser to Emperor Nero, engaged in this kind of rapacity.

The growth of economic inequality also meant that the plebeians were cowed by the patricians due to their indebtedness to them, as falling into arrears could lead to debt servitude. Marx records a passage from Jhering about how this constrained plebeian political opposition to the upper classes: "In order to comprehend the plebeians' complacent attitude and their political apathy at this time, influence of this means of coercion to be noted."

While the small plebeian farmers were losing their economic position, a parallel change affected the artisanal portion of the plebeian class. Where small farmers could not withstand the economic pressures of war and crop failure in the face of large landowners who employed slave labor, the plebeian artisans were thrust into direct competition with slave laborers. This led to status as well as economic degradation, as Marx records, again from Jhering:

> All *common labor*, completely or preferably assigned to the *slave*; whoever performed it lost his honor; artisanal skills themselves became *unworthy of a free man*. The *coarse manual labor*, all that belonged to the regular, vital necessities of life, with very small exceptions, was taken care of in the big estates by slaves.

Such status degradation did not apply to tending one's own farm, however, which was still considered to be honorable.

In the cities, plebeian artisans faced the commercial aristocracy of the equestrian class, who also held slaves on a large scale. This applied to freed slaves—freemen—as well as to other plebeians, as in this passage Marx records from Jhering: "The freeman meets the hereditary enemy— the slave—*in shipping, in trade, in fiscal matters*, even *in the lower positions of the national and communal administration*."

As a result, as seen in this passage Marx records from Jhering, the plebeians increasingly became an urban, largely non-productive class, existing by the "generosity" of those who had expropriated their forebears:

> For Rome *proletariat* therefore an unavoidable result of its institutions; from Italy all rushed preferably to Rome; city for proletarians, as existed never before; without work, in a way a comfortable existence; constant distractions—games, festivals, charity donations from the government and from the rich; *splendid* misery, Roman citizens the "haughty attitude" of the beggar; could *exercise their right to vote* in the comitia tributa, *and sell it* (255, 56). *Aristocratic generosity*—considered

to be a duty of the upper ranks in Rome . . . served in Rome to supplement the system of circulation of goods . . . a flowing back of wealth into the empty spaces (!) (257, 58). *Generosity*—was *customary expenditure for the upper ranks.*

Thus, once the proletarians lost any connection with economic production, their political power dwindled further and they became an abject class. Their formal rights to vote in the tribunate, a very powerful political institution, did not change this in any fundamental sense.

Colonization and military pay offered other means of quieting the proletarians, as in this passage from Jhering that Marx records, which is full of quotations from the first-century CE historian Livy:

> *From the standpoint of the state*: 1) *allotment of landed property to the propertyless masses by founding of colonies or assignment from the ager publicus* [[*Livy* X, 6: "In Rome, too, the many people sent to the colonies have quieted down the plebeians and lessened their burden." V. 24: "There were multiple instances of strife and in order to calm the situation they recommended that 3,000 Roman citizens be removed and their names entered for a colony among the Volsci."]] 2) *Introduction of soldiers' pay* [circa 405 BCE] the ruling class gave in to demands by the poorer class Livy IV. 59, Livy IV. 36: "Hope was held out for the division of public land and the introduction of colonies and . . . *for raising money for the payment of the soldiers.*"

Jhering and Marx suggest that such responses by the state left these plebeians, as mentioned above, a greater sense of status honor than those living on the generosity of the upper classes as proletarians inside the city of Rome. For their part, the patricians, equestrians, and wealthy plebeians prospered through the Republic and the Empire, albeit with fewer political rights once the Republic ended.

Rome: Technological Development and Increasing Class Polarization

Marx also analyzes Rome's economic and technological development. In his notes on Friedländer, Marx also takes up the German historian's thesis that the level of Roman luxury was exaggerated by modern historians, as in this passage:

> The Roman Empire had not even 2/3 of the area of Europe and only a small part of the rest of the world was accessible. The countries of the East, as with the barbarian countries in general, supplied the Roman Empire with only a small portion of their luxury products. In the greater part of its provinces, where cultivation had just begun, their productive capacity still not highly developed, etc. (91, 92). The reason for the relatively limited development of Roman luxury—the relatively small size and poverty of the ancient world.

The last sentence above is Marx's summary of Friedländer's main thesis.

Marx records specifics about luxury imports for the upper classes from India and other parts of Asia, as in this passage from Friedländer:

> The prices of the Oriental luxury articles in those days sometimes unbelievably high and generally higher than today. *Silk* in the 2nd half of the 3rd cent. still weighed out in gold . . . These imports nevertheless very small . . . essentially limited to Rome and some of the larger cities. (50, 51) . . . In the 4th century as a result of completely changed trade relations, the use of silk became common in all ranks of society.

He also records passages from Friedländer on the high level of technical development evidenced by Roman waterworks:

> *Luxury of cleanliness. Public nature of the waterworks.* In a number of Italian cities plumbing pipes imprinted with municipal seals indicate the existence of public aqueducts (in Trieste, Bevagana, Circello, Pozzuoli, Canosa etc.), whose water, when not needed for municipal purposes, was used to provide returns benefiting the municipal treasury. Contributing *to this municipal income* were "the wealthier homeowners, who

let the water be piped into their houses, and the landowners, who (insofar as this was possible from the aqueduct) watered their fields in the same manner, likewise the *artisans*, who needed water for their industries, esp. *the fullers*; then also those who at their own expense built baths (whether for private use, or out of public spirit for poorer individuals)."

In addition, he incorporates into his notes Friedländer's argument to the effect that Roman levels of technological development in terms of water-works sometimes surpassed that of even the more developed parts of nineteenth century Europe, like France:

> Also in the provincial cities *the supply of good and abundant water a main concern of the communities* [Communen]. *Boissieu* (of Lyon) *"Inscriptions de Lyon"* p. 446 notes: "that our time proud as it is of the advance of machinery and possessing wholly different means than had the ancients, for example steam power, has not, even for the big cities, accomplished anything close to *what the Romans did, even for the smallest localities under the most difficult conditions. Ancient Lyon rested on an elevation* and was abundantly supplied with clear and healthy spring water; the *new city lies on a plain between 2 rivers* and must be content with foul-smelling water, polluted sewers and unhealthy air." . . . Likewise in Avenches and *in Cologne, excellent drinking water was supplied from the heights of the Eifel* [mountains] *and ran through a 17-league pipeline almost completely under the earth's surface.* (96)

These remarkable achievements rested upon vast supplies of slave labor, however, an issue Marx also takes up at some length in his notes on Rome.

Returning to slavery in the time of the late Republic, Marx records material from Karl Bücher's 1874 *Die Aufstände der unfreien Arbeiter* (Uprisings of unfree labor, 143–129 BC):

> Particularly with the Romans *slave markets* everywhere, with seemingly inexhaustible *supplies* of human resources from the barbarian countries, every new war provided the Romans with a new mass of captured enemies at rock-bottom prices; *as long as the labor supply could not yet be completely replenished by means of reproduction, the substitution of free labor for the convenient unfree labor* remained a pious wish.

Marx also incorporates into his notes Bücher's description of the scope of the slave-based agricultural economy:

> In Rome *intensive slave economy* with the rise of the large estate complexes, so-called plantation economy. Pervades all lines of business connected to agriculture, wholesale [trade], and the many-sided area of leasing land from the state. With Romans also the *"closed household economy,"* in which the whole cycle of manufacturing from production to consumption takes place independently within the economic unit of the household. (*Pliny XVIII, 40:* "Whoever buys what his farm can supply him with is in no way a farmer." *Petronius, 78:* "Everything originates at home.")

Marx seems to follow Bücher's characterization of Rome as having a far larger and more developed system of slave plantation agriculture than earlier societies.

Marx also takes an interest in the origins of slavery and its relationship to the Roman family [*famulus*], as in this material he records from Lange:

> *Slavery* arises from *capture of prisoners of war* in battles between *different* peoples; therefore with the *Roman jurists*, the *"servitus* [slavery]*" is a "disposition of the jus gentium," "by which, against nature, one man has been subjected to the dominium* [mastery] *of another."* . . . Slaves (prisoners of war) as *booty in general*, belong first of all to the *state*, are therefore *public slaves*; state keeps some for its own use, the rest are sold *"under the wreath."* (The wreath means the gift of life.)

The reference to the wreath connotes that the slave is "given" life; that is, is spared from death. Moreover, slave property was among the oldest forms of legally recognized Roman property. Thus, slavery was tied to both the origin of the family and that of property relations, as in this further passage from Lange Marx incorporates into his notes:

> *Rights of the dominus* [master]: can *use* slaves for whatever purpose he deems fit, *punish, adjudicate life and death, sell*; ownership rights to all that slave earns, also even to his children; dominus *liable for any harm that the slave inflicts on a third party*. In the *most ancient period, as famulus, slave belongs to the sacrificial community of the family*; could

even carry out certain sacrifices in place of the dominus; received *peculium* to use for himself; is transferred, however, with the rest of the *res mancipi* to the authority of the successor.

Marx records another brief passage on the somewhat less oppressive earliest practices of Roman slavery:

The further back one goes *into the ancient period*, the *more humane* the *slavery* appears; slave as servant [*famulus*] member of the family, could participate in their sacrifices, and stood under the family's divine protection; later even the *vernae* [slaves born in the master's house], who grew up with the children [*liberis*], were treated in a more humane way than the newly-acquired slaves.

Thus, the brutality of slavery increased as Rome grew and developed economically. This is in keeping with Marx's notion that modern capitalist slavery was the cruelest version of all, as seen in this passage from Marx's economic notebooks of 1861–65, which comprised draft material for *Capital*:

It is therefore among commercial peoples that slavery and serfdom take on their most hateful form, as e.g. among the Carthaginians; this is even more pronounced among peoples that retain slavery and serfdom as the basis of their production in an epoch when they are connected with other peoples in a situation of capitalist production; thus, e.g. the southern states of the American Union. (MECW 30: 197)

Marx also records from Lange considerable material on the legal evolution of the concept of manumission and the rights of freedmen.

Throughout his notes on Rome and Greece, Marx stresses the cruelty and brutality of slavery, sometimes contrapuntally to the sources he is studying, as in this excerpt he records from Lange and from which he has eliminated language presenting a softer picture:

Gruesome treatment of slaves, when they were not house and table companions any more, but *forced laborers* and held in *ergastulis* [workhouses]. In *Republic* no protection from the cruel master, except for the *censor's reprimands. In Imperial Period legally restricted:*

after *lex Petronia* [61 CE] . . . [[But *Constantine still* recommends to judges mild treatment of masters who killed slaves while administering warranted correction.]] *Master compelled to sell slave* who because of cruel treatment sought refuge with the gods (*Gaius* 1, 53). *Slavery was not abolished*; there arose alongside it in the *last period of the Roman Empire, colonate*, a type of serfdom [bonded slavery], where the *peasants* [coloni] *being bound to the soil were inseparable from landed property* and *passed with it from the ownership of one patron to that of another. If a master is murdered, according to ancient custom all of his slaves are executed* in order to protect the master's life against the slaves (*Tacitus Annales* 14, 42–5). This *ancient custom* confirmed by *the Senatus Consultum Silananium*; under Nero [early second century CE] made even harsher, since *even those slaves* who *would otherwise have been freed by testamentary stipulation were to be executed.*

Here as elsewhere, Marx condemns slavery unstintingly.

In addition to the patrician-plebeian and master-slave relationships, Marx records material on a third hierarchical relationship, that of patron to client. In his notes on Jhering, Marx incorporates material on the origin of Roman clientelism in the position of guests from outside a clan (gens), often traders, who could reside in peace within clan territory only under the legal protection of a clan member:

> Whoever wished to settle within the domain of the state, without having established himself in a binding gentile relationship, was from the very beginning—legally—in the position of the hostis; he could gain protection only by putting himself under the protection of the *patronage* of a Roman citizen as a client . . . with hospitium the quid pro quo lies in the return of the promised protection; with clients, this was naturally omitted, its place is taken by an *obligation of service*, and this meant that the relationship was actually more one of dependence. This dependence was particularly evident in the terms *patronus* and *cliens* . . . "Patronus" . . . denotes this relationship as a *reproduction of paternal power* (230).

This relationship involved mutual albeit hierarchical obligations and could lead to grants of land to a client by a patron:

The *granting of land*—itself alien to the essence of this arrangement, (in contrast to vassalage of the Middle Ages, that had its legal foundation not in the defenselessness of the vassals, but in granting him a fief) was a very effective means of keeping the client interested in the perpetuation of the relationship and as such it was able to come into general use and to even produce the effect that Dionysius witnessed, the carrying over of this relationship from generation to generation on both sides.

Marx excerpts the above passage in a way that makes Jhering's rejection of the "feudal" hypothesis concerning vassalage a bit more emphatic than in the original.

In the notes on Lange, Marx records material on a second, perhaps later origin of clientelism, the relationship of manumitted slaves to their former masters or their descendants:

A further analogy to the *patrician-client relationship* is in the general Roman legal relationship between the *manumittor as patron* and the *manumitted freeman as client*; the latter relationship was modelled on the former; but the client relationship did not evolve from manumission.

But this led to a loss of status for the clients, as Marx also records from Lange:

The *manumitted freedman* entered into a clientele relationship, but only because based on direct manumission, and *not heritable*. The more this sort of clientele proliferates, the *scarcer become the instances where the old clientele persisted*; many patrician lineages died out and with that the clients were rid of their personal duties. The newer relationship affected the older, since the older clients had more dignity than the freedmen recently released from slavery. Therefore it was later considered improper to accept monetary gifts from clients.

But it is in the notes on Friedländer that Marx takes up in greater detail the declining status of the clients.

Marx incorporates some scathing descriptions of the degradation of the patron-client relationship in the late Republic and the Empire into his notes on Friedländer: "*Clients*: only the name in common with the old clientele; no longer a reverential, but a landlord-tenant relationship; *a poorly paid and disdainfully treated person.*" As he also records from Friedländer, the status of the clients sinks as the Empire begins:

> *In the last period of the Republic* the clientele had preserved some of its earlier character. (207) The patron's personal interest in the client subsides to the extent that it became usual in the first century to have hordes of clients, etc. In order to enhance their credit even those land-owning tradesmen who were not wealthy (*Juvenal* VII. 144) had to retain a number of clients to gather around their sedan chair. *Thus, the clientele already had a way of earning a living in the early imperial period*; large numbers of needy people worked for low pay at the bidding of the wealthy and the noble just for the purpose of building a following or enlarging the numbers of those at their disposal in their courtyard.

Not only was their economic position degraded, but the clients had to perform a series of humiliating duties just in order to earn a meager living, if that, from their relationship with their patrons.

This is seen in another passage Marx records from Friedländer on the heavy woolen cloak and other markers of degradation:

> The fellows had to present themselves before the master in *toga*, the national ceremonial dress, *a hot and heavy cloth cloak*, that . . . became *the distinctive garb for clients*, besides that, a not inconsiderable expense for a poor person. "In summer four or more togae are being worn out here." (Mart. IX. 100. X 96. 11.) "*Toga that causes sweating*" (XII. 18. 5) [211]. First, the "*morning visit*" [[called therefore "salutatores" and because of their dress "togati" (toga wearers)]]. But otherwise also in demand throughout the larger part of the day and even well into the evening, since they form, at all public appearances of their master, an entourage. They had to walk in front of his sedan chair or follow it, accompany him on all his visits, finally maybe around the 10th hour of the day, escort him to the thermal baths of Agrippa etc.; create space in crowded places, even through cursing and elbowing; if lord went to the countryside or on trips, they also had to be prepared to take an empty seat in his carriage; if he read his poetry aloud, they had to encourage applause from the audience by standing up or by gesturing admiration; if he testifies in court, "the crowd in togas" shouted bravo. Always singing praises, always submissive etc.

As Marx further records from Friedländer, the relationship was degraded further by the second century BCE into a *"slave-like humility of the lowly before the lofty."*

Thus, as with the proletariat (poor plebeians) and the slaves, the position of the clients deteriorated as Rome became increasingly polarized along economic lines. This constituted a potentially combustible situation.

Roman Slave and Plebeian Revolts, and Something Akin to White Racism

Marx considers slave and plebeian uprisings in Rome and the areas it governed in his notes on Bücher's book. In terms of slave revolts, Bücher takes up the Sicilian slave war of 135–32 BCE and the anti-Roman uprising of 133–30 in Anatolia in which both slaves and peasants participated. These two revolts outside Rome occurred around the time of the 133 Tribunate of Tiberius Gracchus, whose land reforms mobilized Roman plebeians against the aristocracy. All these revolts and dissensions met with severe repression and ultimately, defeat.

But what differentiated them from the later and more famous Spartacus slave uprising of 73–71 BCE was that they involved several kinds of subordinated classes: slaves, peasants, and urban proletarians, as well as leaders drawn from dissident wings of the aristocracy. Marx zeroes in on this aspect in an excerpt he incorporates into his notes on Bücher:

> *Earlier slave revolts.* Wide gulf between the free proletarian and the slave. "Not until the *Roman mob uprisings of the first centuries BC*, where dregs of the whole world had come together in Rome, was there any noticeable joint effort of both under the leadership of high-ranking aristocrats." (20)

The phrase "free proletarian and the slave" is Marx's formulation, giving more emphasis to the different class positions of these subordinated groups than Bücher, who refers in more aggregate terms to "free" and "unfree" proletarians.

In the Sicilian slave war, some 70,000 slaves recently imported from Syria and destitute local peasants rose up under the leadership of Eunus, whom the rebels termed a prophet and a king. Eunus claimed to draw inspiration from a local cult of the Roman fertility goddess Demeter, whom he claimed had appeared to him. Marx incorporates material on this issue in his notes on Bücher:

> In Enna (Sicily) . . . , a city in the mountains, used to have well-attended semi-annual festivals for the *Earth Mother* (Demeter) at sowing time and for *Persephone* when the grain started to ripen. "When the cattle are moving south in November, a small trade fair is held, and when the cattle are moving north in May, the largest cattle market on the island is held there, a *remnant of the ancient festival gatherings*" . . . Demeter took the same place for the religious Sicilians as the Madonna today.

This above paragraph may well be connected to the slightly later discussions of goddesses and gender in Marx's notes on Morgan, in which the stress is on their psychosocial role in the Greco-Roman world, as discussed in chapter 2. But here, unlike in the notes on Morgan, the fertility goddesses Demeter and her daughter Persephone are connected to a popular uprising of slaves and peasants. After this point, Marx skips seven pages of Bücher's text, in which the latter makes further references to "the vista from the heights of the temple of Demeter . . . the goddess . . . the universally beneficent earth mother . . . the Syrian goddess."[1]

Marx singles out a second influence on the Sicilian uprising, the Roman political structures, which allowed a degree of popular participation: "The Romans had left to the provincial cities as a kind of plaything, the forms of a free community association. [[they lay in the hands of the local money aristocracy in those provincial cities.]]" Marx does not incorporate into his notes anything from the rest of Bücher's text on this issue, in which he writes that Eunus used these structures to call a people's assembly.

Marx records more briefly Bücher's description of the slave and peasant uprising in the kingdom of Pergamon, by then a Roman dependency in Anatolia. King Attalus III (r. 138–33) had been allowed to maintain a degree of independence and in return his will ceded the kingdom to Rome upon his death. Thus, at his death in 133, Pergamon

---

1   Karl Bücher, *Die Aufstände der unfreien Arbeiter 143–129 v. Chr.* (Sauerländes Verlag: Frankfurt am Main, 1874), pp. 53–4.

was slated to become a Roman province. Aristonicus (d. 129), who claimed royal descent, defied the Romans and proclaimed himself King Eumenes III. He founded a movement for a free city of the sun—Heliopolis—promising liberation to all slaves serving in his army. This revolt, put down in 130, encompassed not only slaves but also free peasants and proletarians across Anatolia.

Back in Rome, the attempts by Tribune Tiberius Gracchus to redistribute land to the Roman proletariat had been repressed a year earlier, in 133. Gracchus had the people of Rome vote to distribute the revenues from the acquisition of Pergamon to his land commission, which was attempting to redistribute—in violation of legal niceties—large holdings of *ager publicus* lands (based on the Licinio-Sextian Law limit of 300 acres) to poor Romans. This vote over the bequest of Pergamon precipitated the assassination of Gracchus by an outraged senatorial mob, since he had not only challenged their landholdings but also violated the long-standing custom of leaving foreign affairs to the Senate.

Marx incorporates Bücher's chronology linking these three rebellions and dissensions—in Sicily, in Anatolia, and in Rome—into his notes on Bücher, who gives the beginning of the Sicilian uprising erroneously as 143 rather than 135 BCE, which placed it in even closer proximity to the other rebellions of the era. I have added some other clarifications in single square brackets:

> 143 BC beginning of the *Sicilian Slave War* Eunus king. Uprising in Minturnae and Sinuessa combated by Metellus.
>
> *143–41* Victories of *Achaeus* [commander under Eunus] over the praetors [Roman officials]
>
> *141 Consul Servilius Caepio* suppresses the rebellion in *Southern Latium.*
>
> *140 Cleon's uprising* [ally of Eunus in western Sicily]. Conquest of Acragas. Cleon and Eunus united. [Praetor] L. Plautius Hypsaeus defeated.
>
> *139–35.* Victorious *struggle of united slave leaders against the Roman praetors*
>
> [[*Uprising in (Rome?), Attica, Delos, Macedonia.*]] Tauromenium, Catana, Syracuse
>
> Messana conquered; Eunus ruler of the whole country. [of Sicily]

134. Consul G. Fulvius Flaccus fights in Sicily with no luck.

133 The *agrarian law of the Gracchi.*

L. Calpurnius Piso storms Messana and besieges Enna. Attalus III [[Pergamum]] [died].

Eudemos in Rome.—Aristonicus appears and conquers the coastal cities.

Tiberius Gracchus assassinated.

Battle near Kyme. [Anatolia]

Aristonicus founds the Association of the Heliopolites.

132 [Consul] *P. Rupilius in Sicily.* Tauromenium and Enna conquered.

Eunus captured.

Roman ambassadors in Asia Minor. Nasica [died].

131 Laws *of Rupilius* [in Sicily]

[Consul] P. Licinius Crassus [defeated] near Leukae. Crassus †.

Aristonicus, defeated by M. Perperna, surrenders in Stratonikeia.

129 Perperna *[died].*

M. Aquilius metes out punishment, restores order in the province of Asia.

Aristonicus garroted in Rome. [died]. [129 BCE]

Thus, by recording the entire chronology, including the mention of Tiberius Gracchus, Marx seems to link the three large rebellions together in these notes, but without drawing explicit connections among them.

The last passage Marx records from Bücher does make a more substantive link between the supporters of Tiberius Gracchus and the slave/peasant revolt in Anatolia during the same years:

> Blossius [[*Blossius*, Stoic philosopher from Cumae, friend of Tiberius Gracchus. He was also brought before the special punitive court in *132* [[assigned to the Consuls by the Senate]] took revenge against the Gracchans. He was asked if his friendship for Tiberius Gracchus could have induced him to torch the Capitol. Said: "Gracchus would have never ordered that." When asked: "And if he had ordered it?" Answer: "Then I would have obeyed him. For he would never have demanded it unless it would have been for the good of the people." (*Plutarch* Tiberius Gracchus)]] [[*Niebuhr:* This brave answer did not disgrace

Blossius but those who had forced him to give it. He (Blossius) then set
out to Aristonicus, etc.]] (111)

Gaius Blossius, who had been the philosophy tutor of both Tiberius
Gracchus and his younger brother Gaius (assassinated while leading a
second plebeian land reform movement in 121), was never found guilty
of anything and was thus free to go to Asia Minor, although Bücher writes
that he saved his neck by escaping from Rome. After Aristonicus was
defeated, Blossius committed suicide.

Most important here is the indirect link between the Gracchan revolt
in Rome and that of the slaves and peasants of Anatolia through the
person of the philosopher Blossius. Since Marx records Bücher in detail
on Blossius, it is quite likely that the wider possibility of solidarity between
the slaves and the Roman proletariat—and the link not only to dissident
aristocrats like Eunus or Tiberius Gracchus, but to a philosopher like
himself—would have been on his mind.

Here we have three elements that would have made a real social revolution possible, slave and peasant revolts in the provinces, a plebeian
struggle inside Rome, and the presence of leaders educated by a critical
philosopher who was also part of the struggle. Why did this not take
place? On this question, Marx offers a highly original explanation, not
found in Bücher or his other sources, who tend to see the plebeians and
slaves as antagonists and/or potential allies but did not highlight as much
as did Marx the vastly superior position of the plebeians, also treating
relatively uncritically their hostility toward the enslaved population.
Recall that Marx recorded from Jhering a sentence that seemed to sym-
pathize more with the plebeian than the slave: "The freeman meets the
hereditary enemy—the slave—*in shipping, in trade, in fiscal matters*, even
in the lower positions of the national and communal administration." The
stress here is on the declining position and economic fears of the plebeians, not on problems in the social consciousness of the plebeians that
undercut solidarity with the slaves.

For his part, Marx appears to view the slave-plebeian relationship from
a different angle, one that targets something akin to racism in the hostility of the plebeian to the slave. As shown above, Jhering almost blames
the slave for the lack of solidarity, similar to those today who blame the
influx of immigrants to the richer countries for the decline in white
working class support for the left. Bücher does not use that type of

language, but he seems to see slaves and plebeians rather unproblemati-
cally as potential allies, kind of a "unite and fight" position, thwarted by
the plebeians eventually being bought off in various ways by the dominant classes. This is seen in a passage Marx does not record from Bücher:

> Thus money oligarchy, pauperism, slavery encompass the entire life of
> the ancients, a repellent tripartite ring, from which no element may be
> separated without the others slipping out of position. The social ques-
> tion that emerged from the dual contradiction of the proletarian and
> the slave vis à vis the money oligarchy was dual, as it logically had to
> be. In spite of this, only the struggle of the free yet propertyless masses
> against the rich minority comes into view politically because those
> persons who have been reduced to objects, legally subsumed under the
> rubric of private property, have been completely excluded from the
> established organism of the state . . . Feeling their political importance,
> the [free but] unstable and dissatisfied masses constituted a persistent
> danger to the state and to the rule of the rich. In Athens and Rome these
> [rich] [. . .] tried to keep the masses happy with cheap food and
> amusement.[2]

In the above, despite placing slave revolts at the center of his book, Bücher
almost seems to deny slaves a real subjectivity due to their extremely
degraded position and the concomitant lack of records left behind by them.

Taking a different tack, Marx compares the Roman class alignment to
something under modern capitalism: the US South around the time of
the Civil War. He does so by inserting the parenthetical phrase "poor
whites" into the following passage he excerpts from Bücher: "Political
struggle only on the part (the poor whites) of the *proletarians*; in Athens
and in Rome they attempted to humor them by providing them with
cheap food and entertainment when it was no longer possible to relieve
the *pressure on the capital* through . . . *colonies*." Bücher's second point,
about the opening of emigration to the colonies, seems to have interested
Marx more than the more obvious one about bread and circuses. Probably the most dramatic example of this kind of colonization was seen in
Julius Caesar's apportioning of land to his largely plebeian soldiers after
the conquest of the vast territory of Gaul (roughly modern France).

---

2   Bücher, *Die Aufstände*, pp. 14–15.

Let us look at little deeper at Marx's analogy to the poor whites of the nineteenth-century American South. During the US Civil War, in an article from October 25, 1861, for *Die Presse* (Vienna), he avers that the possibility of becoming slaveholders themselves bound the poor whites to the small dominant class of largescale slaveowners. This channeled their class resentment in a harmless direction. Here, he also mentions the Roman plebeians:

> Finally, the number of actual slaveholders in the South of the Union does not amount to more than 300,000, a narrow oligarchy that is confronted with many millions of so-called poor whites whose numbers have been constantly growing through concentration of landed property and whose condition is only to be compared with that of the Roman plebeians in the period of Rome's extreme decline. Only by acquisition and the prospect of acquisition of new Territories, as well as by filibustering expeditions, is it possible to square the interests of these "poor whites" with those of the slaveholders, to give their restless thirst for action a harmless direction and to tame them with the prospect of one day becoming slaveholders themselves. A strict confinement of slavery within its old terrain, therefore, was bound according to economic law to lead to its gradual extinction, in the political sphere to annihilate the hegemony that the slave states exercised through the Senate, and finally to expose the slaveholding oligarchy within its own states to threatening perils from the "poor whites." (MECW 19: 40–1)

Thus, both the Roman and white Southern slaveholding classes held off revolt by their formally free but impoverished popular classes via the prospect of colonization.

This was connected to a sense of higher status on the part of members of these formally free popular classes compared to the enslaved population. Marx outlines this in another context, the address he drafted on the part of the First International in December 1864 in response to Abraham Lincoln's victory in the US election:

> While the working men, the true political power of the North, allowed slavery to defile their own republic; while before the Negro, mastered and sold without his concurrence, they boasted it the highest

prerogative of the white-skinned laborer to sell himself and choose his own master; they were unable to attain the true freedom of labor or to support their European brethren in their struggle for emancipation. (MECW 20: 19–20)

Here, Marx is suggesting that "whiteness" and "freedom" as statuses prevented white workers—and here also in the North—from seeing their class interests more clearly. Recall that the 1869 Fifteenth Amendment to the US Constitution bars denial of suffrage based upon "race, color, or previous condition of servitude." This is of course bound up with the issue of white racism, but here the Radical Reconstructionists who authored the amendment were also careful to single out, with the phrase "previous condition of servitude," the discrimination associated with what we could call slave "status." With all this in mind, I would argue that, for Marx, it is very important that the Roman plebeians' sense of superiority toward the enslaved population, while obviously not based upon race as such, was based upon a kind of status difference that functioned in ways akin to race in the United States. Moreover, in the United States itself, the sense of white racial superiority was bound up with status, with not having been enslaved or descended from slaves.

Finally, there is Marx's 1877 letter to a Russian journal, discussed in chapter 3, in which he again links the class situation in Rome with that of the racialized class relations of the United States. Concerning the Roman plebeians, he writes:

They were originally free peasants, each tilling his own plot on his own behalf. In the course of Roman history, they were expropriated. The same movement that divorced them from their means of production and subsistence involved the formation not only of large, landed property but also of big money capitals. Thus, one fine morning there were, on the one side, free men stripped of everything but their labor-power, and on the other, in order to exploit their labor, owners of all the acquired wealth. What happened? The Roman proletarians became, not wage-laborers, but an idle "mob" more abject than those who used to be called *poor whites* of the southern United States; and what unfolded [*se déploya*] alongside them was not a capitalist but a slave mode of production. (SHN: 136; MEGA2 I/25: 116–17)

Here, the stress is on the Roman plebeians, by now turned into an urban proletariat, but without either ownership of their own means of production or work as wage laborers, for the labor they might have carried out was performed to a great extent by urban slaves.

Putting these passages together, it seems that Marx saw the Roman plebeians as similar in their social and political consciousness to the poor whites of the US South, as well as, though to a lesser extent, to white labor in the North. As mentioned above, I think that, for Marx, animus toward slave "status" on the part of the Roman plebeians operated similarly to the racially charged animus of white labor toward enslaved Black labor in the United States, where "previous condition of servitude" or former slave status was also a key factor. In this sense, something akin to racism was, for Marx, present in the attitudes of the Roman plebeians toward the enslaved population: They took away jobs the plebeians could have performed; they were "servile" in their behavior, something repugnant to the plebeians; they were outsiders for the most part, without Roman "culture." For all these reasons, it was not only a question of "unite and fight" against the aristocracy but also the case that the plebeians would have needed to really acknowledge the vastly worse position of the slaves, and, most importantly, their humanity.

That is of course one side, albeit a very important one, of the relationship between Roman plebeians and slaves. But as Marx stresses, plebeians' hostility and their utter sense of superiority did not solidify all at once, or even in one generation. He seems to indicate that the most serious forms of misdirection of plebeian consciousness occurred over time. The 130s/120s BCE, when the plebeian unrest associated with the Gracchi brothers and the Sicilian and Anatolian slave revolts all took place in the same period, was a period when the plebeian animus toward the enslaved may not yet have fully solidified. This is the other side of the dialectic, the real possibility of solidarity across the lines of free/unfree, just as Marx never stopped hoping for an alliance of Black and white labor in the United States, or of Irish and English workers on the other side of the Atlantic. It is impossible to tell from his notes if the passage Marx excerpts about links through the philosopher Blossius between the Roman proletariat and the Anatolian slaves and serfs, all of them in a state of rebellion against the Roman dominant classes in the late 130s, led him to consider this period as a real opportunity for a radically democratic transformation of Roman society through an alliance of the main oppressed classes.

But even if Marx did consider a combined plebeian/peasant/slave revolt a real possibility in the 130s/120s BCE, it would have been a missed opportunity, albeit a very interesting and important one. Be that as it may, Rome weathered the crisis of the 130s/120s, and in the next century politicians like Julius Caesar and his predecessors, all of them aristocrats, put down the large slave uprising led by Spartacus and destroyed the aristocratic Republic, all the while courting plebeian support to create an Empire that preserved the society's basic class divisions among aristocrats, plebeians, clients, and slaves.

So far, I have examined Marx's Rome notes conceptually rather than chronologically, in the order in which he studied these issues. If they are viewed in the order Marx made the notes, the above interpretation is solidified. The notes begin with Bücher's book on class antagonisms and unrest in the Republic, then move to Friedländer's descriptions of the wealthy upper classes and their clients during the Empire, then to Jhering's accounts of economic decline of plebeians and clients during the Republic and the Empire, and finally, to Lange's study of gender and family law from the earliest days through the late Empire. In this sense, the unrest of the 130s/120s BCE is dealt with and then Marx moves on to the Roman Empire at its zenith, after it had contained the possibility of unrest along similar lines, essentially by bribing the free proletariat and stoking their hostility toward the enslaved population.

In addition, it is important to mention that the Lange notes, by far the longest of those on Rome, cover similar issues to the notes on Morgan on gender relations that were at the center of chapter 2. In this sense, they represent a bridge to the Morgan notes, which Marx apparently began some months after the completion of those on Lange.

Finally, it is also significant that Marx's notes on Rome are interspersed with those on India. As discussed in the introduction, Marx begins to annotate Sewell's chronological study of India, then annotates Bücher, Friedländer, and Jhering. At that point he begins annotating Kovalevsky's anthropological study of Indigenous America and then India, but he goes back to Sewell's book on India before finishing with Kovalevsky on India and then Algeria. The notes on Lange on Roman family and gender relations come after all this. Thus, India is as much at the center of these 1879 notebooks as is Rome.

It is to these notes on India from Kovalevsky and Sewell—plus some later ones from Phear and Maine—that I now turn, in order to examine

Marx's consideration of another great agrarian civilization in flux and change, as it came under British colonial domination.

The Rise and Fall of India's Marathas: Indigenous Resistance to the Mughals and the British

As mentioned above, Marx devotes more words to India than to any other society in the 1879–82 notes on non-Western and precapitalist societies. As discussed in chapter 1, he takes up at great length the evolution of communal social forms in Indian clans and villages, based upon the chapters on India in Kovalevsky's *Communal Landownership*. The Kovalevsky notes do not deal with opposition and resistance very much, however. I took up Marx on Indian resistance to British colonialism in chapter 4, analyzing his notes on Sewell's *Analytical History of India*. These notes focused heavily on the Sepoy Uprising of 1857–59, the largest anti-colonial uprising anywhere until the twentieth century.

In the following pages, I will return to Marx's notes on Sewell's *Analytical History of India* and examine them from another angle, that of Indigenous clan and communal structures as potential loci of rebellion. I will focus on the most important clan-based form of opposition to central authority in the early modern history of India, the Maratha resistance against first the Mughals and then the British, in the two centuries preceding the Sepoy Uprising. Marx's notes on the Maratha resistance, which draw mostly on Sewell, show (1) the power of Indigenous Indian clan structures as loci of resistance; (2) their eventual defeat by the British; and (3) their implicit possibilities for further resistance and rebellion.

The Mughal Empire, first established in 1526 under Babur (r. 1526–30), was the most economically developed and powerful of the precapitalist Indian state forms. Babur, a Turkic warlord who claimed descent from both Genghis Khan and Timur (Tamerlane), entered India from Afghanistan and overthrew the Delhi Sultanate. The Mughals came to power in part via new technology, bringing gunpowder and cannons into India for the first time, while also using older techniques like archery, as illustrated by the following passage from Sewell that Marx incorporates into his notes: "Babur used gunpowder along with arrows; mentions his *mortars*, and *matchlockmen* and *his bowmen*; was himself a fine shot with bow and arrow" (MSW: 30). They conquered most of northern India but were

hampered by dissension among the royal princes and military commanders in the generation after Babur's death.

The Mughal Empire reached its highest point of economic and political power under Akbar (r. 1556–1605), who consolidated power by 1585
over most of northern and central India. Akbar tolerated all major reli-
gions and even fostered debate among them at court, while refraining
from attempts to impose Islam on the largely Hindu population. In this
passage he incorporates from Sewell, Marx sharpens the British historian's characterization of Akbar as "impartial" in matters of religion, making
him "indifferent" [*gleichgültig*[3]] toward religion. For Marx, this would
have been a high compliment:

> Was himself indifferent [*gleichgültig*] in religious matters, therefore toler-
> ant; his chief religious and literary advisers *Faizi* and *Abul Fazl.* Faizi
> translated old Sanskrit poems, including: "*Ramayana*" and "*Mahabharata*"
> (later, after Akbar brought a Roman Catholic Portuguese priest *from Goa*,
> Faizi translates the evangelists [Gospels].) *Indulgence toward the Hindus*;
> Akbar only insisted on *abolition of suttee* (burning of widows on the hus-
> band's funeral pyre), etc. *He abolishes jeziah, i.e., capitation tax,* which every
> Hindu had been *compelled to pay to the Muslim Government.* (MSW: 35)

The jeziah was a particularly touchy issue, as will be seen below once it
was reimposed. In legal matters as well, Akbar refrained from imposing
Sharia law on the Hindu population, as in this passage Marx records from
Sewell: "Akbar reformed the *Code of punishments,* founding them *partly
on Muslim custom, partly on the laws of Manu*" (MSW: 35).

Overall, Marx characterizes Akbar's rule as a high point in Indian
history. In the following passage in his notes, he makes a stronger statement than Sewell, who called Akbar's Delhi "one of the largest and
handsomest in the world" (SW: 54): "Makes *Delhi* into the greatest and
finest city then existing in the world" (MSW: 35).

In the decades after Akbar's death, the Mughals maintained their
power over most of the Indian Subcontinent, as seen under Shah Jahan
(r. 1628–58), famed for having had the Taj Mahal constructed in memory
of his beloved widow. But after Akbar's great-grandson Aurangzeb
(r. 1658–1707) came to power, the policy of tolerance was revoked in

---

3   Could also be translated as "nonchalant."

favor of one that imposed Sharia law on India. This was one of the factors
that led to powerful forms of resistance, most notably on the part of the
Hindu Maratha Confederacy, based in central and southern India, but
chiefly in what is today the western coastal State of Maharashtra.

Aurangzeb's reign also saw the gradual rise of the British East India
Company as a factor in Indian society and politics. The Mughal emperor
largely kept the British in check, limiting them to a number of port cities,
and, on occasion, winning military confrontations with them. But
Aurangzeb's heirs inherited a much-weakened empire, to a great extent
due to Maratha resistance.

Marx notes that the Marathas began to form as an entity in the late
sixteenth century in Bijapur-Ahmadnagar, a Muslim-ruled kingdom in
the Deccan plateau, located in the inland regions of the present-day states
of Maharashtra and Karnataka. This area had held out for many decades
before being incorporated somewhat uneasily into the Mughal Empire. As
Marx records in his notes on Sewell, Malik Amber, an official of the sultanate of Ahmadnagar, led several revolts against the Mughals in the early
seventeenth century. His forces included many local Hindus. By the late
seventeenth century, as Marx records from Sewell, the legendary Maratha
leader Shivaji (ca. 1627/1630–1680) emerges in this borderland region:

> One of *Malik Amber's officers* named *Madhoji Bhonsle* has a son named
> *Shahji*; the latter marries a daughter of *Jadu Rao*, an officer in high
> command; issue of this marriage a son: *Shivaji*; latter always in contact
> with the rude soldiers of his father's "*jagir*" [[or *jaghire*, tract of land
> given by the sovereign to an individual as a reward for special merit]],
> acquires habits of a robber, which he practices early in company of his
> retainers. Seized his father's own territory, captured many forts; then
> begins *open rebellion* by seizing a convoy of imperial treasure; his
> lieutenant takes the *Governor of Konkan* prisoner, occupied the whole
> province with its capital, *Kalyan* [near today's Mumbai]. (MSW: 42)

In this way, the semi-warlord Shivaji moves north, closer to the eastern
coast and the Mughal heartland.

As Marx records further from Sewell, Shivaji comes under attack by an
army led by Shah Jahan's son and future successor, Aurangzeb. At this
juncture, Shivaji exhibits cunning as well as audacity, managing to avoid
repression by the Mughals long enough to gather more strength:

After this success, *Shivaji* makes overtures to Shah Jahan, which are not received unfavorably. He then seizes *South Konkan* and *1655* went on extending his authority. Aurangzeb sent there to humble the pride of the Maratha. Shivaji intrigues and cajoles, forgiven; immediately after departure of the imperial force he repeats his attacks on Bijapur. Afzal Khan, governor of the Province of Bijapur, agrees to—unattended— private interview with Shivaji, who murders him with his own hand, then defeats the Khan's panic-stricken army. (MSW: 42–3)

This victory and humiliation of the Mughals set Shivaji on his future course. But his next move, with Aurangzeb now emperor, really shocks the Mughals, as he seizes briefly their chief port and link to the Middle East, Surat:

1662: Shivaji begins again to ravage Mogul territory. *Aurangzeb* sends against him *Shaista Khan*, who marches from *Aurangabad* to *Poona* and takes it; he stays there in winter quarters throughout the winter; one night Shivaji steals his way to him to murder him; Khan escaped, however. After the rains, *Shaista Khan* to *Aurangabad*, and *Shivaji* at once sacks *Surat*. *1664: Shahji*, father of *Shivaji*, *[died]*, and in right of his father became possessed of *Tanjore* and *Madras*, as well as the *Konkans*, which he himself had conquered. He now assumes the title: "*Rajah of the Marathas*," plunders the country far and wide. (MSW: 43)

As Marx records from Sewell above, Shivaji now controls a vast territory, having become the most formidable Hindu power on the Subcontinent in centuries.

Marx incorporates into his notes Sewell's summary of the Maratha's consolidation of their rule over a large territory, in the face of the weakening of Mughal power under Aurangzeb:

1668 and 1669: Shivaji settles his kingdom; makes advantageous treaties with the Rajputs and other neighbors. 1669: Thus the Marathas a nation, governed by an independent sovereign. 1670: Aurangzeb breaks the treaty; Shivaji first commences operations by seizing Poona, sacks Surat and Khandesh, while Muazzam, Aurangzeb's son, inactive at Aurangabad. Mahabat Khan sent, terribly beaten by Shivaji. Aurangzeb recalls his armies and suspends hostilities. From then on, decline of Aurangzeb's influence; all parties irritated against him; his *Mogul soldiers* furious over his futile Maratha campaigns; *the Hindus, because he renews the "jeziah" and persecutes them on all sides. 1678: Finally he alienates the best warriors of his army, the Rajputs,* by his *conduct toward widow and children* of their great chief: *Rajah Jaswant Singh*, who [died] in *1678. Durga Das*, the rajah's son, plotted with *Prince Akbar*, Aurangzeb's son, marched on Delhi with *70,000 Rajputs*. The combination broken by intrigue and defection, and the army disbanded before any action; *Akbar* and *Durga Das* fled to the *Marathas* under *Sambhaji*, son of the famous *Shivaji*. (MSW: 44)

Marx thus notes that Shivaji's rise coincides with, among other things, the new Emperor Aurangzeb's sectarian renewal of the jeziah, as well as his alienation of his most militarily powerful Hindu allies, the Rajputs.

After Shivaji's death in 1680 the Marathas continue to advance. The following passage Marx records from Sewell marks this period as the real end of the Mughal Empire:

From then on, *Aurangzeb afraid of his own sons*, total suspicion of everyone; his fear becomes: *1687* half madness; without any provocation he shuts up his son *Muazzam* in prison, for seven years. *Fall of the Mogul Empire* dates *from that time*; Deccan in confusion, *the native states were broken up*, country covered with bands of marauders; the *Marathas* were a great power; the *tribes of the North,—Rajputs and Sikhs*—permanently alienated. (MSW: 45)

On the eve of Aurangzeb's death, as Marx records from Sewell:

In the last 4 years of his life whole government disorganized; *Marathas* began to recover their forts and gather strength; a terrible famine exhausted the provisions for the troops and drained the treasury; soldiers mutinous over want of pay; hard pressed by the Marathas *Aurangzeb* retreated in great confusion *to Ahmadnagar*, falls ill, *February 21, 1707, Aurangzeb* [died] at 89. (MSW: 46)

By 1737, Maratha forces were able to threaten Delhi.

As discussed in chapter 3, the Marathas reached the apex of their power in the mid-eighteenth century, but the gigantic 1761 Battle of

Panipat with Afghan invaders under Ahmad Shah Durrani undermined both of these forces from the region, clearing the pathway for British colonialism. As Marx records from Sewell on this point, the "Marathas never recovered from the blow" they received in 1761.

Marx establishes a clear—if brief and almost cryptic—link between his preoccupation with Maratha resistance to both the Mughals and the British and his notes on Kovalevsky's anthropological study of Indian communal structures and clans. Marx does so by slightly bending a passage in Sewell about one of the key Maratha leaders, Raghoba, and his relations with another Maratha group in Gujarat. Sewell's original passage reads:

> In 1774 Raghoba took the field against the Regents and gained a signal victory. But instead of following this up by marching straight to Poonah [Pune], he went off to Burbanpore and then to Guzerat [Gujarat], where he begged for the co-operation of his countrymen the Gwickwar. It happened that at this time the kingdom of Guzerat was suffering under domestic troubles. Govind Rao and Futteh Sing (brothers, sons of Pilaji Gwickwar, the first sovereign), were disputing for the possession of the throne. (SW: 122)

Marx shortens this passage as follows:

> *1774*: *Raghoba* utterly routs the two regents; but instead of marching *on Poona*, he goes to *Burhanpur* and from there to *Gujarat* to ask cooperation of his countryman, the *Gaekwad*. The *House of the Gaekwad* of *Gujarat*: Clan founder [*Stammvater*]: *Pilaji Gaekwad*. (MSW: 83)

Here, Marx alters Sewell's text in an important manner, inserting the term "clan founder" [*Stammvater*[4]] to designate a key Maratha leader, replacing Sewell's term "sovereign." Whereas the latter implies some type of royal or aristocratic status, Marx's term "clan founder" indicates that he believed that the Marathas were part of a clan-based society, a communal social form. This is at variance with the uncritical use of the term "Maratha Empire," language that they themselves used to enhance their prestige but that did not accurately reflect their loose and shifting clan confederation.

---

4   Could also be translated as "clan ancestor."

Marx's reference to a Maratha "clan founder" suggests that he saw the Marathas, at least in part, as an Indigenous, clan-based group that practiced forms of communal solidarity. Two dialectical points emerge here as well. First, while the Mughal Empire constituted the strongest of the precapitalist political and social systems that emerged in India, it was riven with deep contradictions, a major one based upon the fact that as a Muslim dynasty, it ruled over predominantly Hindu populations. This contradiction deepened once the Mughal emperor Aurangzeb revoked Akbar's policy of tolerance in favor of imposing Sharia law, relegating the Hindu majority to a second-class status. Out of this contradiction, and others as well, the Maratha clans grew rapidly as an Indigenous, internal opposition. While the Marathas were ultimately unable to hold together and they certainly lacked a social vision of a better, more egalitarian society, they nonetheless seemed to constitute, at least in Marx's eyes, an internally generated alternative to a centralized, despotic state in the period prior to British hegemony.

A second aspect of this contradiction is that it decisively weakened the Mughal Empire at the very time that British colonialism was beginning to appear on the Indian Subcontinent. Thus, the unresolved struggle between the Marathas and the Mughals, a deep internal contradiction within Indian society, paved the way for the British.

It is also possible, based on Marx's brief evocation of the Marathas as a clan-based society, one that was an important point of resistance to both the Mughals and the British, that he was also ruminating over whether the Marathas could have constituted a progressive force—with communistic tendencies rooted in their egalitarian clan structures. If so, could the Marathas have helped transform India in a positive direction, away from the religious sectarianism of the later Mughals but without conceding anything to British colonialism, which the Marathas also fought against in a determined fashion? These considerations, left implicit by Marx in this brief reference to Maratha clan structures, suggest that he was preoccupied with Indigenous communal forms not only historically and anthropologically, as was Kovalevsky, but also as a political and social factor in contemporary society. And as was taken up in chapter 4, several Marathas emerged as key leaders of the Sepoy Uprising of 1857–59, long after their power had been largely broken by the British.

In the next section of this chapter, on Marx's late writings on Russia, these kinds of issues will be considered anew, based on writings that suggest some real possibilities of positive, emancipatory change—in fact communist possibilities—coming from the communal village structures of another large agrarian empire.

Agrarian Russia: Decay and Regeneration

At this writing, most of Marx's notebooks on Russia during his last years are not yet accessible to scholars. However, it is important to note once again that, while far briefer than those on India, his writings on Russia in his last years that are presently accessible are not confined to notebooks but take the form of letters and draft material in which he is clearly speaking in his own voice—to the dozens of Russian intellectuals and revolutionaries with whom he interacted in person and in correspondence, from the 1840s onward. This gives them a different character than the notes on India and Rome, in that here one can gain a clearer sense of what he was developing from his research on non-Western and precapitalist societies. Finally, throughout his life Marx was preoccupied with the Russian Empire as the major counterrevolutionary power in Europe, a view he never abandoned. What he did abandon over time was his assessment in the early 1850s of the Russian people themselves as lacking in revolutionary consciousness and possibilities. This shift began already in the late 1850s as he wrote about vast peasant unrest and the possibility of a violent social revolution in the wake of Russia's defeat at the hands of Britain, France, and Turkey in the Crimean War of 1853–56.

How did Marx alter his attitude toward Russia in his last years? First, he became even more interested in Russia in the 1870s and, among other things, gained a good reading knowledge of the Russian language. To his great surprise, the 1872 Russian translation of *Capital* was published before the French (1872–75) or English (1887, after his death) editions, one cause of his intensified interest. In addition, the Russian edition generated more debate inside Russia than had the two German editions (1867 and 1872–73) inside Germany. Marx engaged the debate over *Capital* in Russia at some length in his postface to the second German edition.

Second, Marx may have believed that the defeat of the Paris Commune and the collapse a few years later of the First International were indications that Western Europe was entering a quiescent period, after the more progressive and revolutionary years 1861–71, which saw the Civil War in the United States, the Polish uprising of 1863, the founding of the International, and then the Paris Commune of 1871. This may have led him to concentrate his attention upon revolutionary possibilities in Russia, as well as other agrarian societies outside the core capitalist countries of Western Europe and North America.

As Marx reports in an 1877 letter, discussed previously, intended for the Russian journal *Otechestvennye Zapiski* (Notes of the Fatherland) as a response to his critics: "In order to reach an informed judgment on Russia's economic development, I learned Russian and then for many years studied official and other publications" (SHN: 135). As taken up in chapter 3, in this letter and his other late writings on Russia, Marx is at pains to refute the notion that he has developed a unilinear theory of historical development according to which Russia was bound to follow the pathway of Britain from a premodern agrarian to a modern society. As also discussed previously, he writes, "The chapter on primitive accumulation claims no more than to trace the path by which, in Western Europe, the capitalist economic order emerged from the entrails of the feudal economic order" (SHN: 135; MEGA2 I/25: 115), after which he quotes a key passage in the 1872–75 French edition of *Capital* that had not been included in the Russian edition:

> But the basis of this whole development is the expropriation of the cultivators. *So far, it has been carried out in a radical manner only in England . . . But all the countries of Western Europe are going through the same development.* (SHN:135; MEGA2 I/25: 115–16)[5]

This 1877 letter, dated as late October or November (MEGA2 I/25: 655), has survived only in the form of Marx's handwritten draft in French found among his papers after his death by Engels. Engels sent it to Vera Zasulich along with his own letter of March 7, 1884, writing, "It bears the stamp of a piece done for publication in Russia, but he never sent it to Petersburg for fear that the mere mention of his name might compromise the existence of the review which published his reply" (MECW 47:112–13). Thereupon, it was published in Russian (1886) and German (1887), but promptly forgotten, as it—like the passage in the French edition of

---

5   See also see also Marx, *Le Capital. Livre I.* Sections V-VIII, pp. 168, 169; MEGA2 II/7: 634.

Capital, which was similarly ignored in the German, English, and other editions of the book—contradicted the essentially unilinear perspectives of most post-Marx Marxists.

As discussed in chapter 3, Marx's 1877 letter is concerned mainly with refuting the notion of unilinear determinism in the sense of Russia being destined inevitably to follow the pathway of Western Europe, which would have meant uprooting the peasantry and beginning the road toward capitalism by way of the primitive accumulation of capital. Here, Marx poses the alternative for Russia at a very general level:

> I have come to this conclusion: If Russia continues to develop along the pathway it has followed since 1861 it will lose the finest chance ever offered to a people in order to suffer [*pour subir*] all the inevitable vicissitudes [*péripéties fatales*] of the capitalist regime. (SHN: 135; MEGA2 I/25: 115)

In short, Marx believes that Russia has a real chance to avoid capitalism, which at this juncture was only lapping at its edges. Were Russia to enter the capitalist mode of production, however, it would then be subject to the harsh laws of capitalism, as he warns: "Once brought into the fold of the capitalist regime, she will suffer under [*en subira*] its pitiless laws like other profane peoples" (SHN: 135; MEGA2 I/25: 116).

Missing here is any discussion of the means by which Russia might avoid such a fate. As is shown by the next round of Marx's writings on Russia, his drafts for an 1881 letter to Vera Zasulich, this could only come about through a Russian revolution. Since the 1877 letter was intended for publication in a journal subject to Tsarist censorship and its editors were under a constant risk of political repression, Marx probably decided to abstain from the language of revolution, even by implication. No such strictures applied to his letter to Vera Zasulich, in exile in Switzerland by 1881.

One element running through Marx's late writings on Russia is the non-identity between Russia's agrarian social relations and those of Western European feudalism, as discussed in chapter 3. And as seen above, in the 1877 letter, he notes that his discussion of primitive accumulation only traces the route from feudalism to capitalism in Western Europe. In the latter, communal social relations once existed but capitalism did not arise from their dissolution, as he writes in his 1881 drafts for the Zasulich letter:

First of all, in Western Europe, the death of communal property [and the emergence] and the birth of capitalist production are separated by a huge interval which covers a whole series of successive economic revolutions and evolutions, of which capitalist production is but [the last] the most recent. (SHN:100; MEGA2 I/25: 232)

In short, the earlier agrarian communal social relations evolved into feudalism over many centuries in Western Europe, and only afterward did the process of negating feudalism in favor of capitalism truly begin. Nowhere had capitalism developed directly out of communal social relations.

Under British colonialism, that development was beginning to transpire in India, but Russian society possessed two strengths that gave it a better chance at a positive alternative to capitalism. First came Russia's strong geopolitical position and social cohesion within a system of communal agrarian relations centered on the *artel* or work cooperative:

Russia is the only European country in which the "agricultural commune" has maintained itself on a national scale up to the present day. It is not, like the East Indies, the prey of a conquering foreign power . . . On the one hand, communal land ownership allows it directly and gradually to transform fragmented, individualist agriculture into collective agriculture and the Russian peasants already practice it on the undivided prairies; the physical configuration of the land makes it suitable for large-scale mechanized cultivation; the peasant's familiarity with the *artel* relationship [*contrat d'artel*] can help him to make the transition from labor on particular parcels of land [*travail parcellaire*] to cooperative labor; and, finally, Russian society, which has for so long lived at his expense, owes him the credits required for such a transition. (SHN: 110; MEGA2 I/25: 224–25)

Thus, its non-colonial position gave Russia more room to maneuver than India, while its agrarian communal forms encompassed wide swathes of territory and population.

Characteristically, Marx refrains at this point from advocating anything like a Maoist type of autarky for Russia, or what Stalin was to call "socialism in one country"—quite the contrary. This leads to his second point concerning Russia's connections to the outside world:

Nor does it live in isolation from the modern world . . . On the other hand, the contemporaneity of Western [capitalist] production, which dominates the world market, enables Russia to build into the commune all the positive achievements of the capitalist system, without having to pass under its Caudine Forks.[6] (SHN: 110; MEGA2 I/25: 224, 225)

He details these possibilities at another point in the drafts:

Did Russia have to undergo a long Western-style incubation of mechanical industry before it could make use of machinery, steam-ships, railways, etc.? Let them also explain how they managed to introduce, in the twinkling of an eye, that whole machinery of exchange (banks, credit companies, etc.) which was the work of centuries in the West. (SHN: 106; MEGA2 I/25: 220)

Why then, he implies, must Russia reinvent and be subjected to the primitive accumulation of capital?

In yet another passage in his drafts, Marx connects these two points together with greater determinacy:

My answer is that, thanks to the unique combination of circumstances in Russia, the rural commune, which is still established on a national scale, may gradually shake off its primitive characteristics and directly develop as an element of collective production on a national scale. Precisely because it is contemporaneous with capitalist production, the rural commune may appropriate all its *positive achievements* without undergoing its hideous vicissitudes [*péripéties affreuses*]. Russia does not live in isolation from the modern world; still less is it prey to a conquering foreign power, like the East Indies. (SHN: 106; MEGA2 I/25: 219–220)

This passage suggests an alternative, non-capitalist pathway of develop-ment rather than integration into global capitalism.

Marx also connects his discussions of Russia to his notes on Morgan on Indigenous American and ancient communes. He seems to view

---

6 "Caudine Forks" refers to a humiliation imposed upon a defeated army of the early Roman Republic.

Morgan's book not only as a major contribution but also as a sign of the times, in the sense that even a non-socialist scholar was discussing the transcendence of modern capitalist social relations:

> In short, the rural commune finds [modern capitalist society] in a state of crisis that will end only when the social system is eliminated through the return of modern societies to the "archaic" type of communal property, a form which, in the words of an American writer who, supported in his work by the Washington government, is not at all to be suspected of revolutionary tendencies, "the new system" to which modern society is tending "will be a revival, in a higher form, of an archaic social type." We should not, then, be too frightened by the word "archaic." (SHN: 107; MEGA2 I/25: 220)

This passage in the Zasulich draft is surely connected to a similar one in Marx's notes on Morgan, composed not long before this and that I discussed in chapter 1:

> The termination of a career of which property is the end and aim; because such a career contains the elements of self-destruction . . . It [a higher plan of society] will be a revival, in a higher form, of the liberty, equality and fraternity of the ancient gentes [clans]. (EN: 139; MG: 552)

All of this assumes that the Russian village commune would be able to sustain itself, at least for a while. This was by no means guaranteed, a point Marx also makes in the drafts of the letter to Zasulich, writing that "the present situation of the commune is no longer tenable" (SHN: 116; MEGA2 I/25: 228). He sums up the dangers facing the Russian village commune as follows: "What threatens the life of the Russian commune is neither a historical inevitability nor a theory; it is state oppression, and exploitation by capitalist intruders whom the state has made powerful at the peasants' expense" (SHN: 104–5; MEGA2 I/25: 233).

Moreover, these kinds of pressures would open the way to the elimination of the communes, which need not happen in the manner of English primitive accumulation of capital to succeed in its destructive purpose:

> In order to expropriate the agricultural producers, it is not necessary to drive them from the land, as happened in England and elsewhere; nor

to abolish communal property by a ukase. If you go and take from the peasants more than a certain proportion of the product of their agricultural labor, then not even your gendarmes and your army will enable you to tie them to their fields. In the last years of the Roman Empire some provincial decurions, not peasants but actual landowners, fled their homes, abandoned their land, and even sold themselves into bondage—all in order to be rid of a property that had become nothing more than an official pretext for exerting quite merciless pressure over them. (SHN: 114; MEGA2 I/25: 226)

Again, Marx indicates the relationship of his studies of Rome to those of Russia, as a way of illustrating the variety of historical possibilities facing Russia, versus the unilinear interpretation of an English-style primitive accumulation of capital as its inevitable future. In the above example, however, a multilinear development would not end in a liberatory manner, any more than in the fate of the free Roman peasantry.

Marx details the threats facing Russia's village communes at an empirical level at the historical juncture of the early 1880s. As mentioned above, the threat is twofold, coming from both capital and the state:

Leaving aside all questions of a more or less theoretical nature, I do not have to tell you that the very existence of the Russian commune is now threatened by a conspiracy of powerful interests. A certain type of capitalism, fostered by the state at the peasants' expense, has loomed up [s'est dressé] against the commune; it is in its interest to destroy it [il a l'intérêt de l'écraser]. It is also in the interest of the landowners to develop the more or less well-off peasants into an agricultural middle class, and to transform the poor peasants—that is, the mass of them— into mere wage laborers. This means cheap labor! How can a commune resist, ground down [broyée] as it is by state exactions, plundered by trade, exploited by landowners, and undermined from within by usury! (SHN: 104; MEGA2 I/25: 234)

As Marx stresses, while state despotism would have been a long-standing problem, the penetration of capital into rural Russia is a new and dangerous phenomenon, especially since the state is working in tandem with it.

Here, Marx is also attacking the notion that communal social forms wither away spontaneously as societies progress and develop. He underlines this in a remark about India and his intellectual antagonist Maine. As discussed in chapter 1, Marx castigates the British anthropologist in notes taken in spring 1881, a few months after the Zasulich letter, for writing of the disappearance of the Indian communal villages as a natural process, whereas British colonialism was in reality the main engineer of this outcome. Here in the drafts for the Zasulich letter, Marx writes: "As regards the East Indies, for example, everyone except Sir H. Maine and those of his ilk are aware that the suppression of communal property was nothing but an act of English vandalism which drove the indigenous population backward rather than forward" (SHN: 118; MEGA2 I/25: 234). In another passage, Marx is more emphatic:

> One has to be on guard when reading the histories of primitive communities written by bourgeois authors. They do not even shrink from falsehoods. Sir Henry Maine, for example, who was an enthusiastic collaborator of the English government in carrying out its violent destruction of the Indian communes, hypocritically assures us that all of the government's noble efforts to maintain the communes succumbed to the spontaneous power of economic laws! (SHN: 107; MEGA2 I/25: 230)

These passages also offer evidence that Marx was connecting his studies of Russia to those of India.

In an earlier passage in these drafts, cited above, Marx stresses the discontinuity between India and Russia, which was "not, like the East Indies, the prey of a conquering foreign power" (SHN: 110; MEGA2 I/25: 224). Sometimes too much has been made of the latter passage. Even Paresh Chattopadhyay, an astute theorist who took the late writings on Russia most seriously, viewed them as something of an exception, arguing that for Marx, Russia had nothing in common with India in terms of revolutionary possibilities based upon communal social forms in the villages.[7] Few would hold to Chattopadhyay's position today, now that the 1879–82 notebooks have become better known. As Saito writes more recently, "There is no need to limit the argument to Russia. The same logic can be applied to other agrarian communes existing in those

---

7   Paresh Chattopadhyay, "Passage to Socialism: The Dialectic of Progress in Marx," *Historical Materialism* 14:3 (2006), pp. 45–84.

areas that Marx intensively studied at the time in Asia, Africa, and Latin America."[8]

As to the Russian commune itself and its positive and negative future prospects, Marx points to a "dualism" within the commune. This occurs in a passage from an earlier draft of the Zasulich letter, but which in this later version makes the dialectical structure of Marx's argument visible:

[The] Russian rural commune . . . conceals an inner [*intime*] dualism which, given certain historical conditions, may bring on its ruin. Property in land is communal, but each peasant cultivates and works his field on his own account, like the small Western peasant. The combination of communal property and small-plot cultivation, useful in more distant times, becomes dangerous in our own epoch. On the one hand movable possession [*avoir*], playing an ever more important role in agriculture itself, gradually differentiates the fortunes [*la fortune*] of the commune members in terms of wealth and gives rise to a conflict of interests, above all under the fiscal pressure of the state; on the other hand, the economic superiority of communal property—as the basis of co-operative and combined labor—is lost. But it should not be forgotten that the Russian peasants already practice the collective mode in the cultivation of their undivided prairies; that their familiarity with the *artel* relationship could greatly facilitate their transition from small-plot to collective farming; that the physical configuration of the Russian land makes it suitable for large-scale and combined machine farming; and finally, that Russian society, having for so long lived at the expense of the rural commune, owes it the initial funds required for such a change. What is involved, of course, is only a gradual change that would begin by creating normal conditions for the commune on its *present* basis. (SHN: 104; MEGA2 I/25: 233–34)

Notably, this dualism was rooted not only in external factors like state and capitalist pressures but also in the very structure of the Russian communes themselves.

In a still later draft, Marx restates some of the above but with a greater focus on communal labor relations than property relations. Here, he highlights dualities within communal production relations:

---

8 Saito, *Marx in the Anthropocene*, p. 196.

Clearly, the *dualism* inherent in the constitution of the agrarian commune was able to endow it with a vigorous life. Emancipated from the strong yet narrow ties of natural kinship, the communal land ownership and resulting social relations provided a solid foundation; while at the same time, the house and yard as an individual family preserve, together with farming based upon small parcels of land and private appropriation of its fruits, fostered individuality to an extent incompatible with the framework of the more primitive communities. It is no less evident, however, that this very dualism could eventually turn into the seeds of disintegration. Apart from all the malignant outside influences, the commune bore noxious elements within its own womb [*flanc*]. As we have seen, private landownership had already crept into the commune in the shape of a house with its own country-yard that could become a stronghold for an attack upon communal land. But the key factor was labor on parcels of land [*travail parcellaire*, that is, on individual parcels] as source of private appropriation. It gave rise to the accumulation of movable goods such as livestock, money, and sometimes even slaves or serfs. Such movable property, not subject to communal control, open to individual trading in which there was plenty of scope for trickery and chance, came to weigh ever more heavily upon the entire rural economy. Here was the dissolver of primitive economic and social equality. It introduced heterogeneous elements into the commune, provoking conflicts of interest and passion liable to erode communal ownership first of the cultivable land, and then of the forests, pastures, wasteland, etc., which, once converted into *communal subsidiaries* [*annexes communales*] of private property, will also fall in the long run. (SHN: 120; MEGA2 I/25: 237–38)

In this dialectical framework calling attention to internal "dualism," outside influences are minimized, but with internally generated contradictions emerging as more central to Marx's analysis. At this juncture, Marx's argument about the Russian commune connects to that concerning the decline of clan-based communal forms in the notes on Morgan that I discussed in chapter 1, where he saw the clans as being weakened by incipient class divisions between leaders and masses.

Ultimately though, Marx writes that Russia will need a revolution to preserve the commune in a positive sense:

To save the Russian commune, a Russian Revolution is necessary. For their part, the Russian government and the "new pillars of society" are doing their best to prepare the masses for such a catastrophe. If the revolution takes place in time, if it concentrates all its forces to ensure the unfettered rise of the rural commune, the latter will soon develop as a regenerating element of Russian society and an element of superiority over the countries enslaved by the capitalist regime. (SHN:116–17; MEGA2 I/25: 230)

I will discuss Marx on the possibility of a Russian revolution on this basis in the next chapter.

6

New Concepts of Revolutionary Change and of Alternatives to Capitalism

This chapter will draw some conclusions about new concepts of revolution Marx was developing in his last years. If one accepts the argument that he was normally not engaged in pure economic or historical research but was most interested in uncovering the structures of capitalism and the forces of liberation arrayed against it, then it is hard to see his concern with agrarian, colonized, and Indigenous societies during his last years as pure research. Thus, I have argued that Marx, throughout his life, continued to focus on the forces of resistance and liberation, the revolutionary subjects, that grew inside and alongside modern capitalist society, even as he analyzed the structures of that mode of production.

The three new concepts of revolution Marx sketched in his last years centered on (1) colonialism, ethnicity, and the working class in Ireland, Britain, and France; (2) communism and abolition of the state in the programs of socialist groups and in the Paris Commune; and (3) revolution in the Russian communal village in relation to the Western European working class. He develops these new concepts of revolution and, to a degree, of the alternative to capitalism, only briefly, but with sufficient detail to allow us to discern at least some of the new directions in his thinking in his last years. While he never moves away from the Western proletariat as a key force of revolutionary change, by 1869–82, he sees its relationship to the peripheries of capitalism and to the state in new ways. Not only does he pose the modern state alongside capitalism itself as the enemy of human liberation in a new manner, but he now sees revolutionary change in Western Europe emanating from the periphery—in the cases of Ireland and Russia—and moving to the core. This reverses the directionality of revolutionary change in his earlier writings, such as the *Communist Manifesto*, in which he and Engels maintained that the "advanced" industrially developed West would also develop the most advanced radical revolutionary ferment, and then spread it outward to the peripheries of capitalism. In addition, whereas in the 1850s he scorned the collectivism of communal villages in Russia and India as socially stagnant formations that blocked economic progress and undergirded "Oriental despotism," by now he was defending those social forms and the people living under them as important allies of the European industrial working classes. He also saw, within limits of course, the compatibility of these precapitalist communal social forms with the communist aspirations of the modern working class.

Let us begin with Marx's "classic" concept of revolution, the notion of a united working-class uprising that forms the conclusion to his major work, *Capital*, Vol. I. In text kept with few alterations from the 1867 edition, he writes of working-class revolution. In the penultimate chapter, "The Historical Tendency of Capitalist Accumulation," he describes a revolution in an industrially developed capitalist society similar to Britain in his own day.

> Along with the constant decrease in the number of capitalist magnates, who usurp and monopolize all the advantages of this process of transformation, the mass of misery, oppression, slavery, degradation and exploitation grows; but with this there also grows the revolt of the working class, a class constantly increasing in numbers and trained, united and organized by the very mechanism of the capitalist process of production. (CAP: 929)

Here, the development of the productive forces and, concomitantly, a united working class "become incompatible with their capitalist integument," which "is burst asunder." Next comes the death knell of "capitalist [private]¹ property," in which the "expropriators are expropriated" and the workers establish a democratic, communist system. This, he adds,

---

1   In an important change in the 1872–75 French edition, the word "private" is removed.

forms "the negation of the negation," an evocation of his overall dialectical framework rooted in Hegel (CAP: 929).

In this conclusion to *Capital*, Marx is writing at a high level of abstraction, and necessarily so.[2] There is nothing wrong with this, as it gets at the whole, the totality, in a unique way, showing capitalism as not only an all-encompassing system of domination but also as one riven with contradictions so total and deep that they are threatening to break out in a revolution that would constitute both the negation of capitalism and its second negation, the establishment of communism by the proletariat.

At the same time, one needs to particularize this kind of universalist theorization once one steps into the concrete analysis of any given society or region at any given time. Thus, that rigorously dialectical though necessarily very abstract model does not deal directly with race, colonialism, gender, the state, or other concrete factors discussed in some of Marx's other writings on revolution.[3] Along these lines he concretizes his concept of revolution in new ways in his last years.

Ireland and the Wider European Revolution: Interplay of Ethnicity, Nationalism, Colonialism, and Class

According to the last section of the chapter in *Capital* on the "General Law of the Accumulation of Capital," Ireland was the victim of a particularly ruthless capitalist form of colonialism, resulting in very bitter class conflicts, especially between British landlords and Irish peasants. These divisions threatened to weaken Britain as a world power.

During 1869–70, after completing the first German edition of *Capital*, Marx works out a theory of a European-wide revolution focusing on Ireland, Britain, and France, which intertwines peasant and worker, and landlord and capitalist. He shows that anti-Irish prejudice weakens and

---

2   As Bertell Ollman shows in *Dialectical Investigations* (New York: Routledge, 1993), Marx writes at different levels of abstraction, which might include capitalism as a whole but also particular levels such as a single capitalist society or a group of them.

3   Elsewhere, I have shown that despite the abstract character of these concluding pages of *Capital*, hints of these other factors, and sometimes more, appear in the book's earlier chapters: "Five Explicit and Implicit Notions of Revolution in *Capital* I, as Seen from a Multilinear, Peripheral Angle," *Marx's Capital after 150 Years: Critique and Alternative to Capitalism*, ed. Marcello Musto (New York: Routledge, 2019), pp. 197–207.

divides the British working class, but that the super-oppression of the Irish peasant could spark an agrarian revolution that spilled over into Britain, the center of global capitalism. This, in conjunction with a revolutionary outbreak on the Continent, most likely in France, would be a pathway leading to a European revolution.

Because the new concept of revolution arose directly from Marx's participation in the First International, some of that context is important, not least because this key text on revolution constituted not only a theoretical argument but also a political and organizational intervention intended to affect the labor, nationalist, and revolutionary movements of the time. Marx's brief but very significant theorization of revolution was the product of a subcommittee, other members besides Marx unknown, of the London-based General Council (GC) of the First International. The subcommittee met on January 1, 1870, to issue a response to attacks on the GC over Ireland and other issues by a Bakunin-led faction of the International based in Geneva. Half of their letter, which runs about 2,400 words total, is taken up with the new theory of revolution with Ireland at its center, with the other half dealing with Bakunin's objections to the GC's authority over the sections. Written in French and authored by Marx, it has been known as the "Confidential Communication."

In the weeks leading up to the Confidential Communication, the GC debated and approved in November 1869 a very strong resolution supporting Irish political prisoners, something that gained the International both publicity and notoriety in a society deeply prejudiced against the Irish and fearful of the insurrectionary Fenian movement that over the past several years had been convulsing Ireland and Britain. Marx refers in a passage—crossed out and not included in the letter actually sent—to "difficulties and even personal dangers that face General Council members who take such a stand," that is, come out publicly in support of Ireland (MECW 21: 89). These difficulties emanated not only from hostile accounts in the London *Times* and other establishment organs but also from sections of the British trade union movement and some newspapers associated with them. Probably most galling of all to Marx was the polemical attack by the Bakunin faction from within the International itself.

Nonetheless, Marx evidently thought that the resolution on Ireland and the Confidential Communication offered an important basis for solidarity between British and Irish workers, thus uniting the best-organized part of the international working class—the English workers and their trade unions, who formed a core part of the International—and one of Europe's most revolutionary and oppressed working class and peasant sectors, the Irish masses, both in Ireland and abroad. As he stated at a meeting of the GC, referring to two parts of the working classes that had difficulty uniting, the resolution "may bring the English and the Irish together" (MECW 21: 411–12).

This would impact not only the European class struggle but also the situation in the US, as he writes to two German members of the International in New York, also conveying the contents of the Confidential Communication:

> You have wide field in America for work along the same lines. *A coalition of the German workers with the Irish workers* (and of course also with the English and American workers who are prepared to accede to it) is the greatest achievement you could bring about now. This must be done in the name of the International. The social significance of the Irish question must be made clear. (Letter to Meyer and Vogt, April 9, 1870, MECW 43: 476)

Not only was Marx theorizing the relationship of Irish workers to the labor, nationalist, socialist, and revolutionary movements, but he was also developing a position on Ireland and Britain that would be able to expand the International's base among Irish workers, who, along with their country's more revolutionary intellectuals, were engaged in the most militant anti-systemic struggles anywhere at the time. This was nothing easy or automatic, for in the US, both German immigrant and US-born workers tended to look down on the Irish, who, in turn, distrusted them, even their socialist sectors. As the Italian political theorist Mario Piccinini notes, for Marx here, it is also strategy that is at stake, for "it is not a question of putting together the pieces of a puzzle, but of setting forces in motion."[4]

---

4   Mario Piccinini, "England as the Metropolis of Capital: Marx, the International and the Working Class," in *Global Marx: History and Critique of the Social Movement in the World Market,* ed. Matteo Battistini, Eleonora Cappuccilli, and Maurizio Ricciardi (Leiden: Brill Publishers, 2022), p. 238.

While this organizational and political context is important, it should not overshadow the theoretical originality of what amounts to an essay on the European revolution, which not only breaks new ground but still speaks to us today on issues often considered under the term "intersectionality."

Let us turn directly, therefore, to the text of the Confidential Communication of January 1, 1870. First, Marx writes that the wider European revolution would likely start in France, and so he gives this matter only half a sentence: "Although revolutionary initiative will probably come from France . . ." (MECW 21: 86).[5] The economy of language here is telling. Evidently, given 1789, 1830, and 1848, such an assumption was so widespread that there was no need for further elaboration. In this sense, Marx was repeating what was obvious to his comrades. But, in retrospect, it is also telling that another major French revolutionary uprising, the Paris Commune of March 18, 1871, was just over the horizon.

Marx finishes the sentence by moving from political to economic and class issues: "England alone can serve as the lever for a serious economic Revolution" (MECW 21:86). He details this point as follows:

It is the only country where there are no more peasants and where landed property is concentrated in a few hands. It is the only country where *the capitalist form*, that is to say, combined labor on a large scale under the authority of capitalists [*des maîtres capitalistes*], has seized hold of almost the whole of production. It is the only country where the *vast majority of the population consists of wage laborers*. It is the only country where the class struggle and the organization of the working class by *trade unions* have acquired a certain degree of maturity and universality. Because of its domination of the world market, it is the only country where any revolution in economic matters will have an immediate effect on the entire world. If landlordism and capitalism have a classic place in this country, their ricochet means [*par contre-coup*] that the *material conditions* for *their destruction* are also the most mature here. (MECW 21: 86–7)

---

5   Although I reference the most accessible version of the Confidential Communication in MECW, I have often altered the translation based upon the French original in "Le Conseil Générale au Conseil Fédérale de la Suisse romande," *General Council of the First International. Minutes, 1868–1870* (Moscow: Progress Publishers, 1966), pp. 354–63.

The word "ricochet" above could also be translated as "their destruction," but my use of the more literal "ricochet" may convey better that for Marx this is a dialectical process, that the very strength and size of the capitalist system in Britain and Ireland mean that its contradictions, which could easily "ricochet" back upon the system, would also be of huge power and consequence. He adds that "England is the metropolis of capital" (MECW 21: 87).

Thus, while Marx is shifting the angle of his revolutionary gaze to Ireland and the Irish workers inside Britain, he is by no means writing off the English workers, a powerful and growing social class, and one that has also succeeded more than elsewhere in organizing itself. As he wrote only three years earlier in the first edition *Capital*, Vol. I, in reference to the struggle for a shorter working day, "The English factory workers were the champions, not only of the English working class but of the modern working class in general" (CAP: 413). Moreover, as he now writes, the GC, with so many trade union leaders among its members, has a chance to push things forward because "it is in the happy position of having its hand directly on this important lever of the proletarian revolution" (MECW 21: 87).

By no means, however, is this a flawless or exemplary revolutionary class ready to burst out in revolution at the appropriate time: "While the English have all the material necessities for social revolution, the spirit of generalization and a revolutionary passion are lacking" (MECW 21: 87). However, the GC is pushing them toward a better direction, "into revolutionary socialism" (MECW 21: 87).

One crucially important aspect of this turns around the International's relation to the Irish revolutionary movement. Ireland is a weak point wherein British landlords and capitalists, the two principal wings of the ruling class, can be attacked most effectively:

> In the first place, Ireland is the *bulwark* of English landlordism. If it fell in Ireland, it would fall in England. In Ireland this is a hundred times easier because *the economic struggle there is concentrated exclusively on landed property*, because this struggle is at the same time national, and because the people there are more revolutionary and more infuriated than in England. Landlordism in Ireland is maintained solely by *the English army*. The moment the *forced Union* between the two countries ends, a social revolution will immediately break out in Ireland, though in *backward* forms. (MECW 21: 87–8)

Thus, the "normal" class struggle between peasant or tenant and land-lord in Ireland is enhanced because of the "national" element, wherein English landlords represent an outside, colonial power, as well as part of an exploitative ruling class. Their power, and that of the dominant classes inside Ireland more generally, relies less on any kind of political or cultural legitimacy than on sheer military force, with revolution ready to burst out the moment such force weakens. Moreover, as Marx writes elsewhere, the aristocratic landowning classes, in both Britain and Ireland, are more reactionary than the industrial bourgeoisie. In addi-tion, as he knows well, the sons of the landowning classes form much of the officer corps of the military, crucial not only for colonial rule in Ireland and the rest of the British Empire but also for the defense of capital and the state in Britain itself in case of an internal, class-based uprising or revolution. And, in this regard, Ireland is both external and internal to Britain, so intertwined were the two societies.

The current upsurge in the Irish revolutionary movement, and the support it is gaining among British workers and intellectuals, is already weakening the power of the landlord class and encouraging revolution. Thus, English landlordism in Ireland is a double-edged sword. Ever the dialectician, Marx bifurcates this social relationship as follows: in "normal" times it is a factor that strengthens class rule in both Britain and Ireland, while in revolutionary times its deep contradictions, which include nationalist grievances, not only express but exacerbate the "normal" class struggle. Implicit here is also the notion that a revolution in Ireland would spread into Britain as well.

A second and equally crucial aspect of this theorization of revolution is the presence of a large Irish immigrant subproletariat inside England, many of them famine refugees, through which an Irish revolution would spread to England. In "normal" times, however, the presence in England of Irish workers, and the quasi-racist antagonism they face from their English coworkers, has a different effect. As with English landlordism in Ireland, this serves to strengthen and even stabilize the rule of capital over labor in England:

In the second place, the English bourgeoisie has not only exploited Irish poverty and suffering [*la misère irlandaise*] to keep down the working class in England by *forced immigration* of impoverished Irishmen, but it has also divided the proletariat into two hostile camps . . . *In all the big industrial centers in England*, there is profound antagonism between the Irish proletarian and the English proletarian. The common [*vulgaire*] English worker hates the Irish worker as a competitor who lowers wages and the *standard of life*. (MECW 21: 88)

So far, this could have been about "divisions" between two parts of the working class, who would need to, as the venerable socialist slogan goes, "unite and fight."

But Marx's critique runs deeper than that, as he compares the attitude of English workers to racism in the US context. This quasi-racism does not appear entirely spontaneously but is stirred up by the dominant classes. Marx continues on the English worker, who is victim of bourgeois propaganda about the Irish:

He feels national and religious antagonism toward him. He views him similarly to how the poor whites of the Southern states of North America viewed the Black slaves. This antagonism among the proletarians of England themselves is artificially nourished and kept up by the bourgeoisie. It knows that this split is the true secret of the preservation of its power. (MECW 21: 88)

In his subsequent letter to New York comrades reiterating these points, Marx indicates some of the mechanisms involved: "This antagonism is artificially kept alive by the press, the pulpit, the comic papers, in short, by all the means at the disposal of the ruling classes." (Letter to Meyer and Vogt, April 9, 1870, MECW 43: 476). He is evidently referring not only to widespread anti-Catholic bias and legal strictures but also to popular illustrated magazines like *Punch* that were portraying Irish people with ape-like features, as they did with Black people.

This, especially the remark about "poor whites of the Southern states of North America," is, of course, linked to Marx's writings a few years earlier on the Civil War in the US. He summed up the war's lessons in terms of race and class in *Capital*: "In the United States of America, every independent workers' movement was paralyzed as long as slavery disfigured a part of the republic. Labor in a white skin cannot emancipate itself where it is branded in a black skin" (CAP: 414). He states the same point less fervently in the Confidential Communication: "A people that subjugates another people forges its own chains" (MECW 21: 89). It is clear that he is arguing not for any kind of bothsidesism, with both the English and the Irish equally at fault for the divisions inside the working class, but for the notion of an English quasi-racism toward the Irish as the key factor in that division.

Of course, Marx concedes that Irish workers felt antagonism and suspicion toward their English counterparts, but this was a response to a history of condescension and worse, as he notes in the version of the argument he sends to his New York comrades: "The Irishman pays him back with interest in his own money. He sees in the English worker both the accomplice and the stupid tool of *English rule in Ireland*" (Letter to Meyer and Vogt, April 9, 1870, MECW 43: 475).

He adds this pungent remark, also in the letter to his New York comrades: "This antagonism is the secret of the English working class's impotence, despite its organization," referring to its having birthed the world's largest-by-far trade union movement to date (MECW 43: 476). Again, Ireland is, to Marx, a question of paramount importance.

Recall, as discussed in chapter 3, that Marx had written to Engels a few months earlier, on December 10, 1869, concerning his change of position on the directionality of revolution in Britain and Ireland:

> For a long time, I believed it would be possible to overthrow the Irish regime by English working class ascendancy. I always took this viewpoint in the *New York Tribune*. Deeper study has now convinced me of the opposite. The English working class will never accomplish anything before it has got rid of Ireland. The lever must be applied in Ireland. This is why the Irish question is so important for the social movement in general. (MECW 43: 398)

Viewing the last two sentences above in the context of the Confidential Communication, it is evident that Marx is pointing to an incipient social revolution in Ireland, or at least a great uprising there, as the forerunner or vanguard of a possible revolution in Britain.

In this sense, Ireland is not a side issue, let alone one of human rights or democracy alone, but a central factor in the wider European revolution, as important as France. Below are two versions of the argument with a slightly stronger one in the private letter to his New York comrades:

Thus, the position of the International Association with regard to the Irish question is very clear. Its first concern is to advance the social revolution in England. To this end the great blow must be struck in Ireland. (Confidential Communication, Jan. 1, 1870, MECW 21: 89)

After studying the Irish question for years I have come to the conclusion that the decisive blow against the ruling classes in England (and this is decisive for the workers movement all over the world) cannot be struck in England but in Ireland. (Letter to Meyer and Vogt, April 9, 1870, MECW 43: 473)

We have here a complex dialectic of revolution, which recognizes nations and ethnic sectors, which is truly international, and which sees the revolution in a many-sided manner. Summing up:

1. France will probably spark the revolution but, unlike Britain, it is too underdeveloped economically to have a large enough working class to win against global capitalism.

2. Irish peasants will also step in at the beginning, challenging both landlordism and colonialism in their pro-independence and anti-landlord struggle.

3. This will weaken the position of the British ruling classes, since landlords stand alongside capitalists as one of the two major wings of the ruling classes; moreover, the sons of aristocratic landlords dominate officer corps of the military, part of the hard core of the state.

4. In England, the power of the country's burgeoning trade union movement is attenuated by the fact that English workers—in quasi-racist fashion, similar to the attitude of poor whites toward formerly enslaved Blacks in the southern United States—despise the subproletariat of immigrant Irish workers. Revolution in Britain is impossible until this is overcome.

5. As the Irish struggle spills over into Britain, and with the help of agitation by the International in favor of Ireland and for class

solidarity across the Irish-English divide inside Britain, the dialectics of revolution will come to the fore, as the consciousness of English workers will undergo a radical transformation, giving them a greater sense of solidarity with their Irish counterparts and therefore making them more amenable to revolution.

6. Thus, both materially and ideologically, an Irish social revolution will be the lever that pries open the British and the wider European revolution, which will probably begin in France.

This is a richer and more complex framework than the young Trotsky's notion of permanent revolution, which saw primarily agrarian countries like Russia as the weakest links in the chain of global capitalism and therefore likely starting points for a wider revolution. Alluding implicitly to Trotsky's theory, the French communist Auguste Bianchi writes concerning the Confidential Communication: "The position defended here is a long way from subsequent debates within Marxism to figure out if the communist revolution will take place in the most advanced capitalist nation, or rather where capitalism is weakest."[6] First, while Marx acknowledges peripheral agrarian Ireland versus Britain as the center of production and class struggle, he shows their interrelationship via Irish immigration into Britain. Second, France, a different type of a country in the "metropole," is brought in, and, in this way, the framework becomes international in a wider sense, one that also simply assumes the spread of revolution across national borders. Third, industrial labor in the British metropole is not seen as an undifferentiated, unified force but as one riven with ethnic and racial prejudices on the part of workers from the dominant group.[7] In Marx's framework, quasi-racism toward the Irish not only attenuates the revolutionary consciousness of the largest part of the English working class but also estranges it from an oppressed minority of workers, the Irish immigrants, who are characterized by a greater intensity of revolutionary passion. Fourth, the importance of the national struggle is emphasized, with no intimation

---

6   Auguste Bianchi, "Marx aux confins de l'eurocentrisme," *Agitations* (April 21, 2019).

7   To be fair, the mature Trotsky showed great insight into race and class in his conversation in the 1930s with C. L. R. James on Black people in the US.

that such issues are either receding amid advanced capitalism, or that they distract from the "real" class struggle. Fifth, Marx's model shows both accelerants and blockages to revolution inside Britain, thus dealing with both objective and subjective elements rather than stressing either in a one-sided fashion.

What is the relationship of this theorization of revolution in 1869–70 to Marx's research on communal social organizations in precapitalist clan societies—or non-Western agrarian communal villages—that has been so central to the present study? First, at a more general level, Marx begins to learn Russian in 1869, something he pursues for the rest of his life and that was to assist him in his studies of the village commune. While not directly connected to Ireland, this illustrates how he is turning his gaze away from the center of global capitalism in Britain, not only toward colonial Ireland in the far west but also toward Russia, located at Europe's eastern edge. Second, it should be noted that even as Marx was writing to Engels in Manchester about developments and controversies within the GC in London over Ireland, Engels was writing back about his own historical research on Ireland, including discussion of the ancient Celtic Brehon laws and their suppression by the English colonial state. A third link to Ireland can be found in Marx's 1868 letters to Engels about Maurer, discussed in chapter 1, in which he ruminates about ancient Germanic communal social forms lying just under the surface of feudal and even modern villages. There, he holds, contra Maurer, that all this could be connected to Ireland, remarking that "Maurer knows nothing about the Celts" and is unaware of new research on them (Letter to Engels of March 16, 1868, MECW 42:549). This letter is from about eighteen months before Marx elaborates his new theorization of Ireland, England, and revolution. Fourth, Marx finally researches Irish clan and communal forms in detail in 1881, less than two years before his death, in his notes on Maine, which were discussed in chapters 1 and 2. As noted in chapter 1, and will also be discussed in the present chapter, Marx tied his research on Russian communal forms to prospects for revolution and an alternative to capitalism in that country in his own time.

Had Marx addressed prospects for revolution involving Ireland again in his very last years, he would very likely have drawn connections to Irish clan and communal social forms. Recall that, close to the end of his 1880–81 notes on Morgan, as discussed in chapter 1, Marx incorporates Morgan's assessment that "the Celtic branch of the Aryan family (except that in India) held onto their gentile organization longer than any others" (EN: 238). As also discussed in chapter 1, in the still later 1881 notes on Maine, Marx discusses communal "rundale" landholdings in rural Ireland, focusing on their persistence in his own time. And note that, in addition to this, as discussed in chapter 2, Marx takes up in the Maine notes how British judges nullified ancient Irish law's inheritance rights for women in seventeenth century. But if communal forms like rundale continued underneath British feudal and then capitalist colonialism, would not some of these precolonial gender dimensions have also survived, not only inside rural Ireland but also among Irish communities in urban centers, including in Britain and the US? Another issue to consider is how, as discussed in chapter 5, in addition to the comparisons Marx drew in 1870 between anti-Black racism in the United States and English attitudes toward Irish workers, in his notes on Rome, he saw something similar going on in how the free proletariat despised the enslaved proletariat, making connections difficult even at a time when revolt against the aristocratic ruling classes was bursting out in both of these sectors. Surely, Marx would have brought these considerations to bear on future discussions of the revolutionary potential of rural Ireland as seen in the Fenian movement and would likely have sought out lingering influence of these communal forms in the Irish proletariat inside Britain itself.

But, while the Russian revolutionary Zasulich wrote to him in winter 1881 about revolutionary prospects in Russia, and a new Russian edition of the *Communist Manifesto* appeared in 1882, requiring a new preface, no similar invitations seem to have arrived that would have afforded him a ready opportunity to address Irish matters in similar ways in his last years. Moreover, the International had fallen apart in the wake of the reluctance by the English trade union leaders to support the Paris Commune of 1871, an uprising whose militantly secular character also drove down support for the International in Ireland. Thus, the conjuncture of Britain and Ireland looked very different in 1881 than in 1870.

Another more general point to remember from Marx's 1869–70 theorization of revolution in Ireland, Britain, and France is that he explicitly acknowledges a change of position on Ireland. He is therefore espousing a new theory of revolution in 1869–70, beyond that of his earlier years. In this new theory, the directionality of revolution now moves from France and Ireland to the industrial core, Britain, even though, in

economic terms, the latter is the most advanced both in both the development of the productive forces and trade union organization. In
particularizing and therefore complicating the notion of a class revolution put forth at a high level of abstraction in *Capital*, as cited at the
beginning of this chapter, the 1869–70 writings on Ireland show some of
the complex possibilities that emerge from Marx's concept that "capital
is not a thing but a social relation" (CAP: 932).[8]

Anti-Statist Revolution alongside the Anti-Capitalist Revolution

Turning now to Marx's writings on the Paris Commune of 1871 and
other writings of the 1870s on the European revolution, we will see
another explicit acknowledgment of a conceptual turn, toward a clearer
notion of the need to destroy the state as well as the capital relation. At
the same time, these writings show that Marx was continuing to place
the struggle for the emancipation of labor against capital at the center of
his concept of revolution, but with a new twist concerning the state.

In his last years, Marx concentrated more than before on alternatives
to capitalism, including agrarian and clan forms of precapitalist communalism and communist and communal social forms inside the
industrialized capitalist societies of his own day. As Löwy sums up,
concerning "capitalism's 'separation' of human beings from the land, that
is, from nature":

> Marx thought that in precapitalist societies, a form of unity between
> the producers and the land existed, and he considered one of the tasks
> of socialism to be the re-establishment of that original unity between
> human beings and nature, which had been destroyed by capitalism,
> but at a higher level (negation of the negation). This explains Marx's
> interest in precapitalist communities.[9]

---

8   This complexity can be obscured by looseness of expression, as in the rendition
of this as "capital is not a thing but a class relation," which makes discussion of race,
gender, or other differentiations harder to include within Marx's framework. Such an
"amended" version appeared recently in the French historian Julien Vincent's "Aux origins du 'capitalisme racial,'" a review of Sylvie Laurent's *Capital et Race* (*Le Monde*,
February 7, 2024).

9   Michael Löwy, "De Karl Marx à l'Eco-marxisme," *Actuel Marx* (forthcoming).

The late Marx also moved even further away from the notion that communism, in abolishing capitalism, would involve any form of the state, instead of its complete abolition.

In the commodity fetishism section of *Capital*, developed in its final form in the 1872–75 French edition after the Paris Commune of 1871, Marx writes of the dialectical opposite to the distorting lens of commodity fetishism, which hides the actual exploitative relations of labor: "Let us finally imagine, for a change," he writes, "an association of free human beings [*Menschen*], working with the means of production held in common" (CAP: 171). He goes on to describe going beyond the wage system to a new form of remuneration based upon labor time, eliminating much of the hierarchical division of labor under capitalism and previous class societies:

> We shall assume, but only for the sake of a parallel with the production of commodities, that the share of each individual producer in the means of subsistence is determined by his labor-time. Labor-time would in that case play a double part. Its apportionment in accordance with a definite social plan maintains the correct proportion between the different functions of labor and the various needs of the associations. On the other hand, labor-time also serves as a measure of the part taken by each individual in the common labor, and of his share in the part of the total produce destined for individual consumption. The social relations of the individual producers, both toward their labor and the products of their labor, are here transparent in their simplicity in production as well as in distribution. (CAP: 172)

He concludes that this would constitute a society "based upon production by freely associated human beings ... under their conscious and planned control" (CAP: 173). But, as with his conclusion in the same work about the working-class revolution quoted at the beginning of the present chapter, there is no mention of the state. Discussion of the state can be found, however, in two other major writings of the 1870s.

In the *Critique of the Gotha Program* (1875), Marx famously outlines the two phases of communism, something that continues to spark much discussion.[10] His description of the second or higher phase, often quoted,

---

10   In *Marx's Concept of the Alternative to Capitalism* (Leiden: Brill, 2012), Peter Hudis sums up and develops a critique of this discussion, which he develops further in

outlines an utterly free association based upon voluntary labor and remuneration based solely on need:

> In a higher phase of communist society, after the enslaving subordi-nation of the individual to the division of labor, and thereby also the antithesis between mental and physical labor, has vanished; after labor has become not only a means of life but life's prime desire and neces-sity [*erste Lebensbedürfniss*], after the productive forces have also increased with the all-round development of the individual, and all the springs of cooperative wealth flow more abundantly, only then can the narrow horizon of bourgeois right be completely transcended [*überschritten*] and society inscribe on its banners: From each accord-ing to his abilities, to each according to his needs![11]

But this not the immediate outcome of the transition from capitalism to communism; far from it.

It is preceded in the *Critique of the Gotha Program* by a first phase of communism, similar to that outlined in the fetishism section of *Capital*, as discussed above. Marx begins by noting:

> Here we are dealing with a communist society, not as it has *developed* on its own foundations, but, on the contrary, just as it *emerges* from capitalist society; which is thus in every respect, economically, morally, and intellectually, still stamped with the birthmarks of the old society from whose womb it emerges.[12]

In this account, wages have been abolished in favor of a remuneration from the community based upon labor time, but Marx specifies, in a formulation not yet found in *Capital*, that "labor, to serve as a measure, must be defined by its duration or intensity, otherwise it ceases to be a standard of measurement."[13] Thus, labor like taking care of autistic children, caring for the sick during epidemics, heavy construction work,

---

his introduction to Marx, *Critique of the Gotha Program*, revised translation and anno-tation by Kevin B. Anderson and Karel Ludenhoff, with an introduction by Peter Hudis and an afterword by Peter Linebaugh (Oakland: PM Press, 2022).

11   Marx, *Critique of the Gotha Program*, p. 59.

12   Ibid., p. 57.

13   Ibid., p. 58.

or heart surgery, each of which involve intense physical or mental stress, would count more quantitatively than less taxing forms of labor.

After elaborating his two phases of communism, Marx attacks any notion of the existence of a state under communism and also opposes vehemently various socialist arguments in favor of controlling or even strengthening the state for communist purposes. The state had to be abolished, just as did capital. In particular, he attacks relentlessly the Lassallean German socialists and their statist concept of socialism: "The German Workers' Party . . . treats the state rather as an independent entity that possesses its own *'intellectual, ethical, and libertarian bases.'*" He also attacks their illusions concerning the Prussian state: "a state that is nothing but a police-guarded military despotism, embellished with parliamentary forms."[14]

Thus, Marx's vision of communism here does not include a state, although he does speak of practices "analogous" to state "functions," presumably those such as healthcare, education, provision for emergencies, irrigation, and other forms of social protection:

> The question then arises: What transformation will the body politic [*Staatswesen*] undergo in communist society? In other words, what social functions analogous to present state functions [*Staatsfunktionen*] will remain at that juncture? This question can only be answered scientifically, and one does not get a flea-hop nearer to the problem by a thousandfold combination of the word "people" with the word "state."[15]

It is important to note that the first sentence of the above paragraph has been rendered incorrectly in most English translations, rendering "body politic" as "state." But here Marx is not speaking of the state as such, as seen also in his term "state functions [*Staatsfunktionen*]" in the same paragraph. Such a mistranslation undercuts Marx's attack throughout the *Critique of the Gotha Program* on the state and on statist notions of socialism in particular.

As Peter Hudis shows, Lenin also muddied these waters. To his credit, Lenin was the only major Marxist thinker of the generation after Marx

---

14   Ibid., pp. 67–8, 69.
15   Ibid., p. 68.

to place *Critique of the Gotha Program* at the center of Marxist theory. But, in his *State and Revolution*, in which he did so, often to good effect, Lenin unfortunately made the error of equating the first phase of communism with the dictatorship of the proletariat, a still earlier stage in Marx's discussion of the road toward communism. As Marx writes on this score in *Critique of the Gotha Program*, in a passage at some remove from his discussion of the two phases of communism: "Between capitalist and communist society there lies the period of the revolutionary transformation of the one into the other. Corresponding to this is also a political transition period in which the state can be nothing but *the revolutionary dictatorship of the proletariat.*"[16] Failing to distinguish the latter, which still had a state, from Marx's totally anti-statist vision of communism, Lenin wrote of a "first phase of communist society," in which "all citizens are transformed into hired employees of the state, which consists of the armed workers."[17] This type of society was "usually called socialism," Lenin added at another point.[18] This unfortunate slip on Lenin's part allowed Marx's *Critique of the Gotha Program* to be used to suggest that he supported statist communism as the first phase of communism, even though Lenin himself roundly attacked the state throughout most of the *State and Revolution*, calling for its abolition and attacking the social democrats for not having placed that at the center of their theorization of revolution.

In *The Civil War in France* (1871), Marx also attacks the state as well as capital and landed property. He writes of the Paris Commune's policies: "It wanted to make individual property a truth by transforming the means of production, land, and capital, now chiefly the means of enslaving and exploiting labor, into mere instruments of free and associated labor. But this is communism, 'impossible' communism!" (MECW 22: 335). He also highlights the intertwining of capital and the state, and the need to destroy both the state and the capital relation, an issue not expressed explicitly in *Capital*. He declares: "But the working class cannot simply lay hold of the ready-made state machinery, and wield it for its own purposes" (MECW 22: 328).

---

16   Ibid., pp. 68–9.
17   Vladimir Lenin, *State and Revolution, Collected Works*, Vol. 25 (Moscow: Progress Publishers, 1964), p. 478.
18   Ibid., p. 472.

As the Commune practiced it, a modern social republic of the working class needed to abolish the standing army, the police, and other organs of state repression, substituting a direct proletarian democracy based upon an armed citizenry. Thus, Marx advocates not the destruction of all state functions, which could result in a reactionary outcome like warlordism, but its positive abolition and replacement by a social republic dominated by a revolutionary working class. Marx extolls "the destruction of the State power which claimed to be the embodiment of that unity [of] the nation itself, from which it was but a parasitic excrescence" (MECW 22: 332) and writes further that the Commune "breaks with the modern state power" (MECW 22: 333). This formed the basis for the takeover of some factories by workers committees, a precursor of what would emerge later in the Russian revolution as soviet power.

While the Paris Commune did not abolish capitalism, Marx writes that its abolition of the state created the political form for such a task: "It was essentially a working class government, the product of the struggle of the producing against the appropriating class, the political form at last discovered under which to work out the economical emancipation of labor" (MECW 22: 334). Engels also thought the Commune, which worked toward communism, was an example of the dictatorship of the proletariat.

In addition, as discussed in chapter 2, Marx singles out as "heroic" the "real women of Paris" who assumed their part in the civil war (MECW 22: 341). A year later, in 1872, Marx indicates that the Commune has caused him to change his position on the state, compared to that articulated in the *Communist Manifesto* of 1848. Thus, in their 1872 preface to a new edition of the *Manifesto*, he and Engels write of several aspects that had become outdated. One of these outdated features was the "revolutionary measures" (MECW 23: 174–5) proposed at the end of Section 2. In 1848, these included "centralization of credit in the hands of the State" and "centralization of the means of communication and transport in the hands of the State" (MECW 6: 505). Referring to "the Paris Commune, where the proletariat for the first time held political power," they write: "One thing especially was proved by the Commune, viz., that 'the working class cannot simply lay hold of the ready-made state machinery, and wield it for its own purposes'" (MECW 23: 174–5).

Here, as with his 1869–70 theorization of Ireland and the wider revolution, Marx is explicit about having changed his position, and he does so publicly. To be sure, he kept the core concept of the self-emancipation of labor, but with an important modification concerning the state. How would Marx have further modified his vision of communism, of abolition of the state as well as capital, in light of his research on Indigenous communism and communal villages in his last years? The former usually existed without any kind of state, whereas the latter self-governed in a manner that was in major ways independent of the state.

Both of these themes connect to the next type of revolution to be considered in the present chapter. This is a revolution that emanates from communal societies on the periphery into what was then the heart of global capitalism: Western Europe. On this issue, however, especially concerning Russia, the change of position on Marx's part is left implicit.

Communal Villages as Loci of Revolution, in Russia and Beyond

Two years before his 1879–82 notebooks on communal social forms around the world, Marx begins to see an uprising in Russia as the most likely starting point for a wider European revolution. For example, in remarks on the Russo-Turkish War (the "oriental crisis") in a letter of September 27, 1877, to the New Jersey communist Friedrich Sorge, Marx views Russia as a cauldron of revolution:

> That crisis marks a new turning point in European history. Russia— and I have studied conditions there from the original Russian sources, unofficial and official (the latter only available to a few people but got for me through friends in Petersburg)—has long been on the verge of an upheaval. The gallant Turks have hastened the explosion by years with the thrashing they have inflicted, not only upon the Russian army and Russian finances, but in a highly personal and individual manner on the *dynasty commanding* the army (the Tsar, the heir to the throne and six other Romanovs). The upheaval will begin *secundum artem* [according to the rules of the art] with some playing at constitutionalism and then there will be a fine row. If Mother Nature is not particularly unfavorable toward us, we shall still live to see the fun! The stupid nonsense which the Russian students are perpetrating is only a symptom, worthless in itself. But it is a symptom. All sections of Russian society are in complete disintegration economically,

morally, and intellectually. This time the revolution will begin in the East, hitherto the unbroken bulwark and reserve army of counterrevolution. (MECW 45: 278)

In this period, the last years of Marx's life, I know of no other consideration of revolutionary possibilities in any other country equivalent to what he is expressing here concerning Russia. This is illustrated in how, in the very same letter, Marx dismisses the prospects of revolution in France, still suffering under the wave of reaction that set in after the defeat of the Paris Commune, and where the republicans were battling the threat of a military dictatorship: "The *French crisis* is an altogether secondary affair compared with the oriental one. Yet one can only hope the bourgeois republic wins" (MECW 45: 278). In the event, Russia defeated Turkey the following year, thus attenuating for the moment the internal crisis Marx foresaw in 1877. But he did not alter his position on the underlying issues eating away at the Russian social order. This is seen in a letter to Wilhelm Liebknecht four months later, in which he remarked that, while Turkey's defeat had for the moment forestalled a revolutionary outbreak, he continued to believe that "all the elements are present in abundant measure" for a "social revolution" in Russia "and hence radical change throughout Europe" (Letter of February 4, 1878, MECW 45: 296).

Fifteen months later, in a letter to French socialist Jules Guesde dated May 10, 1879, which has come to light only recently, Marx writes in a similar vein concerning the world revolution starting in Russia. But, here, he details how it might reach Western Europe and the obstacles it would face there:

I am convinced that the explosion of the revolution will begin this time not in the West but in the Orient, in Russia. It will first impact the two other harsh despotisms [*illegible word*], Austria and Germany, where a violent upheaval [*bouleversement*] has become a historical necessity. It is of the highest importance that at the moment of this general crisis in Europe we find the French proletariat already having been organized into [*constitué*] a workers' party and ready to play its role. As to England, the material elements for its social transformation are superabundant, but a driving spirit [*l'esprit moteur*] is lacking. It will not form up, except under the impact of the explosion of events

on the Continent. It must never be forgotten that, however impoverished [*misérable*] the condition of the greater part of the English
working class, it takes part nonetheless, to a certain extent, in the
British Empire's domination of the world market, or, what is even
worse, imagines itself to be taking part in it.[19]

As in the 1877 letter to Sorge and the 1878 one to Liebknecht, Marx sees
the revolution breaking out first in Russia.

But, here, sounding notes similar to those in the Confidential Communication on Ireland of 1870, he expresses strong, perhaps even
stronger, reservations about the level of class consciousness among
English workers, here stressing their affective ties to the Empire. This
should not, however, be taken to mean that Marx has given up on the
English working class, any more than in the Confidential Communication of nine year earlier. Also, as in 1870, he sees France in a crucial role
but provides more details. His failure to mention the Paris Commune in
a letter that would likely have been read by the French police may be due
to ongoing political repression of those associated with it. And, in a way,
Russia is now a replacement for Ireland, as the land where the revolution
is most likely to detonate first. Different, of course, is the lack of
Russian working-class immigration, of anything similar to the Irish
subproletariat in Britain, and the fact that Russia is not under colonial
domination. The letter constitutes a multifaceted sketch of how the next
European revolution would likely break out and move forward, written
from a seamlessly internationalist perspective that also takes very specific account of local and national circumstances. Editor Jean-Numa
Ducange is absolutely correct to refer to "France," the "Orient," and the
"West" in his title for the article containing the letter. It should also be
noted that, in his response, Guesde shows a narrow focus on France,
responding only to remarks by Marx about various socialist tendencies
in his country, not even mentioning Marx's key point about the European revolution breaking out first in Russia. Here, not only can we
discern a Western disinterest in revolutionary movements emanating
from the non-industrialized societies to the East, but we are also on the
road toward the Second International's focus on socialist parties in each

---

19   Jean-Numa Ducange, "Une lettre inédite de Karl Marx à Jules Guesde sur la
France, l'"Orient" et l' 'Occident' (1879)," *Actuel Marx* 73 (2023), p. 112.

nation operating quite separately from each other, joined together only in a loose federation.

In this 1878–79 correspondence, Marx does not mention Russia's communal villages. It is only in his very last publication that Marx finally combines these two elements, Russia as starting point for a new round of revolution in Europe and the Russian village commune as source of resistance to capital, of revolution, and of communism. He does so in a new preface, coauthored with Engels, to the 1882 Russian edition of *Communist Manifesto*. This brief preface, drafted in December 1881, adds discussion of both the US and Russia, each of them hardly mentioned in 1848 but since then having risen to great prominence, the US for its surging industrial economy, and Russia for its plethora of revolutionary movements.

Without being aware of the letter to Zasulich and other discussions by Marx of the Russian village commune, all of which lay unpublished in 1882, the reference to these communes as loci of revolution might have been easy to miss, especially given its brevity:

> Can the Russian *obshchina*, a form, albeit heavily eroded, of the primeval communal ownership of the land, pass directly into the higher, communist form of communal ownership? Or must it first go through the same process of dissolution that marks the West's historical development? The only answer that is possible today is: Were [*wird*] the Russian revolution to become the signal for a proletarian revolution in the West [*im Westen*], so that the two fulfill [*ergänzen*][20] each other, then the present Russian communal landownership may serve as the point of departure [*zum Ausgangspunkt*] for a communist development. (SHN: 139; MEGA2 I/25: 296)

Neither in the above lines in the 1882 preface to the *Manifesto* nor in his correspondence with Russians in his last years does Marx acknowledge a change of position. Still, the changes since the 1840s and early 1850s are clear. For, in the earlier period, he viewed Russia as an utterly reactionary power, but, by now, Russia had become for him the likely starting point of a wider revolution.

---

20   Could also be translated as "complement" or "complete," the latter a stronger term that I have rendered here a bit more colloquially as "fulfill."

Interestingly, the last clause of the above was altered in the hand-written original, with a different wording crossed out, presumably at the end of the process of writing the preface. With the crossed-out text intact, the preface would have ended with the phrase "communal land-ownership's ruin may be avoided" (MEGA2 I/25: 974). If, as is then likely, the substitute phrase about the commune "as the point of departure for a communist development" was added at the last minute, this heightens the possibility that the final wording constituted a theoretical innovation on Marx's part.

The above sentences—in what was Marx's last publication—exhibit a complex and intricate dialectic that needs to be unpacked. It is important to note that the quest for the free development of the Russian commune is not unconditioned, a point that is made explicit here, versus being left only implicit in the 1881 drafts of the letter to Zasulich. Russia can avoid the dissolution of its rural communes and the destructive process of the primitive accumulation of capital if the effort to do so is accompanied by a "proletarian revolution in the West."

There are two contingencies here, which form part of a totality riven with contradictions and various possibilities. Were a Russian revolution to break out ahead of one in the West—likely on the basis of a revolution rooted in the rural communes and their resistance both to the state and to capitalist incursions—then a wider European revolution would be touched off not in Western Europe but in Russia. In this case, Russia's Indigenous form of rural communism would become the spark, "as the point of departure" for a wider revolution and transition to a modern, positive form of communism. Thus, there could be no successful transformation of the Russian communes into a modern communism without a proletarian revolution in Western Europe, but the strong possibility also existed that a revolution in Russia could touch off such an event in the West.

Despite being published in Russian and soon after in German, the 1882 preface was almost completely forgotten. This forgetting—by the "post-Marx Marxists, beginning with Frederick Engels,"[21] in Dunayevskaya's

---

21 Raya Dunayevskaya, *Rosa Luxemburg, Women's Liberation, and Marx's Philosophy of Revolution*, second edition (Urbana: University of Illinois Press [1982] 1991), p. 175. This is particularly poignant given the fact that the original manuscript of the 1882 preface is in Engels's hand (MEGA2 I/25: 297). Engels quotes the 1882 preface in full in his 1890 preface to a new German edition but does not discuss its implications, and

pungent formulation—can be seen in Engels's letter to Karl Kautsky two years later, on February 16, 1884:

> [In Java] today, primitive communism (so long as it has not been stirred up by some element of modern communism) furnishes the finest and broadest basis of exploitation and despotism, as well as in India and Russia, and survives in the midst of modern society as an anachronism (to be eliminated or, one almost might say, turned back on its course) no less than the mark communities of the original cantons. (MECW 47:103)

In the above, Engels places so much emphasis on the need of these pre-capitalist communes, whether the village communes of Java or the traditional German/Swiss "mark community" or village commune, to be "stirred up by modern communism" that the 1882 preface recedes almost to the vanishing point. Instead, unlike Marx, he seems largely to have maintained their Eurocentric positions of the 1850s, which held that these kinds of communal forms were the foundation of "Oriental despotism." It seems, therefore, that Engels never changed his position on the Russian village commune very much.

The newness of Marx's 1882 formulation can also be seen when compared to the drafts of the letter to Vera Zasulich written nine months earlier, in March 1881. As discussed in previous chapters, in those drafts Marx saw the Russian village commune as something distinct from Western European villages. In the West, individuals and family groups, or agricultural laborers working for wages, worked specific plots of land, which were held as private property or at least with possessory rights held by families. In the Russian village, both work groups and property relations were instead organized communally, with individual families having a share in the commune as a whole but not receiving ownership or even long-term possession of a specific piece of agricultural land.

But the Zasulich texts comprised letters and drafts, not programmatic texts, unlike the 1882 preface to the *Manifesto*. Here, albeit briefly, Marx looks through a wider lens, incorporating the Russian village into the system of global capitalism and its dialectical opposite, the movements

---

he otherwise restricts the rest of his preface to Western Europe and North America (MECW 27: 53–60).

of revolution and resistance by a wide variety of social groups throughout that system, from London and Paris to Saint Petersburg. In this way,
he makes his theorization of revolution in Russia and Western Europe
clearer than anywhere else, despite the brevity of the text.

Some forty years ago, as the late Marx was being first put forward on
an international level as a topic of research by those like Dunayevskaya
and Shanin, three different lines of interpretation could already be discerned. First, in Shanin's 1983 volume, *Late Marx and the Russian Road*,
an essay by the British Marxists Derek Sayer and Philip Corrigan took
the position that there was nothing really new here, "that Marx's late
texts represent not so much a radical break as a clarification of how his
'mature' texts should have been read in the first place" (SHN: 80). This
approach continues today among those who acknowledge the originality
of the late Marx but see it as simply continuous in this respect with the
young Marx and with the mature Marx of *Grundrisse* and *Capital*. In
other words, Marx remains brilliant but there are no fundamental
changes in the period 1869–82.

A second and seemingly more fruitful approach, also found in the
Shanin collection, acknowledges important changes of perspective by
Marx after 1869, so much so that they constitute a break in his thought.
This is the position of Shanin himself in 1983. This approach is also
found in the essay by the Japanese Marx scholar Haruki Wada, who
carries out a deep textual analysis. Nearly a decade before the collapse of
the Soviet Union and even before the ascendency of Mikhail Gorbachev,
Wada had managed to obtain access to some of Marx's papers in Moscow,
something almost invariably denied to researchers from outside the
Soviet bloc. Wada begins by discussing some of Marx's statements in the
drafts of the letter to Zasulich about the possibility of a revolution emanating from the Russian village communes—"a Russian revolution is
required, if the Russian commune is to be saved"—and contrasts them
with Marx's earlier judgments from the 1850s to the effect that the
communes were conservative and that radical change would need to
come from outside, from the Western proletarian revolution (SHN: 67).
Wada also notes that Marx has by now become a supporter of the
Russian Populists and their idea of a peasant revolution and direct
attacks on the autocratic state. Wada writes that this contrasted with
those around Zasulich, who awaited the development of an industrial
proletariat for a revolution. Finally, Wada observes that Engels never

really changed regarding their old view of Russia from the 1850s, and he notes Marx's declining health by late 1881, when the request for a new preface arrived.

Wada also notes that the surviving draft of their introduction to the *Manifesto* was in Engels's handwriting. From all this, Wada concludes Marx must have "asked Engels to make a draft, and put his signature to it" (SHN: 70). This seemingly rigorous argument is less convincing than it seems. I am aware of no case—as seen most clearly early on in their collaboration in 1847–48 on the *Communist Manifesto*, and for which Engels's early draft has been preserved—in which Marx was not clearly the senior author in any of their joint writings. More substantively, Engels never wrote anything similar to the 1882 preface after Marx's death, even though he quoted it on one occasion, as he continued to view the Russian commune as something backward and without any revolutionary potential. Thus, Marx is almost certainly the author of the 1882 preface.

At a more general level, Wada's argument lends itself to the notion that Marx saw the Russian commune as an autonomous force of revolution that could establish a society that could recede from world capitalism and build a viable socialism on its own resources, not only without leadership from the "Western" proletariat but also without even their participation or that of already industrialized societies. In short, we do not need the working class for radical, anti-capitalist revolution. Here too, a variety of thinkers, from Maoists of the 1960s and '70s (as Wada himself was at the time) to radical ecologists in more recent years, have picked up on this strand of argument, not always to good effect.

Dunayevskaya articulates a third kind of argument concerning the late Marx. As a relative outsider to the Marxist intellectual establishment of the time, she was not invited to contribute to the Shanin collection, but, in this period, she addresses not only the late Marx on Russia but also the *Ethnological Notebooks*. Overall, she sees both "new moments" and continuities in Marx's late writings, writing that, in the *Ethnological Notebooks*, "he was completing the circle begun in 1844" and "was diving into the study of human development, both in different historic periods and in the most basic Man//Woman relationship."[22] All this was couched in terms of Marx's concept of "revolution in permanence," as put forth in the 1850 "Address to the Communist League," and which is

---

22   Dunayevskaya, *Rosa Luxemburg,* pp. 188, 190.

seen to have marked his entire work thereafter.[23] The 1844 reference concerns the startlingly radical paragraph from the *1844 Manuscripts* on gender with which de Beauvoir ended *The Second Sex*, as discussed in chapter 2. Whether in Marx's notes on Morgan, as discussed in chapter 1, or in the late Marx on the Russian communal village, Dunayevskaya stresses not only the ways in which Iroquois clans or Russian village communes offered an alternative to capitalism but also how even these precapitalist forms of communism exhibited social contradictions, including over gender. Moreover, these were, for her, not just historical but contemporary issues:

> These studies enabled Marx (*Marx, not Engels*) to see the possibility of new human relations, not as they might come through a mere "updating" of primitive communism's equality of the sexes, as among the Iroquois, but as Marx sensed they would burst forth from a new type of revolution.[24]

In this sense, Marx's exploration of gender in the *Ethnological Notebooks* was connected to those on the Russian village commune, and to gender in other clan and communal societies Marx studies in his last years, with all this connected to "a new type of revolution."

Dunayevskaya also finds deep connections between what was going on in Russia and the capitalist societies of Western Europe. Thus she stresses, with regard to Russia, that it would be

> a capitalist world in crisis . . . which creates favorable conditions for transforming primitive communism into a modern collective society: "In order to save the Russian commune there must be a Russian Revolution." In a word, revolution is indispensable, whether one has to go through capitalism, or can go to the new society "directly" from the commune.[25]

In commenting on the 1882 preface, she writes that it "projected the idea that Russia could be the first to have a proletarian revolution ahead of

---

23   Ibid., p. 186.
24   Ibid., p. 190.
25   Ibid., p. 183.

the West."[26] That is, a Russian revolution could surge ahead of one in the West, forming a starting point, but it could not remain alone if it were to be successful. It could not win out in long-term isolation from the Western proletariat.

I took a position similar to that of my mentor Dunayevskaya on the 1882 preface in *Marx at the Margins*, noting that "a Russian revolution based upon its agrarian communal forms would be a necessary, but not a sufficient condition for the development of a modern communism."[27] It would be necessary, though, to shake the Western proletariat out of the doldrums into which it had descended with the defeat of the Paris Commune, and soon after, of Reconstruction in the US. This amounted to the setting in of a global era of reaction in the West, after the revolutionary period of the 1860s through the early 1870s. That is why I began the present chapter with Marx's Ireland essay on the interrelationship of the agrarian periphery's revolutionary struggles to that of the working class in the metropole. That is also why I took up Marx on the "Western" Paris Commune, also in this chapter, just before considering Marx on the Russian commune. Still, the Russian commune and similar social forms around the world were, in Marx's eyes, crucial "starting points" for global revolution and also points for the conceptualization of an alternative to capitalism. His interest in Russia deepened as it became the first country where *Capital* was translated (in 1872), and where, unlike in Germany, the book was extensively discussed by the intellectuals, and where a vibrant, youthful revolutionary movement—composed of students and young intellectuals who sought to stir up a peasant revolution based upon the village commune—was growing by leaps and bounds.

It must be underlined that Marx, while rejecting unilinear notions of progress and development, was calling neither for the preservation of these village communes nor for their return to a "purer" state than the one presently under capitalist encroachment. Nor was he calling for a revolution based upon rural Russia alone. Instead, all this was part of a broader, global strategic view of revolution, around the "agrarian question," something that dogs the left to this day. This problem is addressed by the French Marxist thinker Isabelle Garo:

---

26   Ibid., p. 187.
27   Kevin B. Anderson, *Marx at the Margins: On Nationalism, Ethnicity, and Non-Western Societies* (Chicago: University of Chicago Press, [2010] 2016), p. 235.

Thus, the traditional commune is to be conceived not as a model to be generalized but as the possible social and, above all, political lever of an alliance between the working class and the exploited peasant class, a lever at once indispensable and extremely difficult to construct.[28]

The young Brazilian economist Guilherme Nunes Pires cautions that for Marx, "only with the Western proletarian revolution and the incorporation in the rural commune of the most advanced techniques of production" could a "transition by a non-capitalist road . . . to a classless society" take place.[29] These are valid points, but, at the same time, it should be noted that Marx is reversing the directionality of the European revolution in his 1877–78 letters and in the 1882 preface to the *Manifesto* when he writes of revolution in Russia based on the commune as such as a revolution's "point of departure."

Looking at the problem in this more general, global sense, I would argue that Marx's writings on the Russian village commune and revolution, especially the 1882 preface to the *Manifesto,* are just the tip of the iceberg. They form part of a vast project in which, as we have seen, he made hundreds of thousands of words of notes on anthropological and social history studies of India, Indonesia, North Africa, precolonial and colonial Latin America, Russia, ancient Rome, precolonial Ireland, and a variety of preliterate societies, from the Indigenous clans of the Americas to the Homeric Greeks. These notes also deal extensively with gender, especially in Greece, Rome, Ireland, and the Americas.

These voluminous notes are deeply connected to Marx's new notions of revolution. To be sure, we cannot know what he would have done with this material, including how he would have incorporated it into subsequent volumes of *Capital.* Still, it may be worthwhile to sketch the kind of globalized theory of revolution and of the alternative to capitalism that might have flowed out of these studies in his last working years, 1879–82.

1. As Marx states explicitly, resistance on the part of Russia's communal villages to capitalist encroachment could form the

28   Isabelle Garo, *Communism and Strategy: Rethinking Political Mediation* (London: Verso, [2019] 2023), p. 214.

29   Guilherme Nunes Pires, "Marx and Russia: The Russian Road and the Myth of Historical Determinism," *Ciencias Humanas e Socais,* Vol. 1 (2023), p. 74.

"point of departure" for a European revolution if it developed links to the Western proletariat. This is connected to the fact that, by the late 1870s, he saw Russia as the country with the greatest level of revolutionary unrest, with the most determined revolutionary movement, with the greatest interest in *Capital*, and therefore the most likely starting point for a wider European revolution. He sees its villages as more communistic in their internal relations than the Western European village under feudalism or capitalism.

2. In his notes on Algeria's clans, communal villages, and their resistance to French imperialism, Marx connects the fear of the metropolitan French ruling classes over this anti-colonial resistance to their fear of the modern communism of the Paris Commune that broke out under their very noses in 1871. Here, something similar to his 1882 preface is evident, the relationship of the Algerian anti-colonial and Indigenous struggles against French colonialism to those in the metropole, which, in this period, experienced the Paris Commune, a unique social revolution that moved toward a non-statist form of communism on the largest scale attempted anywhere up to that point. Moreover, Marx singles out the heroism of the women Communards, as well as the ways in which French colonialism deepened patriarchal domination in Algeria, signs of the importance of women's struggles to revolutionary and anti-colonial movements.

3. In his notes on precolonial and colonial Latin America, Marx singles out the persistence of Indigenous communal social structures even after the establishment of Spanish colonialism, also noting that Spain's relatively underdeveloped capitalism did not undermine these structures as radically as did British colonialism in India. He also notes that these communal societies were much more resilient than modern capitalism in terms of sustainable agriculture and safeguarding food supplies and other necessities of life in anticipation of natural disasters and crises of other kinds. He singles out as well the prominent position of women in these networks of sustainability.

4. In his notes on the Indian Subcontinent, the area of the world he covered most extensively in the 1879–82 research notebooks at the center of this study, Marx writes of the persistence, albeit with important evolutionary changes, of communal social structures that persisted for millennia. Important communal elements remained even after these structures were severely undermined, and sometimes destroyed, by capitalist "modernization" policies imposed in the 1790s under British colonialism. Thus, these clan and communal structures underlay the late seventeenth-century uprising led by Maratha rebel Shivaji against the Mughal Empire, and they continued as the Marathas fought the Mughals and then the British, through Marx's own time. In addition, he points to "rural communes" as sources of resistance to British colonial rule and to its imposition of capitalist social relations. Moreover, despite the long-standing suppression of women's rights on the part of Hindu religious authorities during the precolonial and colonial periods, Marx also notes that women emerged as military leaders during the massive anti-colonial Sepoy Uprising of 1857–59.

5. In his 1881 notes on communal and clan structures in precolonial Ireland, Marx emphasizes the persistence of these social forms through his own time. He also stresses how, even before the arrival of British overlords, who imposed feudal social relations, the ancient communal forms were being undermined by incipient class structures among the Celts themselves. He also singles out the social power women held in the days before the British conquest, and how this was expressed in ancient Irish clan law. Had he taken up Ireland and revolution in the 1880s, he would likely have brought this research on communal forms and gender into his theorization of agrarian resistance to colonialism and class rule by aristocratic landlords.

In any or all these ways, Marx may have been intending to connect his research on communal and clan societies to specific areas of the world that were experiencing struggles against colonialism and class rule, as he did in the 1882 preface to the Russian edition of the *Communist Manifesto*.

Can the extensive notes on Native American societies, especially in the Morgan notes, also befitted into the framework outlined in the 1882 preface? Here, any relationship would have to be seen at a higher level of generalization. In both sets of notes, gender comes to the fore as a central social category. In the case of Morgan and Native American societies of North America, this involves studying how gender subordination was at the root of many other forms of social hierarchy. At the same time, Marx investigates relative gender equality in Indigenous America, while not adhering to the idyllic portraits of these societies found in Morgan, or, for that matter, Engels. One can say, based on our present evidence, that it is likely that, after grappling with Morgan and critically absorbing his data, Marx would likely have centered gender in new ways had he ever written up the results of his 1879–82 notebooks more fully.

The notes on Morgan especially, but also those on ancient Greco-Roman society, as well as those on Ireland, investigate the origins not only of patriarchy but also of slavery and of class society. At the same time, these notes, especially those on Morgan, show alternatives to the forms of patriarchy and class rule prevalent in Marx's lifetime. In this sense, they contribute to his theorization of alternatives to capitalism. Löwy addressed this problem nearly three decades ago: "The idea that a modern communism would find some of its human dimension from the 'primitive communism' destroyed by the civilization founded upon private property and the state" was a major theme for the late Marx.[30]

Finally, it should be noted that, in a number of the cases Marx explores—India after Britain's undermining of the communal village, Latin America after the arrival of Spanish colonialism, Ireland under British rule, Algeria under French rule, or the Russian village commune under pressure from capitalism—he sees the communal forms within these societies as taking on especially revolutionary dimensions in times of social stress and crisis. Thus, it is not the preservation of these communal forms so much as their role in a global revolutionary movement—of English factory workers, of Irish tenant farmers, of impoverished Irish workers in Britain, of Algerians struggling against French domination, of Russian villagers seeking to defend their way of life in the face of capitalist penetration, of Indian villagers and clans using remnants of older communal formations to struggle against dynastic or colonial

---

30   Michael Löwy, "La dialectique du progrès et l'enjeu actuel des mouvements sociaux," *Congrès Marx International. Cent ans de marxisme. Bilan critique et perspectives* (Paris: Presses Universitaires de France, 1996), p. 200.

oppression—that, heterogenous as it was, offered real possibilities of a transformation that was as global as was capitalism itself. It cannot be stressed enough that unrest and uprisings, as in Russia, often broke out only after the communal forms had, to a great extent, disappeared, at least on the surface, and struggles based upon or influenced by these social forms intersected with more modern-facing ones. Thus, it was not so much defense of these forms as they were, as seeing them as elements of revolutionary energy and renewal of society on a totally new basis.

As we have seen in this chapter, in his last years, Marx developed three new concepts of revolution alongside that of a united working-class uprising. First, in 1869–70, he conceptualized a British workers' revolution sparked by an uprising in France and especially by an agrarian national revolution in Ireland, which would shake up the quasi-racist false consciousness of English workers and unite them with their immigrant Irish coworkers. Second, in his writings on the Paris Commune and his *Critique of the Gotha Program*, Marx theorizes working-class forms of revolution against capital that also target and abolish the modern centralized state while moving toward an emancipatory alternative. Third, Marx writes of revolutions beginning in non-capitalist agrarian societies like Russia that were imbued with communal village systems, which, in resisting capitalist encroachments, could become the base for a large social revolution. These movements could also connect to the revolutionary labor movement of Western Europe and North America, and they would, if victorious, be able to build on their archaic forms of communism as part of the struggle for a modern, democratic form of communism. In each of these struggles, groups subject to super-oppression, whether women or oppressed minorities, would likely play leading parts.

These three kinds of revolutions are a most important legacy of the late Marx, with equally important insights for today. This is the case, whether in analyzing the structures of oppression and domination, in conceptualizing all the multifarious forces of liberation that are in a position to challenge them, including all their contradictions with each other, and in theorizing what a real alternative to the exploitative, racist, sexist, heterosexist world of capitalism and its class domination would look like.

Postscript

The following three issues are so important that I do not want to close this book without mentioning them, although a real analysis of them will have to await further studies on the late Marx by those who will surely continue to work in this important field.

1. While I referred occasionally to the ecological dimensions of the late Marx, this topic was not integrated into this study. Partly this is because Saito developed so much on this issue just as the present book was going to press, and I did not want to jump to conclusions about his recent work, although I have made occasional comments in this book. Nor did I want to too hastily try to connect these issues to those at the center of the present book, something that needs to be done in the future.

2. It is a similar story with alternatives to capitalism, an issue taken up most comprehensively of late by Peter Hudis. Even though I refer to this topic throughout the book and have taken it up directly in the present chapter, the late Marx and alternatives to capitalism could be discussed much more in future studies. This is especially the case concerning Russian and other village communes as well as clan societies.

3. While the above two issues have been discussed by other scholars, this last one has not received as much discussion, but it also holds great importance both for our understanding of Marx and for today's struggles. It is notable that the three examples of Marx on revolution taken up in the present chapter, and, to my mind, the most prominent of those Marx developed in his last working years, 1869–82, all involve considerations of revolutionary organization. This is because, in each case, Marx had important organizational ties to those involved in the movements he was analyzing and offering strategic advice on. In Ireland/Britain, his reflections on a new type of revolution in 1870 took the form of a programmatic, organizational intervention in what he saw as a potentially revolutionary situation. All this occurred at a time when the First

International was at its zenith and was able to influence events in Britain, Ireland, the United States, and France. In particular, the International, pressed on by Marx's theoretical and political interventions at its General Council in London, was trying to influence workers from the dominant ethnic groups to overcome their anti-Irish prejudices, to recognize the deeply revolutionary Irish as an oppressed minority, and in this way to attempt to recruit the Irish into an interethnic, class-based revolutionary movement. As to the Paris Commune, it is well known that the First International had members deeply involved in the Commune and that it was identified with Marx after its suppression, in an exaggerated way. His *Civil War in France* was thus a programmatic and an organizational document, which did not even carry his name as author, but that of the International as a whole. Moreover, the *Critique of the Gotha Program* dealt not only with conceptualization of the alternative to capitalism in the form of two phases of communism but also with organizational issues that impinged upon how to get there. In Russia in 1877–82, Marx had many ties both to intellectuals and to the People's Will or Populist revolutionary movement. Here too, Marx's writings were programmatic as well as theoretical, seeking to influence what was at the time the world's most active revolutionary movement.

Acknowledgments

During the writing of this book, I have been helped and encouraged by people too numerous to name.

First of all, this book is a product of years, even decades, of dialogue with a number of scholars who themselves worked on the late Marx, and on whom I have closely relied. Back in the 1970s/1980s, I was able to interact directly with pioneering scholars of the late Marx, among them Lawrence Krader, Teodor Shanin, and above all my intellectual mentor Raya Dunayevskaya, all of them now departed. Not long after that, Peter Hudis and David Norman Smith, as well as the late Paresh Chatto-padhyay, also became closely engaged with these Marx writings at a time when so many were moving away from Marx altogether, not least because of overblown charges of Eurocentrism. Even the intellectual star power of Adrienne Rich, who embraced Dunayevskaya's interpretation of the late Marx as a revolutionary thinker with much to say to contemporary feminists and anti-imperialists, could not stem the anti-Marxist tide of the 1990s on this point.

In the wake of the collapse of the USSR in 1991, Marx's archives slowly became more accessible and as the new century was dawning, I was able to interact with some of the editors of the *Marx-Engels Gesamtausgabe*, especially Jürgen Rojahn and Rolf Hecker. This helped make possible my 2010 book, *Marx at the Margins*, which devoted a chapter to the late Marx. In a sense, the present book is a continuation of that previous one.

Second in terms of chronology but no less important substantively has been my dialogue with a younger generation of scholars who began to take up the late Marx by the second decade of this century: Heather A. Brown, Kohei Saito, Ryuji Sasaki, Marcello Musto, Emanuela Conversano, and Melda Yaman, as well as Tomonaga Tairako from my generation. Their arrival on the scene, as well as the global reception of *Marx at the Margins*, helped inspire me to finish this book. This period also witnessed a burgeoning discussion of the French edition of *Capital* by various scholars around the world. Among them one finds Jean-Numa Ducange in France, Rodrigo Pinho in Brazil, and translator of *Capital* Hassan Mortazavi in Iran. Mortazavi used some of my writings on the French edition to form the preface to Vol. I, not long before that country became the first to issue a translation of *Marx at the Margins*, in 2012.

Especially important in the period since 2010 have been my interactions with Irish scholars like Eamonn Slater and Chandana Mathur at Maynooth University, where in 2016 I gave a lecture that first delineated the chapters of this book. I also had substantial contact with scholars of Marx, slavery, and race, especially Angela Zimmerman and August Nimtz. In addition, I would like to mention my lecture tours in Brazil in 2017 and 2023, where *Marx at the Margins* was translated and where I was able to discuss themes from the present work with numerous other researchers, among them Marcelo Badaró Mattos, Hugo da Gama Cerqueira, Guilherme Leite Gonçalves, and Rhaysa Ruas. Dialogue with scholars in India, Catalonia, Spain, Turkey, and Japan, as well as the Arab world, played no small role in this period, as did those with Francophone intellectuals after the publication of the French edition of *Marx at the Margins*. Most of all, the annual London Historical Materialism Conference became a welcoming place to discuss the issues developed in the present book.

Along the way, I received important help with source material from Soichiro Sumida, Patrick Cabell, and Michael Heinrich, among others.

Sebastian Budgen of Verso has encouraged me, sometimes forcefully, to finish this book, and Verso editors Nick Walther and Daniel O'Connor performed expert editing. I am also grateful to Sean Crommelin of California and Bruno George for proofreading.

Finally, my beloved partner Janet Afary has encouraged this book at every step of the way and has done so as someone deeply knowledgeable about the issues it takes up, especially around gender, colonialism, and precapitalist societies.

Index